ESTABLISHING CONTROLS AND AUDITING THE COMPUTERIZED ACCOUNTING SYSTEM

ESTABLISHING CONTROLS AND AUDITING THE COMPUTERIZED ACCOUNTING SYSTEM

Elise G. Jancura
Robert Boos

VNR **VAN NOSTRAND REINHOLD COMPANY**
NEW YORK   CINCINNATI   ATLANTA   DALLAS   SAN FRANCISCO
LONDON   TORONTO   MELBOURNE

Van Nostrand Reinhold Company Regional Offices:
New York Cincinnati Atlanta Dallas San Francisco

Van Nostrand Reinhold Company International Offices:
London Toronto Melbourne

Library of Congress Catalog Card Number: 80–12622
ISBN: 0–442–80507–1

Manufactured in the United States of America

Published by Van Nostrand Reinhold Company
135 West 50th Street, New York, N.Y. 10020

Published simultaneously in Canada by Van Nostrand Reinhold Ltd.

15 14 13 12 11 10 9 8 7 6 5 4 3 2 1

Library of Congress Cataloging in Publication Data
Jancura, Elise G   1938—
    Establishing controls and auditing
    Includes index.
    1. Electronic data processing departments—
Auditing. 2. Electronic data processing departments—
—Management. I. Boos, Robert, joint author.
II. Title.
HF5548.2.J269   658'.054   80–12622
ISBN 0–442–80507–1

Preface

This book attempts to provide the reader with a complete and realistic treatment of the topic of computer controls and computer auditing. This is done by stating the theory of computer auditing and then illustrating it with examples. The theory is the text, which appears first in each chapter; the example is a case study that uses a fictitious company: Werner Manufacturing, Inc. The case study follows the text in each chapter.

The authors consider computer auditing from the independent and internal auditor's point of view and deal with financial rather than operational auditing. The computer auditing process is divided into six parts, each of which constitutes a separate chapter.

ELISE G. JANCURA
ROBERT BOOS

Contents

ESTABLISHING CONTROLS AND AUDITING THE COMPUTERIZED ACCOUNTING SYSTEM

1
EDP Controls

Accounting is the process of identifying, evaluating, recording, and communicating financial information about an economic entity. Accounting controls may be characterized as a system of procedures designed to facilitate the proper discharge of accounting responsibilities for the protection of company assets and the creation of a satisfactory audit trail. These control procedures should document all transactions and insure that only correct and authorized data enter the accounting records. Further, once the source data is identified and recorded, proper control procedures require that the use of that data be restricted to legitimate needs of the organization. Care must be taken that any operations performed on the data are done accurately and in a time frame that will produce usable results.

These concerns for proper collection and control of data extend beyond just the accounting records. They include all of the information and records that must be collected and organized for operational control of an organization. As organizations grow in size and complexity, the process of management has come to depend less on individual communication between people and increasingly on the formalized recording, organization, and reporting of data. The process of information flow and use encompasses the entire organization, and in dealing with the question of data collection, verification, and control, it is important to recognize that the data processing department or the computer department is only one step in this process. In fact, much information flow never reaches the computer department at all but consists of communications between non-computer departments and between individuals of those departments. Further, even in those areas where the data involved does in fact move through the data processing department, it is important to keep in mind that it is usually generated outside of that department.

The American Institute of Certified Public Accountants has defined internal control as:

> The plan of organization and all of the coordinate methods and measures adopted within a business to safeguard its assets, check the accuracy and reliability of its accounting data, promote operational efficiency, and encourage adherence to prescribed managerial controls.[1]

A good system of internal control should accomplish the following objectives:

---

[1] Auditing Standards Executive Committee, *Statement on Auditing Standards No. 1: Codification of Auditing Standards & Procedures* (New York: American Institute of Certified Public Accountants, 1973), par. 320.09.

1. Provide for the detection and deletion of unauthorized or unexplained transactions from the financial records
2. Provide for the detection and prevention of erroneous processing
3. Insure the completeness and timeliness of data captured and incorporate it into the financial records
4. Provide for appropriate segregation of the functional responsibilities involved in the authorization of transactions, the record-keeping function, and the physical control or custody of the assets

The objectives and primary characteristics of internal control do not change with the method of processing and are equally applicable to both manual and computerized accounting systems.

RESPONSIBILITIES OF MANAGEMENT AND INDEPENDENT AND INTERNAL AUDITORS

Management bears the ultimate responsibility for the successful operation of an organization. It is management which has the primary responsibility for instituting control procedures to insure that all data is properly recorded, that the recording process includes proper verification procedures, that safeguards exist to prevent duplication of proper data or inclusion of extraneous data, and that proper security and classification of the data so recorded is maintained. Management is also responsible for the exercise of continuing supervision to determine that these controls are functioning as prescribed and are modified as appropriate for changes in operating conditions.

Auditing is an attest function involving objective review and evaluation of an organization's records and operations. In a *financial audit* the review and evaluation is primarily concerned with the fairness and authenticity of the records, measurements, and financial reports prepared by and for the management of an organization and for other users of the organization's financial reports. An *operational audit* is the review and evaluation of controls from a management viewpoint, considering such factors as efficiency, economy, and effectiveness of operations. An important part of this attest process is determining the adequacy of the controls in effect and the level of compliance with them, because these controls influence the accuracy and reliability of the resulting financial and operational information.

The audit function can be performed by an external independent auditor or by an internal auditor. The objective of the usual independent audit engagement is an expression of opinion on the extent to which the financial statements fairly represent the financial position of the firm and the results of its operations. The auditor states whether the examination has been made in accordance with generally accepted auditing standards and whether the financial statements are presented in accordance with generally accepted accounting principles, applied consistently from one accounting period to another.

The independent auditor's specific responsibilities regarding internal control are noted in the Second Standard of Field Work which states:

> There is to be a proper study and evaluation of the existing internal control as a basis of reliance thereon and for the determination of the resultant extent of the tests to which auditing procedures are to be restricted.[2]

Thus, an important objective of the study and evaluation of internal control for an independent auditor is to identify those elements upon which to rely in determining the nature, timing, and extent of other audit procedures.

The independent auditor's primary concerns are the financial consequences and risks caused by unacceptable and/or erroneous accounting procedures and failure to protect the organization's assets. Unless engaged for a specific, special-purpose audit, the external independent auditor is usually only incidentally concerned with questions of excessive costs, operational inefficiency (as compared to effectiveness), failure to maximize revenue, instances of unnecessary competitive disadvantages, and instances of erroneous management decisions.

The internal auditor's responsibilities include an evaluation of the accuracy and the efficiency of the record keeping and other activities of the organization. The internal audit function is a service performed by an employee of the organization for the internal use of the organization and covers all of the areas mentioned in the preceding paragraph. The techniques used by external and internal auditors are frequently the same, but their objectives and responsibilities can vary significantly.

IMPACT OF EDP ON INTERNAL CONTROL

Statement on Auditing Standards No. 1, which sets forth definitions and basic concepts for the auditor's study and evaluation of internal control and for correlation with other auditing procedures, indicates that:

> The increasing use of computers for processing accounting and other business information has introduced additional problems in reviewing and evaluating internal control for audit purposes, and closely related to the increasing use of computers is the trend toward integrating accounting information required for financial and other operating purposes into coordinated management information systems.[3]

Transactions can be recorded by manual procedures, by EDP equipment, or by a combination of the two. Transactions in a manual system are usually supported by some kind of visible record such as signed approvals, vouchers,

[2] *SAS No. 1,* par. 150.02.
[3] *SAS No. 1,* pars. 320.03 and 320.04.

and invoices. These visible records may also exist in an EDP system, but are often replaced by machine-readable forms and in some instances may disappear altogether unless adequate controls are developed to properly document the transactions. Because the transactions and the basic accounting records are usually recorded in machine-readable form in an EDP system, the data cannot be easily read without use of EDP equipment. Further, these machine-readable records might be changed without leaving any evidence of alteration. Detection of unauthorized changes is more difficult in magnetic recording media.

The audit trail may also be substantially altered in an EDP system. The documentary evidence of controls in a manual system such as signatures, time stamps, date stamps, initials, and intermediate hard-copy documents may no longer exist. Some provision must be made in the EDP system to deliberately provide a usable audit trail.

Computers can perform complex calculations and logical operations with great speed and reliability involving large masses of data. In many instances a computer can perform all the procedures and calculations that previously had been performed by many different people in a manual system. Because of this new concentration of duties, traditional controls based on the separation of duties can be weakened or destroyed. Compensating controls must be developed to replace those eliminated by the computer.

Computer hardware is inherently very reliable. Computer programs process data consistently, so if programs have been carefully prepared and controlled, there will be consistent processing accuracy. On the other hand, if the computer programs contain errors or are not controlled, processing results may be consistently in error. Computer systems may incorporate numerous control procedures that are not economically feasible in manual systems to help insure proper processing. The use of self-checking digits, consistency checks, and other edit checks are facilitated by the processing abilities of computer systems.

NATURE OF EDP CONTROLS

There are two basic types of internal controls in an EDP environment:

1. *General controls,* which are primarily environmental and span most or all of the accounting applications
2. *Application controls,* which relate specifically to each accounting application

General controls are applied to most or all of the accounting applications processed by an EDP system. Typically their purpose is not directed to any one application but to all applications in general. Effective general controls provide the proper environment for good accounting control. These general controls gain in importance as more control procedures are centralized into the EDP organization.

The effectiveness of many application controls can be significantly impaired without good general controls. For example, in an EDP system where programmed controls are greatly relied on to test and validate transactions for processing, the effectiveness of these programmed controls can be impaired without general control procedures to regulate access and changes to computer programs. If general control within the EDP organization is weak or absent, application controls performed outside the EDP organization should be evaluated to determine if they satisfy the accounting control objectives, since the internal control review encompasses the total system.

General controls encompass the following areas:

1. Plan of organization and operation of the EDP activity
2. Procedures for documenting, reviewing, testing and approving systems or programs and changes thereto (discussed in Chapter 2)
3. Controls built into the equipment by the manufacturer (commonly referred to as "hardware controls")
4. Controls over access to equipment and data files
5. Other data and procedural controls affecting overall EDP operations [4]

Application controls relate to the specific control requirements of individual accounting applications. They are concentrated upon the verification and testing of data and those processing procedures designed to record, classify, and summarize authorized transactions and to update the master files. The application controls depend to a large extent on the existence of adequate general controls. Individual programmed tests of transactions and other accounting data can be ineffectual if the general controls do not provide adequate protection for the program libraries and prevent unauthorized access and changes to the program or unauthorized access to the data.

The tasks of verifying and controlling data generally involve the activities of capturing source data, accurately transcribing non-machine-readable data, and guarding against any subsequent loss or distortion as the data is subjected to the many different manipulations, summaries, and transformations performed upon it in the course of normal processing operations. A variety of techniques, some manual and some computerized, are employed to insure the accuracy of the data used and thus to enhance the value of the information produced for use by management.

Application controls are often categorized as *input controls, processing controls,* and *output controls.* Input controls provide reasonable assurance that data received for processing by EDP have been properly authorized,

[4] Auditing Standards Executive Committee, *Statement on Auditing Standards No. 3: The Effects of EDP on the Auditor's Study & Evaluation of Internal Control* (New York: American Institute of Certified Public Accountants, 1974), par. 7.

converted into machine-sensible form, and identified. These controls also include techniques to assure that data (including data transmitted over communication lines) have not been lost, suppressed, added, duplicated, or otherwise improperly changed. They include controls that relate to rejection, correction, and resubmission of data that was initially incorrect.

Processing controls should provide reasonable assurance that data processing procedures have been performed as intended for the particular application. These controls should insure that all transactions are processed as authorized, that no authorized transactions are omitted, and that no unauthorized transactions are added. The output controls should assure the accuracy of processing results and insure that only authorized personnel receive the output.

Application control procedures can be performed by user departments, groups independent of both the user departments and the EDP organization, supervisory personnel in the EDP department, organizationally separate data control groups, computer operators, or other personnel. Since many application control procedures can be performed outside the EDP department, control weaknesses within the department may be mitigated by control strengths outside the department. On the other hand, control strengths within the department may be compromised by control weaknesses outside the EDP department. Where significant individual or collective weaknesses in application controls exist, the audit impact of these weaknesses on the nature, timing, and extent of other auditing procedures must be determined in order to obtain reasonable assurance that no material, undetected errors or irregularities have occurred.

GENERAL CONTROLS

Plan of organization. The data processing department does not create information, nor does it act as the end user. It is only a processing facility that makes it possible for user departments to increase the efficiency of recording and processing data generated by those departments and to maximize the use or benefit derived from this information. The source or user departments have responsibility for proper authorization of data and in many instances for verifying the accuracy of source data.

EDP should be separated from source and user departments and should have no incompatible functions within the company. For example, the functions of initiating and authorizing transactions, recording transactions, and maintaining custody of assets should all be segregated. Since the EDP department is heavily involved in the recording (processing) of transactions, it should not initiate or authorize them. Except for the computer hardware itself and the other equipment and supplies of the EDP department, it should not be charged with the custody of assets.

Employees who initiate transactions, especially master file changes, can perpetrate errors or irregularities unless there is third-party control or review. The ability to conceal errors or irregularities is ordinarily limited by the extent to which these employees have uncontrolled access to data files or programs. For example, an employee might be able to initiate a pay rate change in a master file. If a list of all these changes is printed and independently reviewed, any unauthorized changes could be detected. An independent review of the payroll register, such as a comparison with supporting documents, might also disclose a pay rate higher than that authorized. If, however, the employee also has unrestricted access to the payroll programs, that employee could suppress the printing of the unauthorized pay change on the change list and could print a pay rate on the payroll register different from that used to calculate gross pay. The responsibilities of initiating, processing, and reviewing transactions should therefore be organizationally segregated.

If possible, an independent review of transaction authorization should be made before processing. Programmed controls can be considered a form of review and, within certain limitations, may be used to test the validity of the transactions. In many cases a comparison of output with properly authorized input may prove an effective control.

Within the data processing organization itself, there should be a basic division between the *systems development function* and the *operations functions*. The systems development function is concerned with planning, designing, programming, and testing a processing system. This function will be discussed in detail in Chapter 2.

The operations functions involve the use of the hardware and processing systems (including the programs that form part of that system) to receive input data from the departments in which it originates, to process that data using approved procedures, and to deliver the output to appropriate users. Generally, the operations functions include the following activities: data control, data conversion, file control, computer operations, and program library control. Depending upon the size of the installation, these activities may be performed by the same individuals or by separate staffs.

An appropriate separation of responsibilities provides for a series of checks and balances, making fraudulent use of the accounting data more difficult and furnishing an automatic review process that can help discover unintentional errors. In a data processing installation, this means that operators who have physical access to the computer should have only controlled access to preselected files. They should not be allowed to participate in the systems design activities nor have an opportunity to make changes in operating programs through uncontrolled access to the program libraries or the program loading procedures.

The control function should be performed independently to check on the results produced by the operating procedures, using the facilities built into the system to balance the data results obtained with the control criteria supplied by the source and user departments. Although the data and file control groups have access to the data, they should not have access to the programs or to the computer equipment. Whenever possible a separate control group should be established which is responsible for receiving data from user departments, checking for proper authorization, verifying or establishing user batch controls, and returning processing results to user departments after verifying that they balance with input and EDP-generated controls.

In very small installations it may not be possible to segregate duties, and alternate or compensating controls must be instituted. In such cases, user departments must assume total responsibility for controlling input and output.

Hardware controls. Modern computer equipment is efficient and generally reliable; however, any piece of equipment is subject to occasional breakdown and malfunction, and it is important for the installation to be aware of such occurrences. All computer equipment has built into it certain checking capabilities designed to detect any condition within the machine that could cause a distortion in the data being handled by that equipment. These hardware or equipment checks have as their sole purpose the detection of malfunction within the equipment. They do not guarantee the accuracy of the data but only the accuracy of the machine operation. Hardware checks make no provision for determining whether the data fed to the equipment is correct or valid. They represent a procedural control that assures proper operation of one important segment of the processing system. Hardware checks take many forms, depending upon the physical characteristics of the individual devices involved. The auditor or other employee responsible for evaluating hardware checks should be acquainted with the specific features of the equipment in use by the organization.

Some of the hardware checks are designed to stop the system. More frequently, the hardware errors detected usually require programmed routines to process the error conditions. Most installations use standard routines written by computer manufacturers. For example, when hardware detects an error while reading magnetic tape, a standard routine backspaces the tape and attempts to read it again. These routines sometimes accumulate statistical information on the number and types of hardware errors and print them on the console typewriter. Excessive read/write errors usually indicate that either the piece of hardware involved needs servicing or that the recording medium is defective.

Quality can be reasonably assured only if the installation properly maintains the equipment. The auditors should determine if the installation adheres to the vendor's recommended maintenance schedule. If it does, the auditor will usually accept the existence of hardware controls without further investigation, unless there is reason to believe a hardware-related problem exists. If the installation does not adhere to the vendor's recommended maintenance schedule, the auditor will usually review console printouts and downtime logs to determine whether read/write errors have been significant. Good control procedures require that hardware error-correction procedures be fully specified and carefully executed. This is particularly important because improperly executed correction procedures can themselves introduce errors.

Controls over access to equipment, programs and data files. To make unauthorized changes, an individual must have access to the data or programs. To prevent these changes, there should be physical and/or computer-based controls over equipment, transaction files, master files, programs and related documentation. If possible, these files should be maintained in a computer file library under the control of a librarian independent of computer operations and programming. Weaknesses here may be mitigated by effective input and output controls, effective use of internal and external file labels, and processing duplicate control copies of programs on a surprise basis.

The physical layout of the EDP facility itself can also act as a control feature. For example, many facilities maintain computer files in the computer room and have a rigidly enforced rule that programmers, data control personnel, and other nonoperators are not allowed in the computer room.

Programmers who have access to the computer, or computer operators who have access to program documentation (source programs, program listings, and detail flowcharts) and know programming can usually circumvent programmed controls. For example, to change the company's master payroll file, an employee might need a code word. If an operator has unauthorized access to the program documentation, he could discover the necessary code word or develop a sufficient understanding of the program logic to alter the program and circumvent this control. Lack of control over program documentation occurs in many small organizations. If unauthorized program changes are not controlled, the impact on operations and therefore on the nature, timing, and extent of other auditing procedures would have to be determined.

There is still a great deal of disagreement about how much training and how much programming knowledge an operator should have. If the operator has no knowledge of the internal logic of a program, he will be unable to make modifications in the program for his own purposes. On the other hand, operators who have inadequate knowledge of the programming system frequently cannot provide appropriate responses when unusual conditions occur. In a large-scale system, unnecessary delays or errors caused by an operator's inability to respond properly can be expensive. One way to handle this situation is to provide several levels of operational skill. Most operators would have minimal program knowledge, but lead operators or supervisors would receive more extensive training. Unusual situations or problems could be handled by the lead operator who is trained to deal with them.

In some installations, copies of the programs can be in the form of punched cards, stored in appropriate filing drawers. Most installations, however, have progressed to some sort of operating system environment in which the machine-language copies of the programs are maintained in a machine-accessible library, usually stored on a disk file. Access to these programming libraries must be controlled, both in terms of execution of the programs within these libraries and in terms of any changes made to the copies of the programs that exist in the working libraries. Periodic examination of the programs stored in the working library (where programs are actually loaded and executed in the computer) is a necessity to prevent any unauthorized changes in the programs as they are executed from the specifications found in the installation's formal documentation.

Unauthorized operator intervention can have the effect of avoiding programmed controls or of otherwise altering the processing results from those for which the program was designed. Whenever possible, a written record of operator activity should be maintained. On many of today's advanced computer systems, communication between the operator and the computer system takes place through a console typewriter. Retention of a console typewriter output log should be a standard procedure, with systematic review and analysis of these logs by the operations supervisor. Rotating processing assignments among the operators is an additional control against certain unauthorized program or data changes. This is particularly effective when manual intervention is required during each processing to avoid discovery of the manipulation.

Many unauthorized changes can only be made by using the computer itself. For example, a programmer who wrote a program to increase his pay rate could suppress all signs of the change. But that program is worthless unless he can use the computer to change the master file. It is important to know how controls over programs, files, and the use of equipment interact. The console log gives a permanent record of all jobs processed by the computer. EDP management (e.g., the operations supervisor) should review this console log and compare it with production schedules; in conjunction with periodic observation of the operators, this can control the operator's adherence to prescribed procedures. The computer, if equipped with a time clock, can record the processing time for each job on the console log. The jobs and processing times can then be read by the computer operator and entered in a utilization log and any downtime caused by hardware breakdown can be entered in a trouble log. Thus all computer time is accounted for. EDP management should, therefore, include the console, utilization, and trouble logs in their review.

EDP typically generates numerous reports and documents. Some are produced on a daily basis, others monthly, quarterly, or even annually. Maintaining a schedule of reports to be produced helps insure that all are generated on a timely basis. Since numerous reports are distributed to various individuals throughout the company, procedures are needed to control the distribution. Operator instructions should specify the number of copies of each report to be produced, and schedules should indicate those who are to receive the reports.

Other data and procedural controls.   Reconstruction of computer files is necessary when, for some reason, original data in its machine-readable format is destroyed or distorted and has to be re-created. If proper thought is given to procedures for saving data in its machine-readable form, this reconstruction procedure can be greatly facilitated. If, however, when machine-readable data is destroyed the installation has to go back to original non-machine-readable forms to reconstruct that information, the process can be time-consuming. Further, transaction records that affect a given version of the master file should be saved until such time as that master file has been used as the input to another updating cycle in which a subsequent generation of the master file is produced. The procedure involves retention of several generations of the master file as well as of all of the intervening transaction files.

When a new generation has been created through an updating procedure, it becomes the input for the next processing cycle. The old generation is retained until completion of the next processing cycle to provide backup in case the current generation is damaged. After two processing cycles there will be three generations of the master file. The most recent is often referred to as the "son"; the file generation used as input to the second processing cycle is referred to as the "father"; and the generation used as input to the first processing cycle is referred to as the "grandfather." Once the son file has been successfully created, the installation no longer needs to retain the grandfather generation or the transactions processed against it for reconstruction purposes.

The grandfather-father-son retention technique is not appropriate, however, in those instances in which the updating process actually destroys the old generation of a master file because the new information is written on the same physical space previously occupied by the old generation. This *destructive updating* is frequently employed in direct-access devices. Because the previous generation of data is destroyed in the process of updating, additional precautions must be taken in this approach. The usual approach is to make periodic copies of the master file, a process referred to as *dumping the file*. All transactions used in updating the master records since the last dump should be retained for reconstruction purposes until the next dump is made. Should any erroneous updating or other damage to the master file occur, it is then possible to reconstruct the proper data by going back to the previous version and updating that with all intervening transactions.

An alternative to periodic dumping of the entire file is the technique of logging changes to the master file as updating is being performed by writing the contents of the transaction and the master record before and after the update on a logging device (frequently a reel of tape). Updating logs or periodic dumps can be made to another recording device similar to that containing the master file, they can be made to magnetic tape, or they can be printed. Making the dump to a machine-readable medium such as disk or tape can help speed the reconstruction procedure.

Good management of an installation requires that carefully planned procedures be developed to handle any error conditions or machine malfunctions that might be expected to occur in the normal course of operation. It is equally important that an installation give thought to the procedures it would follow for recovery in the event of a major breakdown of its information system, including destruction of its equipment and/or records. The need for this protection from major breakdowns is becoming more important as the information flow of organizations becomes increasingly computerized. Companies with large computerized data files representing a substantial proportion of their accounting records or companies engaged in real-time processing applications that directly affect their normal operations must consciously provide for procedures that allow recovery of data and reinstitution of service in the case of a major installation breakdown.

Although security controls do not directly affect the proper processing of transactions, their absence can contribute to a serious breakdown within the processing system, causing interruption or loss of accounting information. Access to the computer room and file library should be granted to the relatively few people with authorized business there. Access can be controlled by locking the doors of the machine room and other areas and by requiring personal identification for authorized personnel. Remote access to data files and computer facilities through the use of terminals and long distance communication lines also poses a problem. If an installation has remote terminals, every effort should be made to control physical access to the terminals and to require adequate identification of the terminal users and their right to use the terminal and to access the data files involved.

Precautions should be taken to minimize physical damage. The computer should be housed in a fire-resistant facility and the files stored in fireproof vaults and cabinets. The fire system should be heat and smoke sensitive and use a nonliquid fire-extinguishing agent. Precautions should be taken against accidental water damage. Formal emergency procedures should be well defined including hardware shutdown procedures.

A formal recovery plan should be developed and responsibility assigned for its maintenance and updating. The data files, application programs, supporting software, and operating instructions which are a part of that plan should be fully documented and stored in an offsite location.

A good recovery or contingency plan must include several elements. First, arrangements must be made to obtain, when needed, a particular hardware-software configuration. Duplicate programs and operating instructions are useless unless the company can provide the same computer configuration (including software support systems) for which these programs and instructions were designed. Since the stresses produced by an emergency situation are not conducive to very effective performance in changing operating procedures and even programs to fit different computer configurations, arrangements for alternative computers should be made well in advance, with frequent review of both the home and alternate systems. Periodic review is important, for the value of the backup plan could be severely limited should the alternate computer be changed without proper notification and without corresponding revisions of the plan. Not only must the backup computer be frequently reviewed concerning its physical configuration, but the arrangements providing for the use of that computer should also be periodically reviewed.

The environmental conditions of the alternate computer are also important. If access time is limited, this can create the same negative impact as a change in physical configuration. Thus, if arrangements have been made to use a particular system, based on the assumption that it will have shifts free during the day, and if the load in that installation has changed so that the computer now has only a few hours free a day, it is important that contingency plans be reorganized to recognize that limitation.

Second, the operating instructions for the recovery procedures must be carefully documented and stored in a safe area away from the primary installation site. These should include not only the actual computer procedures, but also the documentation of all manual procedures, such as data preparation and balancing, that are a critical part of a successful operation. Training individuals who will be involved in the recovery operations is just as essential as the documentation. Vital time can be lost and expensive errors made when personnel are expected to handle unfamiliar activities during a period of stress.

Third, the programs themselves must be copied and stored where they can be properly secured and made readily available when needed. Proper maintenance of the backup program library is as important as its original creation. At a minimum, current copies of the object programs and their related constant or table data should be stored. Additional documentation, such as source programs and diagrams, is also highly desirable once the immediate restart has been accomplished, and the secondary recovery activities, such as reestablishing normal documentation in the main installation, are begun.

Fourth, data files that are essential to continued company operation must be copied and stored in an offsite location. This task more than any other represents an ongoing, continuing effort. Each time one of these critical files is updated, the offsite backup file must also be updated. Provision must also be made for keeping backup records of the transactions that will affect the latest generation on file (or procedures for recapturing the content of those transactions). Emergency alternate procedures for collecting data from currently occurring transactions must also be activated until the main installation is again functioning normally.

Because the contingency plan is so important to the installation, and because one missing data file could cause an entire system and all of the preliminary planning to be nullified, it is essential that the contingency plan be current and executable at all times. For this reason a periodic review and audit of the proposed procedures are highly desirable. The plan of action and the facilities provided for the recovery procedure should be examined regularly. Responsibility for maintenance of the reconstruction plan should be specifically assigned to a knowledgeable employee. An adequate contingency plan helps an installation to minimize its losses and resume normal operations efficiently. It is impossible, however, to completely avoid all losses.

The installation should investigate protection and cost-recovery services provided by insurance programs. Installations usually recognize the value of their computer hardware and have it adequately insured. But they frequently fail to recognize the value of the supporting software and the data files. The cost of reconstructing destroyed files and the loss of revenue and added costs of carrying on normal business activities while the files are being reconstructed should also be recognized. After calculating the dollar value of such losses, the installation should consider obtaining adequate insurance coverage to help recover and minimize such expenses. For organizations such as service centers and time-sharing companies that supply computer time or data processing services for outsiders, such potential losses represent liabilities that must be covered by data processing liability insurance. But these losses are also recognizable expenses for the installation providing in-house service and should not be overlooked in providing for a company-wide insurance program.

APPLICATION CONTROLS—INPUT

Completeness controls.   Control totals (batch controls) are one type of completeness control. User departments should establish control totals before submitting the data to EDP for processing. Some installations, however, establish control totals in the machine room; here, some other form of control, such as prenumbered documents, should be in effect to insure that all documents are processed. If neither of these controls is used, others must be developed.

Although control totals can be taken of almost anything, some that are commonly used include: footing totals of dollar and quantity fields, record counts, and hash totals of account numbers or any other significant numerical fields such as dates. (*Hash totals* are the sum of any numeric field such as dates or account numbers which would be nonsensical in and of themselves). If any of these control totals do not agree with the manually computed totals, an error report should be generated and processing terminated until the user department or the data control group resolves the difference. This is typical with very simple systems.

In many systems today, however, processing of only the erroneous data is terminated while processing of the valid data continues. When the user department or the data control group resolves the differences (perhaps several days later), the corrected data is processed with the next batch. In these situations, it is extremely important that all rejected data be adequately controlled to insure its reentry into the system. The error report can be used to reconcile the control totals to the batch totals when the data is originally rejected, and it can be used to control reentry of the data into the system when corrected.

Programmed procedures that test for missing data within a record are another type of completeness control. Although these tests vary depending on the data being processed, they include checks for the presence of:

1. Quantities, part numbers, and unit cost data in an inventory application
2. Employee numbers, job numbers, data and hours worked in a payroll application
3. Invoice numbers, invoice dates, shipping dates, quantities and unit prices in an accounts receivable application

If any missing item is significant to the application, the entire record should be rejected from processing. Erroneous records should be noted on an error or edit listing for follow-up.

Conversion controls.   The need to convert data into a machine-usable format introduces additional considerations to the control process. Procedures must be developed to insure that the conversion process takes place without error, so that the machine-readable records reflect accurate and complete data. Furthermore, because these records are not usually intelligible to a human being without interpretation from the data processing equipment, the possibility exists that errors in the data will go undetected until a fairly long period of time has elapsed, or until the error is reflected in the final report. The delay in the detection of an error can be costly, particularly if these records are being used to control or otherwise affect the actual operation. In addition, correction becomes more difficult when undetected errors are allowed to mingle with large volumes of other transactions.

Much machine-readable data is created by a manual process, usually a keying operation, in which the operator copies the information from some previously recorded document and produces as output of this operation a machine-readable version of that document. The key-driven device used for this copying or conversion process may be physically located in the data processing department, or it may be located in the user department. These devices vary in nature from traditional keypunches, key-to-tape and key-to-disk devices (all usually located at a central data collection location) to various manually operated terminal devices such as teletype (and other typewriterlike units) and cathode ray tube (CRT) units which are usually located at the individual user sites.

Assuming that the original document is correctly and accurately recorded, control techniques for the conversion process center around comparing the contents of the machine-readable record with the contents of the source record.

Visual verification is useful in those instances where the data being recorded is to be used immediately, as is the case in real-time systems. When an operator is recording information on a terminal for immediate use in updating an installation's files, it is imperative that it be checked for accuracy at the point of recording rather than through some subsequent, more automated technique. In these circumstances the terminals should be equipped with a facility to provide automatic feedback for immediate visual checking. If the terminal has a CRT device, the information being recorded by the operator is displayed on the tube. A similar approach is the attachment of a hard-copy facility to a terminal. This is even more desirable, since it provides an audit trail record as well as an opportunity for the operator to visually check the accuracy of the data as it is being recorded.

Visual checking of the data should usually be limited to situations in which information must be used immediately. It is time–consuming, delaying the operator's ability to record subsequent information, and it is subject to the same fallibility that affects all human activities. A much more common technique for verifying the accuracy of the conversion process is a key verification of the data recorded. This technique essentially involves a duplication of the original keying procedure. The original recording operation in which the operator produces the machine-readable record is followed by a second operation in which another operator rekeys the data from the source document while the device is concurrently reading the previously produced record. The device then compares the information keyed by the operator with the information recorded in the previously recorded machine-readable document. If they agree, the document is passed through as having been properly produced. If they do not agree, the operator is notified so that the record can be corrected.

Use of a *check digit* (or self-checking number) is another common technique employed to verify the accuracy of certain fields. The check digit approach allows verification beyond mere accuracy of the conversion operation, for it checks on the validity of the number itself. If the source data is incorrectly recorded, the check digit approach identifies the error; key verification identifies only conversion errors, not errors in the input data. Check digits can be used to validate fields such as part number, customer number, or employee number, where the content of the field is not subject to change by the processing involved and where the value in the field is predictable.

A check digit can be used in a number of ways. Keypunches can be equipped with a hardware feature to handle check digits. The technique can also be easily implemented through program control in the computer. Any time a data field can appropriately use a check digit, the computer program can calculate and check for it. This can be done whenever a data record is accessed by the computer and is especially useful when original source data is being entered directly—that is, in real-time operations where an operator is keying in source data through a remote terminal.

A self-checking number is also useful where data is being entered through optical scanning techniques that read original documents. Check digits verify more than the accuracy of the conversion process—they also provide a technique for validating the contents of the fields themselves.

If instantaneous reaction to a transaction is not required, it is usually more efficient to collect a group of transactions (and make any necessary corrections) before using the data for processing. When transactions can be held for batching, control totals for a group of transactions can be calculated from the original source data. When the machine-readable records for this group of transactions are created and subsequently read by the data processing equipment, control totals from the machine-readable records can be calculated. If these control totals balance with the control totals accompanying the original source data, the assumption can be made that the conversion process has recorded the data accurately.

Authorization controls. Each application should include a procedure for authorizing input transactions. Authorization is normally evidenced by a signature or a stamp on a source document or by user department approval of a batch of documents. In systems where input is not supported by documents, authorization may be controlled by a program that checks an internal table in the computer to determine if the individual is authorized to both operate the terminal and enter that type of transaction. Terminal and user identification is then stored as part of the input transaction.

Many applications involve a large number of transactions for relatively small dollar amounts. In such cases, management may issue a general authorization for handling all transactions of a given amount or less. This is acceptable when specific authorization for each transaction is not practical. Still another alternative is to use the computer itself to perform part of the authorization function. For example, one could set up a computer system in which remittance checks to vendors would be automatically generated for purchases up to a specified limit, provided certain data are entered in the system:

- Purchase orders, once properly approved, are converted to machine-readable form (e.g., punch cards) and entered on a computerized open purchase order file (e.g., magnetic tape).
- When the ordered items are received, the warehouse enters the receipt in the computer system, identifying it by the applicable purchase order, using an onsite remote terminal.
- The computer matches the receipt to the appropriate open purchase order and deletes it from the file.
- Then the computer, accessing a vendor master file, prints a check payable to the vendor. The amount of the check depends upon the quantities actually received. After the checks are printed the computer

prints a cash disbursements journal. An alternative to this process would be to generate a computerized accounts payable file and print a voucher register. Checks would then be subsequently generated by the computer by programming it to read the accounts payable file periodically. Payables open for a specified length of time would be selected for payment and a check printed, together with a cash disbursements journal.

If input transactions are not approved before processing, control can be provided after processing by a review of the input data by personnel who have the authority to approve transactions. An alternative is review of the transaction output by either an independent group or the user department that originated the input. Still another technique is to print a list of all transactions exceeding a specified value or volume limit or individual authorization on an exception basis.

Reentry controls. In order to properly process transactions initially rejected by the input controls, the following conditions must exist:

1. Positive identification of all rejects
2. Review of the cause for rejection
3. Correction or adjustment of each rejection
4. Review and approval of the correction
5. Prompt reentry of the correction into the system at a point where it will be subject to the same input controls as the original data

Failure to exercise control over the correction procedure can be a serious weakness in a program for data control. There should be formal, carefully prescribed procedures to insure that once errors and data are discovered, corrections are effected and the corrected data is properly reintroduced into the processing activities. One of the observations an auditor should make when reviewing a client's/auditee's system of input controls is the attention paid to the error-correction process and to the assignment of responsibility for its implementation.

The processing cycle in which error correction can be accomplished will vary, depending upon the circumstances of the application and the type of processing (batch or real-time). *Batch processing* is the traditional method of recording transactions in a computerized system. Transactions are gathered into groups and held for processing, generally at specified times. It usually involves gathering transactions into predetermined batches (e.g., fifty), accumulating control totals for later comparison with computer-generated totals and converting the transactions to machine-readable form (e.g., punch cards). In a batch system there is a time lag between when the transaction occurs and when it is processed by the computer.

In contrast, *real-time processing* involves each transaction being entered for computer processing shortly after it occurs. There is a very short time lag (sometimes only a few seconds) between a transaction's occurrence and its processing by the computer, which generally means the results of that processing are immediately available to the user. *Real-time* refers to this immediate availability of results.

In a batch-oriented system the usual procedure is simply to take the corrected items and reintroduce them in the next cycle. In the real-time system, where the erroneous data may have already effected a change in the master record, the effect of the incorrect transaction on the master records must be determined. The effects of the error must then be reversed and the corrected transaction or an adjusting entry made and processed. Processing applications should have built into them, either as a routine of normal programs or as a special correction program, facilities by which properly authorized personnel can make changes in the data files when errors are discovered. Certainly any changes made to correct previous errors should be done with a thoroughly tested procedure and should always be properly logged so there is a clear record of what was done in each instance.

If the control over rejects is inadequate, the value of the control procedure that initially caused the reject is seriously weakened. Unless controls exist to detect improper reentry, transactions can be lost or incorrectly processed. If audit reliance is placed upon input controls, the effectiveness of the control procedures over the reentry of rejects is a critical factor.

APPLICATION CONTROLS—PROCESSING

Programmed controls use the computer's ability to perform logical testing operations. These procedures can either be incorporated into the processing programs or written as separate programs, generally referred to as *data editing programs*. Programmed controls are used to insure that input data is complete and accurate, that input data values are reasonable, that data accuracy is maintained throughout processing, and that proper data files are being used as input. Any errors discovered by the programmed controls or edit checks should be noted on edit reports or logs with the following information included: reason why the transaction was rejected, details of transactions that failed the tests, and the disposition of these items, that is, whether they were processed or rejected.

Reasonableness or validity checks. Although the primary responsibility for insuring the integrity of data rests with the user/initiator departments, there are some techniques that the data processing department itself can employ to check the accuracy or validity of the data. The responsibilities of the data processing group should extend whenever possible beyond mere verification of the conversion and processing procedures and should attempt to establish the accuracy of the data itself before or as it is recorded in machine-readable form and used for processing.

The employment of a check digit or self-checking number is an example of a technique that concerns itself with the accuracy of the data itself. As indicated previously, self-checking digits can be used as a conversion control. In addition, the check digit can be used as a validity check to insure that certain fields within machine records contain valid information. These check digits can be employed during the recording process or during subsequent processing techniques to insure that records being used to update master files are valid. They can be implemented by manual key-driven recording activities or in programmed procedures.

The logical consistency of individual fields within a record can be checked by a processing program designed to edit the data. This editing program can be combined with a balancing operation or, as in batch-mode processing, it may be executed independently as a separate program. In those instances where the computer itself captures the original data, it can be programmed to perform the editing function as it is recording the transaction rather than after it collects the batch of transactions to be edited. Some of the editing functions may also be incorporated in subsequent processing programs.

It is possible to predict the validity of certain classes of data for various applications. For example, if customer numbers in the accounts receivable file should not contain alphabetic data, the customer identification field in these new transactions can be tested for any alphabetic characters when transactions affecting that customer file are being edited. The existence of an alphabetic character signals something wrong with that record. It is possible that a transaction from a different kind of activity has become mixed in with the file, or it is also possible that the customer number for this particular record was incorrectly recorded and somehow escaped the verification procedures associated with the conversion process.

The field containing an action code has certain predefined acceptable actions for a given application. Thus, that field can be edited to make sure it contains only codes that are acceptable or recognizable by a subsequent processing program. Other fields that contain blanks, negative amounts, alphabetic data, or information that exceeds certain values can also be recognized as being inconsistent with data acceptable for a particular application. Frequently, it is not possible to predict what a particular value should be in a field, but it is possible to predict maximum and minimum values. For example, when editing the data records that reflect hours worked in a payroll application, it is quite possible to recognize potential errors in the hours-worked field if the number of hours recorded exceeds a logical maximum for a week or if an employee receiving sick pay receives credit for hours worked during the same time period.

When using a given transaction to effect an updating operation against the master file, it is possible to use certain information recorded in the master file to further verify the transaction before using it for updating purposes. For example, if the employee master records that contain year-to-date earnings also contain a skills inventory indicating the number of hours the employee has worked, it is possible to verify the job code and the transaction record against the skills inventory recorded for that employee. A transaction record directing payment for a job code or compensation rate for which the employee is unqualified can thus be identified and printed out on an exception report for special review by the payroll department.

Sometimes none of the verification procedures in effect will detect an error in a transaction record. It is quite possible to record a valid customer number that happens to be the number for another customer and is incorrect for this particular transaction. But some other tests of logical consistency can be used. For example, if a transaction indicates receipt of cash from a customer whose balance due is zero, this can be an indication that the transaction somehow was recorded with the wrong customer number or that, in fact, there could be an error by the customer and an overpayment. In any event, such a condition can be printed out on an exception report and brought to the attention of the accounts receivable department. It is much more desirable to verify that a customer has overpaid than to neglect to record a receipt from one customer by giving credit to another. It should also be noted that this type of error would not be detected by batch controls.

Maintaining data accuracy.   Once input data has been recorded and every possible effort has been made to insure its accuracy, additional control techniques will be directed at insuring that this data is properly processed to produce accurate and useful reports. Responsibility for controlling the use and movement of data within the organization is shared by the user/initiator and data processing groups. Since data must be frequently transferred from one group to another (including transfers to and from the data processing department) and is therefore subject to many processing steps, procedures must be implemented to insure that no data is lost or distorted by subsequent manipulation.

One technique that is helpful in accounting for data items is the use of serial numbers whenever they are appropriate. Serial numbers can be printed or stamped on source documents or can be generated by the computer as it produces identifiable items of information. One example of a computer-generated serial number is a check number or invoice number assigned by the computer as it processes these documents. Another is a computer-generated transaction number attached to each transaction accepted in a real-time environment. Serial numbers can be used to check for missing data before, during, and after processing. If documents are transferred between groups, the sender can prepare a control document such as a batch control ticket, a transmittal form, or a routing slip. Serial numbers can be used for identification and control of batches as well as individual documents. If the serial numbers are recorded in machine-readable form (e.g., punched into checks in card form or into a field and a transaction record being logged on tape or disk), the computer itself can be used efficiently to search for missing items.

Two other techniques that can be used to guard against the possibility of losing or distorting data during processing are the use of record counts and control totals. These controls have already been discussed as aids in controlling the accuracy of the conversion process, but they are also useful tools for controlling the movement and processing of data during subsequent processing operations. The use of control totals and record counts is primarily useful in a batch processing environment, but they can also be applied in a real-time environment. The use of these control totals will differ in a real-time environment from that in a batch processing environment. The purpose of various processing controls and data controls is, first, to prevent erroneous data from producing incorrect results and to prevent loss and distortion of data through processing errors, and second, to facilitate correction of errors when errors are discovered. Because the batch totals can be calculated and used before the data is actually used to update master records, the batch controls in a batch processing environment allow both goals to be accomplished. This is not possible in a real-time environment because, by definition, in a real-time environment transactions are processed immediately as they occur. It is possible, however, to make good use of control totals in a real-time environment to accomplish the second objective of error control—that is, to facilitate correction and recognition of errors when they occur.

As individual transactions occur and are used to update master records in a real-time environment, a log can be maintained of all those transactions as they are recorded. At the end of the day, hour, or some other appropriate period of time, the total of all of these transactions can be used as a control total to indicate the net change and the balance of a given item over the period of time. The old balance at the time the correction procedure was started and the summary of the net change in the log can be compared with the net balance currently existing in the master records, or the control total of all transactions during the period can be compared against some external total. Any discrepancy would indicate a possible error in the handling of transactions.

Transaction logs can result from a logging operation in real–time systems or can be produced in a batch-mode application as a part of the control total balancing operation. Transaction logs are listings which serve multiple purposes. They can be used as a control and balancing tool; they can be used as an aid in reconstruction if necessary; and they can also aid the auditor without additional expense to the installation, since transaction logs can serve as excellent audit trails.

Input of proper data files.   Each installation should have predetermined procedures for physically identifying and handling data files. With punched cards, identifying different transaction types is frequently accomplished by cards of different color, with varying corner cuts, or with various markings. The process of identifying files becomes more difficult when the files are recorded on magnetic media such as tape or disks, since individual storage units in these media are not distinguishable to the human eye.

The use of carefully created and applied external labels, containing appropriate identification of the data on the tape reel or disk pack, makes physical identification and control of the volumes easier and more reliable.

Because there is room for human error in the use of these visual external labels, many installations also use internal, machine-readable records called header and trailer labels. These header and trailer labels are used to protect the magnetic files by insuring that "live" or actual files are not prematurely destroyed and that proper input files are used.

A *header label* is an identification record at the beginning of each file; a *trailer label* is a control record written at the end of each file. Depending on the type of equipment used and the operating system, header and trailer labels may be written and read by system or application software. Figure 1–1 shows examples of standard magnetic tape labels (DOS/VS).

Magnetic tape also employs another manual technique to protect data

A. One single file, on one single volume:

| VOLUME LABEL SET | FILE HEADER LABEL GROUP | T M | DATA BLOCKS OF FILE A | T M | FILE TRAILER LABEL GROUP | T M | T M |

B. Multi volume file:

All volumes except last one (EOV labels)

| VOLUME LABEL SET | FILE HEADER LABEL GROUP | T M | FILE SECTION OF FILE A | T M | FILE TRAILER LABEL GROUP | T M | T M |

Last volume (EOF labels).:

| VOLUME LABEL SET | FILE HEADER LABEL GROUP | T M | LAST SECTION OF FILE A | T M | FILE TRAILER LABEL GROUP | T M | T M |

C. Multi file volume :

| VOLUME LABEL SET | FILE HEADER LABEL GROUP | T M | FILE A | T M | FILE TRAILER LABEL GROUP | T M | FILE HEADER LABEL GROUP | T M | FILE B | T M |

Figure 1–1. Header and Trailer Labels.

Reprinted by permission from: DOS/VS Data Management Guide © 1973 International Business Machines Corporation, p. 68.

recorded on tapes from accidental destruction. This technique involves the use of a device called a *file protect ring*. The file protect ring is a plastic ring which can be inserted in a mounted reel of tape. It depresses a trigger on the tape drive and engages the writing mechanism of the tape drive. When the file protect ring is missing from a reel of tape mounted on a tape drive, the trigger is not depressed and the tape drive is inhibited from writing. When data that is to be retained for some period of time is written on a reel of tape, the usual operational procedure is to remove the ring from the reel. Thus, the absence of a file protect ring in a reel prevents destruction of the data on that reel if the reel is accidentally mounted on an output drive.

If an incorrect file is input to a processing run or a nonscratch file is mounted to record an output file, label-checking procedures should issue a warning message to the operator. In a generalized label-checking routine the operator can override the warning message. Good control procedures should include a review of the console log to verify that the operator has not over-ridden a warning message. When an operator has ignored such a message, an explanation should be formally recorded describing the reason for the variance. The decision to ignore label messages should be reserved to some senior person in an installation who has both the experience and necessary information to determine whether such a message should be ignored. The consequence of ignoring label warnings could be destruction of data pre-maturely or use of incorrect data as an input file.

Application software can be used to create additional labels which meet the user's unique needs. A common example is the placement of control totals in trailer labels. The objective is to enable the user to write an application program that reads a tape and accumulates certain totals from fields in each record and then compares those totals in a trailer label. The totals in the trailer label were created when the tape was written, that is, when it was created as output from processing an application program.

How header and trailer labels are created and read varies. For example, in IBM System/370 OS, trailer labels created by system software can contain control totals; in System 360/DOS, trailer labels with control totals are created by application software. In OS, this is handled through the job control.

APPLICATION CONTROLS—OUTPUT

Output control functions can be performed by the user department, a separate control group, or the computer itself. Output controls should insure that output data is complete and reasonable, that output reports are distributed only to authorized persons, and that machine-readable output is properly identified. It is also important to remember that output not only consists of reports pro-duced for user departments but also of newly produced data or master files which will be used as input for subsequent processing runs.

Many of the program techniques applied to input data can also be applied to the results of processing. Programs can be developed to test the reasonableness of the results of processing by comparing them with predetermined limits or with flexible limits described by decision rules incorporated in the program. Another technique that can be implemented through programming is the development of control totals that can be balanced against input controls and that can also be used to test the consistency of results. Original input controls such as record counts, control totals, and hash totals can be carried throughout the processing to serve in the verification of processing results. Those performing the reconciliation should be independent of both the department originating the information (the source department) and the EDP department. Where the overall reconciliation is done by the computer, a reconciliation report should be generated for the user department or control group to examine. The user department should review the reasonableness of all the computer's calculations. Lists of master file revisions should be carefully reviewed because incorrect changes and such items as incorrect pay rates and selling prices or uncontrolled changes in credit limits can negate the results of otherwise well-controlled and supervised processing.

For each application, those persons receiving printed reports should be clearly identified. The number of output copies produced should be closely controlled, particularly for those reports containing highly confidential information. In addition to the expected output, error listings and exception reports should be carefully distributed to those individuals having responsibility for the correction of errors or irregularities. A production schedule is one way to provide control over distribution of output reports by allowing recipients to anticipate when such reports should be received and to take corrective action when they are not.

After processing is completed, master files and supporting transaction files should be stored in controlled areas which are protected from physical damage and from unauthorized access. If the installation is relatively large, an independent librarian may control all access to the installation's files. These files should be identified both internally (header and trailer labels) and externally (visible labels). Earlier generations of each file (the grandfather-father-son approach in tape files or a file dump for disk files) should be maintained and stored in the library in case they are needed to reconstruct lost or damaged current files.

WERNER MANUFACTURING, INC.—CASE STUDY

The use and effect of a system of internal control, including both general and application controls, is illustrated by the following description of the system at Werner Manufacturing, Inc.

WERNER MANUFACTURING, INC.

Our review of computer internal control and auditing will use a case study of a very large manufacturer of aircraft engines: Werner Manufacturing, Inc. Werner produces both for special orders and for inventory; special–order business is four times that of standard items from inventory.

Werner's main plant and manufacturing offices (including its computer center) are in Cleveland, but there are three subsidiary plants/sales offices in New York, Houston and Los Angeles. CRT terminals are used at each of these locations to enter production, sales and shipping information; they communicate with the Cleveland data center over leased telephone lines.

This portion of the case study describes Werner's computer situation in general terms and then provides a detailed description of the sales, accounts receivable and cash receipts accounting system, before and after computerization.

Werner's annual EDP budget is approximately $740,500 (Table 1–1).

Its EDP organization chart is shown in Figure 1–2 (number of persons in brackets). Tables 1–2 and 1–3 describe Werner's hardware and software resources.

Figures 1–3 and 1–4 show schematic layouts of Werner's computer hardware and the data processing department at the Cleveland office.

SALES, ACCOUNTS RECEIVABLE AND CASH RECEIPTS SYSTEM

Read the two flowcharts (Figures 1–5 and 1–6) that describe the sales, accounts receivable and cash receipts system in its computerized and precomputerized forms. The roman numerals in circles refer to information in Tables 1–4 and 1–5. The references there describe the internal controls that are or should be present in the system, that is, the application controls. They also refer to the differences one should note in the manual and computerized versions of

Table 1–1. Annual EDP Budget—Werner Manufacturing, Inc.

ITEM	CLEVELAND DATA CENTER	REMOTE LOCATIONS	TOTAL
Hardware	$215,000	$6,000	$221,000
Personnel	445,000	—	445,000
Software	8,500	—	8,500
EDP teleprocessing	10,000	—	10,000
Supplies	26,750	—	26,750
Overhead	21,250	—	21,250
Maintenance	8,000	—	8,000
Total	$734,500	$6,000	$740,500

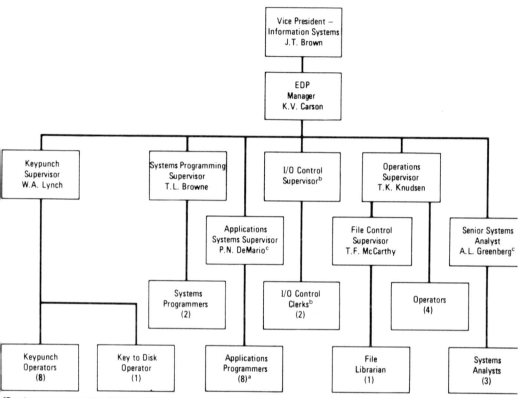

Figure 1–2.   EDP Organization Chart—Werner Manufacturing, Inc.

the system. The general or environmental controls, which so strongly affect the application controls, are discussed below.

For purposes of our illustration, we will assume there are no sales returns, and master file changes (e.g., adding and deleting customers) are carried out through separate processing, not illustrated here.

GENERAL CONTROLS

This section is a review of the general controls Werner has installed. Werner's organization chart (Figure 1–2) shows how the following data processing functions are organizationally separated:

- Systems programming
- Applications programming
- Operations
- Data preparation, (keypunching, keyverification and keying to disk)

- File control
- Input/output (I/O) control (proposed: will presumably be set up in about six months)
- Systems analysis

Table 1–2. Hardware Resources—Werner Manufacturing, Inc.

	CLEVELAND DATA CENTER			REMOTE LOCATIONS		
EQUIPMENT	MFR.	MODEL	QTY.	MFR.	MODEL	QTY.
Central processor	IBM	S/370-145	1	—	—	—
Main memory size	Multi-vendor	1 million bytes [a]	—	—	—	—
Magnetic tape, tracks and density	IBM	3420, 9 track 6250 BPI [b]	7	—	—	—
Disk	IBM	3340	16	—	—	—
Card reader	IBM	3505	1	—	—	—
Card punch	IBM	3525	1	—	—	—
Printer	IBM	3211	2	—	—	—
Terminals	IBM	3275 (CRT)	1	IBM	3275 (CRT)	3
Keypunch	IBM	129	10 [c]	—	—	—
Communications	IBM	3270 Information Display System	1	IBM	3270 Information Display System	1
Key-to-disk data entry	IBM	3760 Dual-Key Entry Station	1	—	—	—

[a] A byte is a unit of computer storage.
[b] BPI means bytes per inch and refers to the amount of data that can be stored on magnetic tape.
[c] One machine is in the computer room.

Table 1–3. Software Resources—Werner Manufacturing, Inc.

	CLEVELAND DATA CENTER		REMOTE LOCATIONS	
LANGUAGE/SYSTEM	MFR.	DESCRIPTION	MFR.	DESCRIPTION
Programming language	IBM	ANS COBOL	—	—
	IBM	FORTRAN IV	—	—
	IBM	BAL	—	—
Operating system	IBM	OS	—	—
Teleprocessing	IBM	SNA: VTAM [a] for 3270	IBM	SNA: VTAM for 3270
Other	Standard IBM card, tape and disk utilities, including SORT, MERGE, and DITTO. Standard IBM library maintenance utilities.			

[a] Systems Network Architecture (SNA) is an integrated structure of equipment and programs designed by IBM to efficiently manage and control teleprocessing systems.

Separation of duties is a basic tenet of internal control in both manual and computerized accounting systems. The discussion which follows deals with the six areas, describing how they operate and interact with each other and with general and application controls to form an internal control "system."

Systems programming. An *operating system* is a group of programs that controls all resources attached to the central processing unit (CPU), manages application programs in process and provides other supporting functions. Werner's operating system is called OS. Although the operating system is supplied by the hardware manufacturer (in this case, IBM) to direct the computer's activities, the user still has the ability to tailor it to his particular needs. This tailoring takes place because the user wants to maximize his computer resources by getting the most power for the least cost. "Power" in this sense describes the things the computer can do, while "cost" refers to the space taken up by the operating system in main and auxiliary storage and the possible reduction in throughput. The more things the operating system can do, the more space it will take up, and this could reduce throughput. If the operating system limits the space available for data and applications programs, this may force the user to either add storage to operate the way he wants to or reduce the size of his application programs and/or data files. Adding storage is generally the less expensive alternative.

Assume that the full OS operating system supplied by IBM enables the user to write and execute programs in ANS COBOL, FORTRAN IV, BASIC, RPG, PL/1 and BAL (Basic Assembler Language). But the user (e.g., Werner) may only intend to write programs in ANS COBOL, FORTRAN IV and BAL. Since the basic operating system contains compiler and assembler programs to translate programs written in each of these languages into object language (which the computer can execute), the size of the operating system can be reduced if the compiler programs for RPG, PL/1 and BASIC are deleted.

Many other options are available. Werner is using teleprocessing, so it elected to retain those programs in the operating system needed to communicate with the terminals at the New York, Houston, and Los Angeles locations. If it did not have teleprocessing, those programs could have been deleted.

Tailoring can take place at three stages:

1. When the various parts of the basic operating system are selected and linked together to form a new operating system
2. When certain portions of the existing operating system are modified to meet changing conditions
3. When completely new programs are written and added to the operating system because the programs supplied by the manufacturer do not meet the user's needs

CLEVELAND DATA CENTER

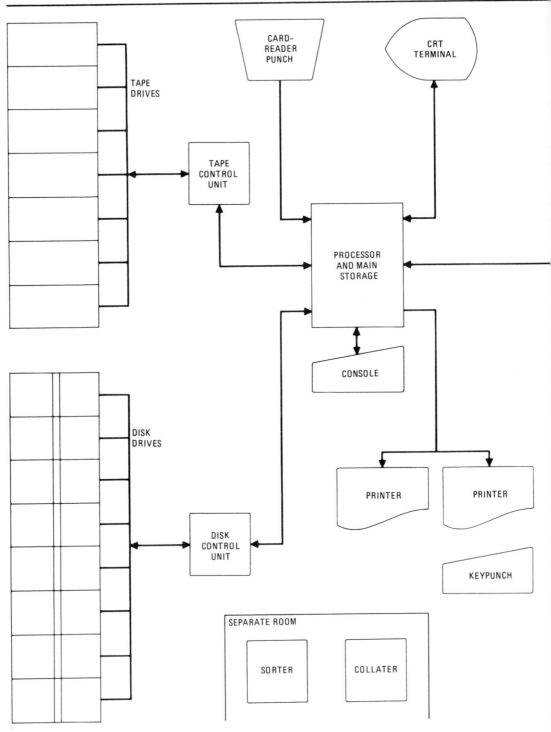

Figure 1–3.   Computer Hardware—Werner Manufacturing, Inc.

Remote Locations: New York, Houston and Los Angeles

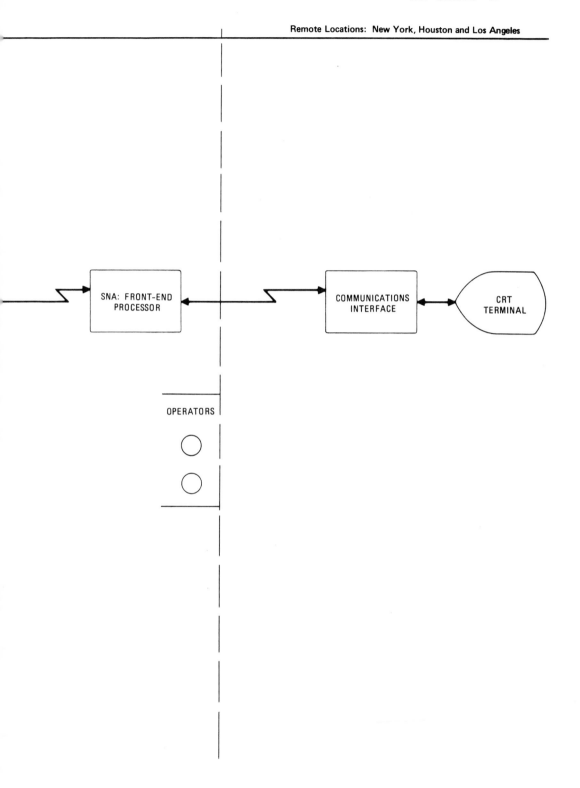

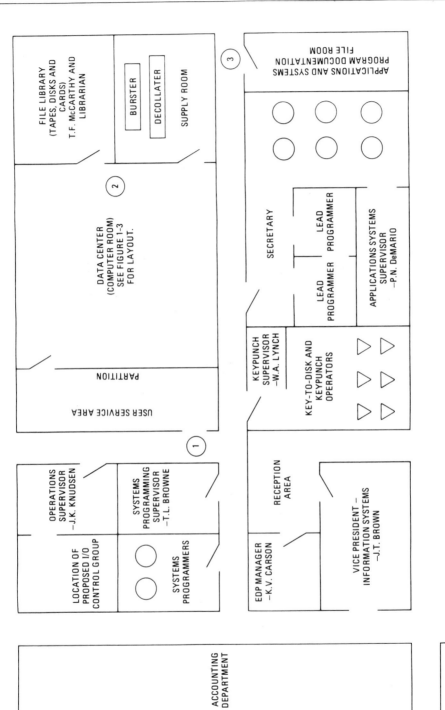

Figure 1-4. Data Processing Department Layout—Cleveland Office—Werner Manufacturing, Inc.

32

When this tailoring takes place, a new operating system is created. Computer specialists call this a SYSGEN, an acronym for System Generation. The people in a user's organization who are responsible for this tailoring, that is, for planning, generating, maintaining, extending and controlling the use of the operating system to improve the installation's overall productivity, are called *systems programmers*.

Werner has three systems programmers, T. L. Browne, the systems programming supervisor, and two under his supervision. Browne and one of the programmers handle enhancements of the operating system; the other programmer is responsible for setting up the *job control language* (JCL): commands which tell the operating system how to process the various applications or jobs, such as processing sales, accounts receivable and cash receipts transactions. Because of the relatively small systems programming group (Werner plans to hire two more programmers), Browne and his two programmers frequently perform each other's jobs.

Werner is acutely conscious of the fact that systems programmers' activities must be closely supervised; Browne keeps a close check on them, requiring that (1) they maintain careful, detailed logs of how they spend their time and (2) all their work be fully documented and presented to him for review *before* any changes are made to the operating system or new JCL implemented. This control is necessary because the systems programmers' potential for damage to the installation is very great. They have computer expertise, and their activities span the *entire* system. This places them in a unique position to affect all phases of computer operations. In general, close supervision is the most effective form of control, aside from the basic integrity of the vast majority of systems programmers. Some firms identify a third group, called *maintenance programmers*. These are responsible for correcting detected errors in applications programs that have been declared operational and implementing the vendor's latest software revisions. At Werner, the applications and systems programmers handle these functions.

Applications programming and systems analysis. Applications programs interact with the operating system to enable the computer to perform its daily "production function." The file inquiry procedures in Werner's sales, accounts receivable, and cash receipts system are performed under the control of an applications program, as are those which update the master files for completed sales (shipments) and cash receipts.

Applications programs are written by programmers who are in a good position to damage their employer's operations. They may do this by writing incorrect and/or inefficient programs, or by inserting special instructions in well-written programs that will cause them to carry out and/or conceal frauds. Although the employer cannot ignore the possibility of fraud, the greatest threat is posed by incorrect or inefficient programs.

To guard against these possibilities, Werner has instituted a number of

Operation	Personnel	Sales Office

1. Customer order is received, and, via CRT terminal, is compared with the customer accounts receivable file (on direct-access storage device) to determine if credit limit will be exceeded or if customer has been put on a cash basis.

   Note: The customer accounts receivable file contains:
   - Open invoices
   - Unapplied cash receipts
   - Credit limit
   - Customer account number
   - Customer address
   - Code for special delivery and/or billing instructions.

   If a sale exceeds the credit limit or if the customer if not allowed credit, it is held pending written approval by the credit manager or is rejected.

   SALES CLERK

2. If the order is accepted, quantities are compared with the inventory file for that location. If an insufficient quantity is available, the other locations' files are queried. Sales orders are filed by number.

   SALES CLERK

3. If a sufficient quantity is not on hand, the item is backordered and a notice sent to the customer; a copy of the backorder is sent to sales for filing by estimated availability date.

   COMPUTER OPERATOR

4. The backorder status is recorded in the inventory file. When stock is replenished, the computer prints a replenishment notice and sends it to the sales office. The sales office may then reenter it as a new order, starting at operation no. 1 above. After the decision is made to order or not, the replenishment notice is filed by date and the related back order notice is removed from its file.

   COMPUTER OPERATOR

NOTE: File Symbols: D = Date
N = Numerical Sequence
S = Shipment Date

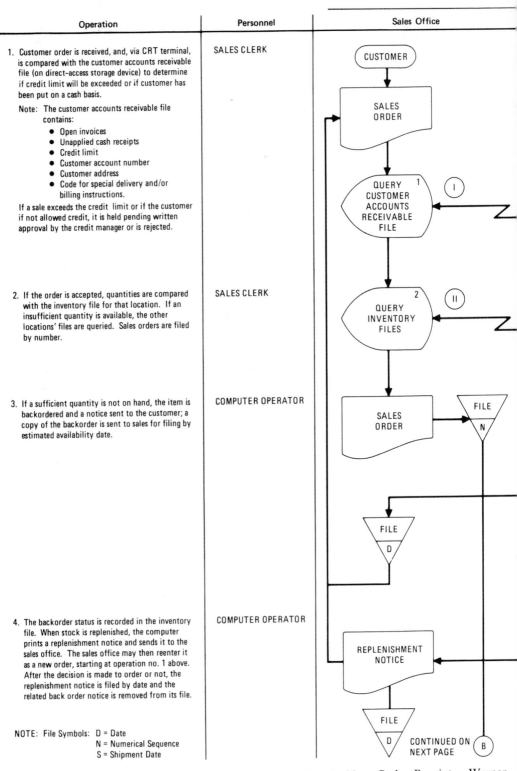

Figure 1–5. Computerized Sales, Accounts Receivable, Cash Receipts—Werner Manufacturing, Inc.

Data Processing Dept.

Sales Office

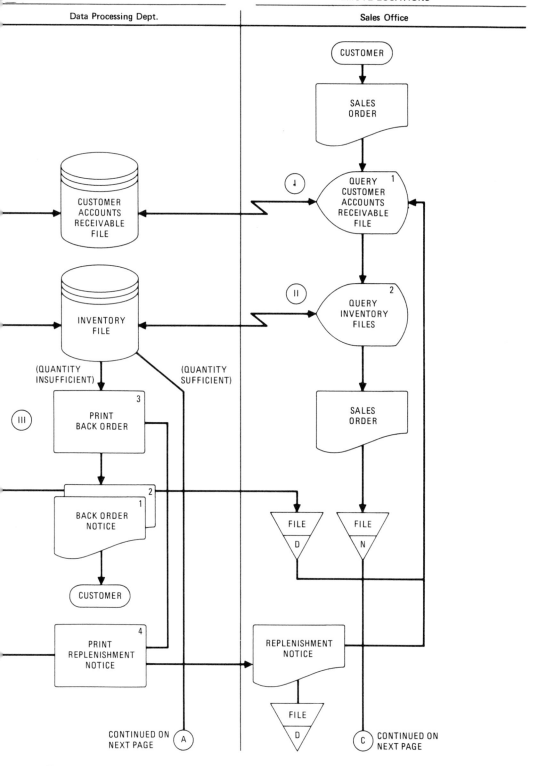

CONTINUED ON
NEXT PAGE (A)

CONTINUED ON
(C) NEXT PAGE

Operation	Personnel	Sales Office

CLEVELAND

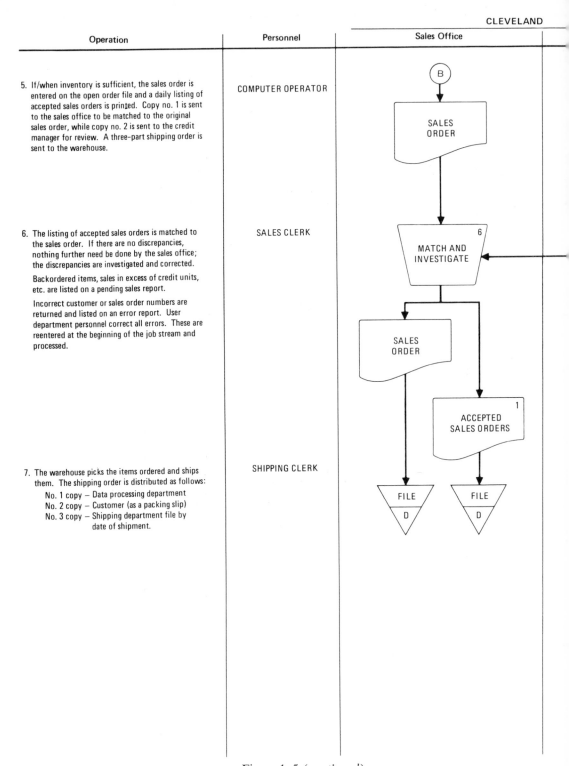

5. If/when inventory is sufficient, the sales order is entered on the open order file and a daily listing of accepted sales orders is printed. Copy no. 1 is sent to the sales office to be matched to the original sales order, while copy no. 2 is sent to the credit manager for review. A three-part shipping order is sent to the warehouse.

COMPUTER OPERATOR

6. The listing of accepted sales orders is matched to the sales order. If there are no discrepancies, nothing further need be done by the sales office; the discrepancies are investigated and corrected.

Backordered items, sales in excess of credit units, etc. are listed on a pending sales report.

Incorrect customer or sales order numbers are returned and listed on an error report. User department personnel correct all errors. These are reentered at the beginning of the job stream and processed.

SALES CLERK

7. The warehouse picks the items ordered and ships them. The shipping order is distributed as follows:

No. 1 copy — Data processing department
No. 2 copy — Customer (as a packing slip)
No. 3 copy — Shipping department file by
            date of shipment.

SHIPPING CLERK

Figure 1–5 (*continued*)

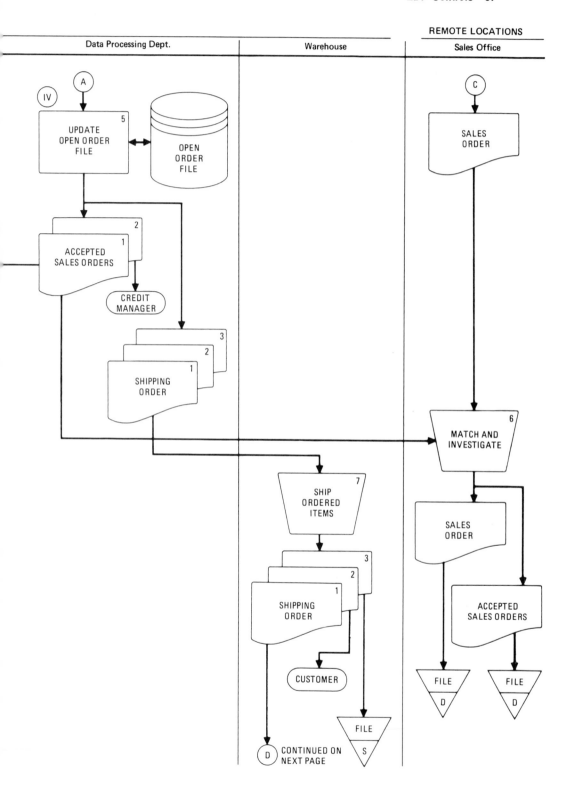

REMOTE LOCATIONS

Data Processing Dept.   Warehouse   Sales Office

IV

A

UPDATE OPEN ORDER FILE   5

OPEN ORDER FILE

C

SALES ORDER

ACCEPTED SALES ORDERS   1   2

CREDIT MANAGER

SHIPPING ORDER   1   2   3

MATCH AND INVESTIGATE   6

SHIP ORDERED ITEMS   7

SALES ORDER

SHIPPING ORDER   1   2   3

ACCEPTED SALES ORDERS

CUSTOMER

FILE   D   FILE   D

FILE   S

D   CONTINUED ON NEXT PAGE

Operation	Personnel	Data Processing Dept.

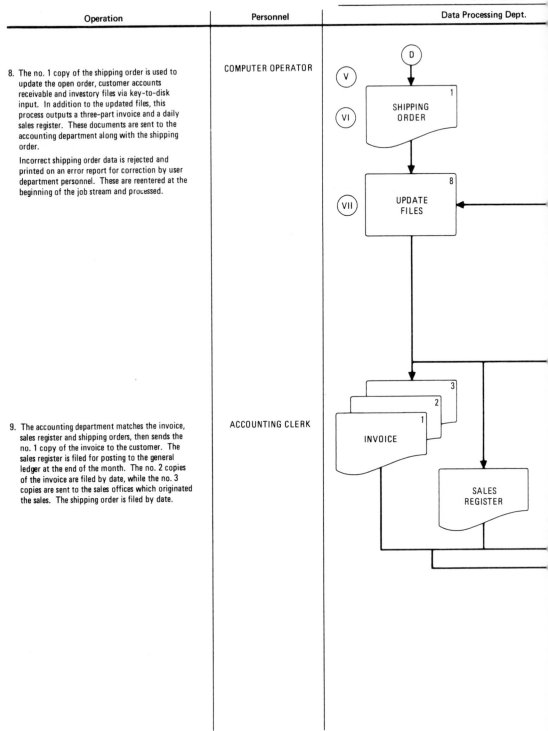

8. The no. 1 copy of the shipping order is used to update the open order, customer accounts receivable and inventory files via key-to-disk input. In addition to the updated files, this process outputs a three-part invoice and a daily sales register. These documents are sent to the accounting department along with the shipping order.

   Incorrect shipping order data is rejected and printed on an error report for correction by user department personnel. These are reentered at the beginning of the job stream and processed.

9. The accounting department matches the invoice, sales register and shipping orders, then sends the no. 1 copy of the invoice to the customer. The sales register is filed for posting to the general ledger at the end of the month. The no. 2 copies of the invoice are filed by date, while the no. 3 copies are sent to the sales offices which originated the sales. The shipping order is filed by date.

Figure 1–5 (*continued*)

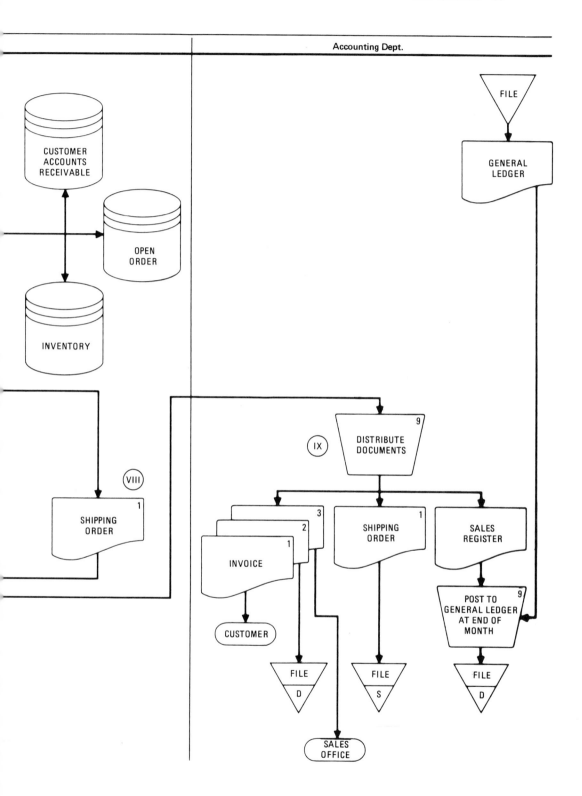

Operation	Personnel	CLEVELAND Mail Room
10. Opens mail and verifies that check amount equals amount on remittance advice. Stamps checks with restrictive endorsement. Prepares a remittance advice (from the check information) if none is included or if check amount does not match invoice amount.	MAIL CLERK	
11. Runs an adding machine tape of all checks, thus establishing initial control over cash receipts. Sends adding machine tape directly to the accounting manager.	MAIL CLERK	
12. Prepares deposit ticket in duplicate and sends checks and deposit ticket to the bank. The bank sends the duplicate copy of the validated deposit ticket to the accounting manager.	ACCOUNTING CLERK	
13. Prepares a cash receipts listing from the information on the remittance advices. The listing is prepared in duplicate and is used to input data to the computer.	ACCOUNTING CLERK	
14. Compares initial control tape to duplicate deposit ticket and cash receipts listing. Initials the no. 2 copy of the cash receipts listing, attaches the duplicate deposit ticket, adding machine tape and remittance advices, and files by date. Sends the no. 1 copy of the cash receipts listing to the keypunch section of the data processing department.	ACCCOUNTING MANAGER	

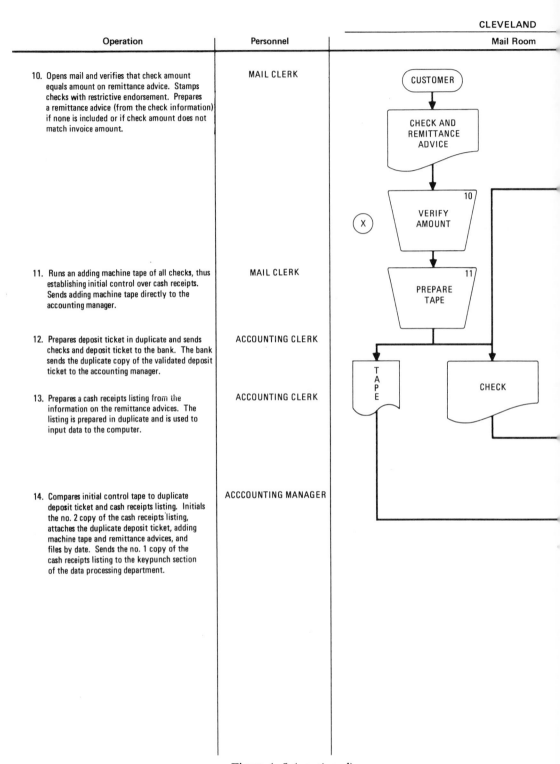

Figure 1–5 (*continued*)

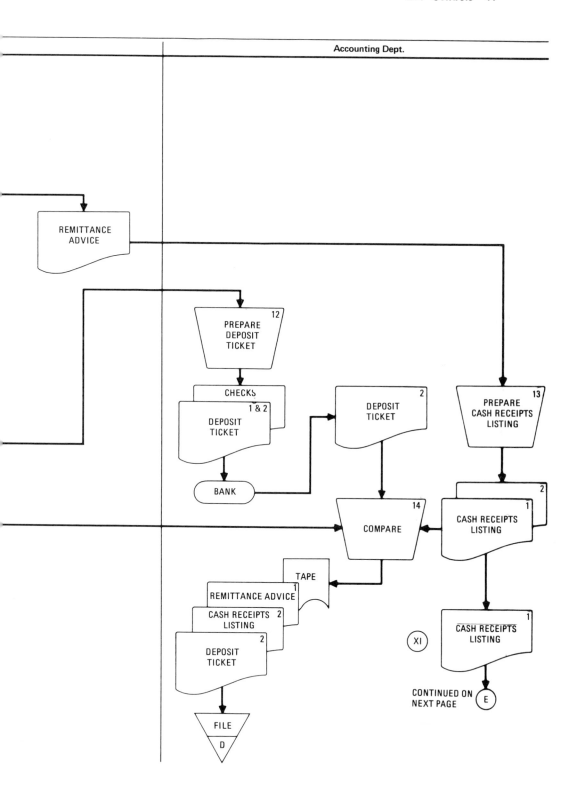

		CLEVELAND
Operation	Personnel	Data Processing Dept.

15. Keypunches and keyverifies cash receipts information from the cash receipts listing.

KEYPUNCH OPERATORS

E

(XII) CASH RECEIPTS LISTING

(XIII) KEYPUNCH AND KEYVERIFY 15

16. Runs a listing of cards punched and compares total with cash receipts listing. Corrects errors. Files cash receipts and transaction listing by date.

COMPUTER OPERATOR

(XIV) RUN TOTALS AND COMPARE 16

17. Runs program to process cash receipts and update customer accounts receivable file. A daily cash receipts book is printed, filed, and posted to the general ledger at the end of the month. The punched cards are kept until the monthly customer accounts receivable trial balance is reconciled to the general ledger; then they are destroyed.

COMPUTER OPERATOR

TRANSACTION LISTING

CASH RECEIPTS LISTING

FILE

D

18. Reconciles bank statement monthly. Bank statements are received unopened directly from the mail clerk.

CONTROLLER'S SECRETARY

19. Approves bank reconciliation and files by date.

CONTROLLER

Figure 1–5 (*continued*)

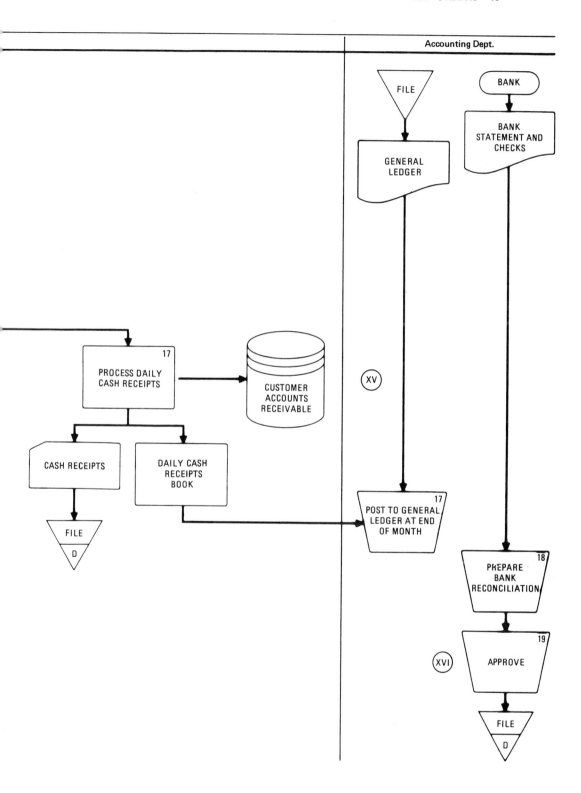

Operation	Personnel	CLEVELAND Data Processing Dept.

20. At the end of every month, prepares a listing of open orders, an aged trial balance of customer accounts receivable and a classified inventory trial balance. Copies are distributed.
Open order listing:
  No. 1 – Vice-President–Sales
  No. 2 – Credit manager
  No. 3 – Controller*
Customer accounts receivable
Trial balance-aged:
  No. 1 – Vice President – Sales
  No. 2 – Credit manager
  No. 3 – Controller*
 	
Inventory trial balance:
  No. 1 – Vice Pres. – Mfg.
  No. 2 – Purchasing Mgr.
  No. 3 – Controller*
 	
*Controller uses as input to monthly accounting report.
	COMPUTER OPERATOR	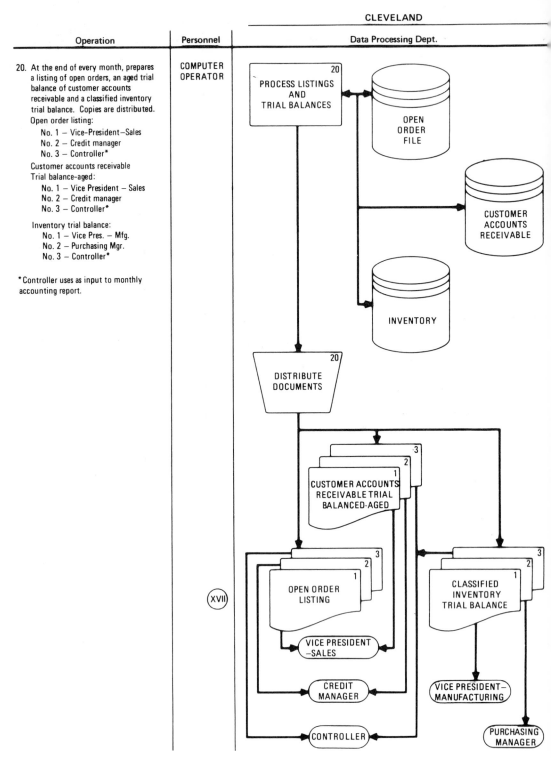

Figure 1–5 (*continued*)

organizational control procedures and safeguards. One important safeguard is unrelated to the programmer's writing even a single line of a program: Werner hires only competent EDP professionals (at all levels) and pays them appropriately. Also, a clear career path is designed for each person through periodic performance evaluation and career counselling sessions. Recognizing that a professional's skills and knowledge must be kept current not only to insure high-quality job performance but to maintain morale, Werner encourages its EDP professionals to attend conferences and formal training programs.

All work done by an applications programmer, even that which involves modifying existing applications, is part of a *development project*. Development projects are described in some detail in Chapter 2. In this section, only those aspects of development projects that illustrate Werner's organizational controls will be presented.

When a project has been approved, the senior systems analyst, A. L. Greenberg, reviews it with the development team and assigns it to one of her systems analysts. The analyst prepares the detailed specifications (system flowcharts, input/output requirements and formats, processing requirements, and so on) and discusses them with the applications system supervisor, P. N. DeMario. DeMario chooses staff members for a programming team by considering the language and programming skills required.

Werner is following the *top-down structured programming approach* to systems development. This enables the analyst to break the development project down into a series of short, logical program modules. These modules are then coded by programming teams (see Werner's organization chart) according to a schedule which enables each module to be tested independently before being accepted.

The programming team works with the systems analyst to be certain they fully understand the project's requirements and objectives. As modules are programmed, they are exchanged so that one team member checks another's work. Then the code is keypunched and processed against test files. All code must bear DeMario's written approval and a job identification code before keypunching will accept it.

As modules are compiled and run against test data files, they are reviewed by DeMario and the systems analyst to be sure that the code accomplishes the project's objectives in the most cost-effective way and conforms to Werner's data processing standards and conventions. DeMario and the systems analyst keep a project evaluation and review technique (PERT) chart of the project's progress to be certain it is on schedule.

Programmers must prepare weekly time reports by project; time spent on nonproject work (e.g., training or personal development projects) must be accounted for on this report.

While the program is being keypunched, the analyst and programmers prepare test files for "debugging" the program. Since test files must cover all

Operation	Personnel	CLEVELAND – Sales Office
1. Customer order is received and a four-part, pre-numbered sales order is prepared.	SALES CLERK NO. 1	
2. Sales orders are distributed: No. 4 copy is filed by number in the sales office where it originated. Nos. 1-3 are sent to Cleveland.	SALES CLERK NO. 1	
3. Prices sales orders.	SALES CLERK NO. 2	
4. Approves sales orders.	SALES SUPERVISOR AND CREDIT MANAGER	

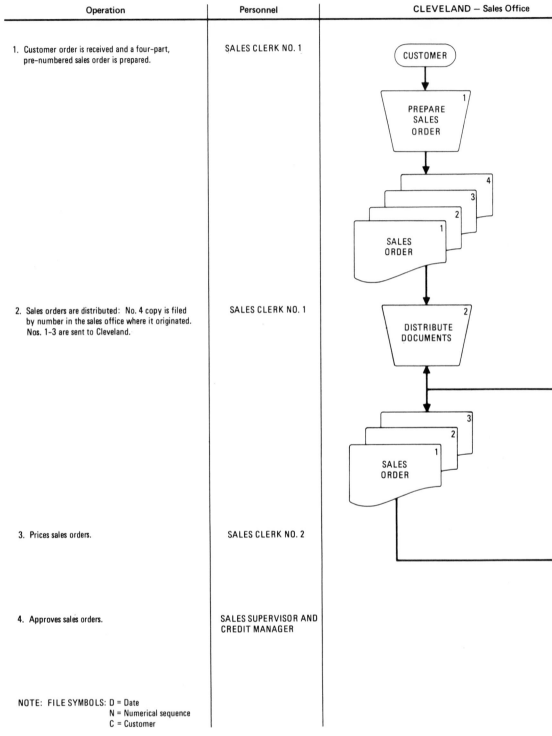

NOTE: FILE SYMBOLS: D = Date
                    N = Numerical sequence
                    C = Customer

Figure 1–6.   Manual Sales, Accounts Receivable, Cash Receipts—Werner Manufacturing, Inc.

Remote Locations — Sales Office

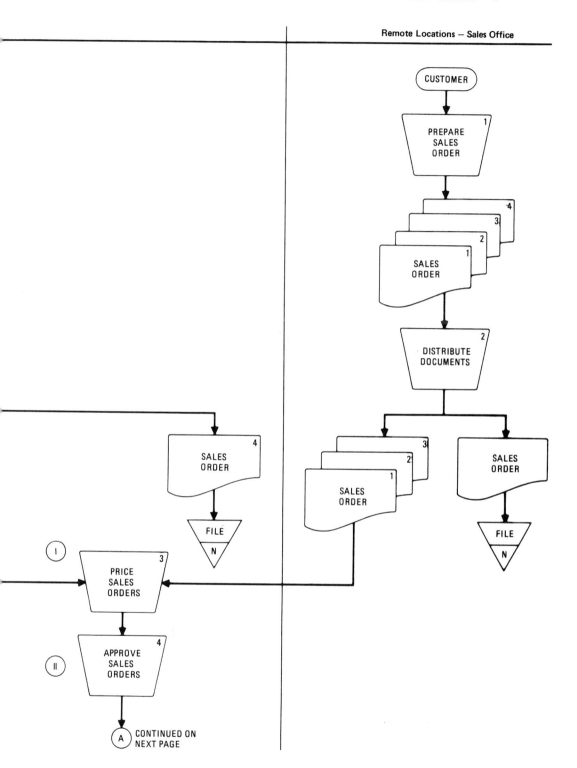

Operation	Personnel	CLEVELAND — Sales Office

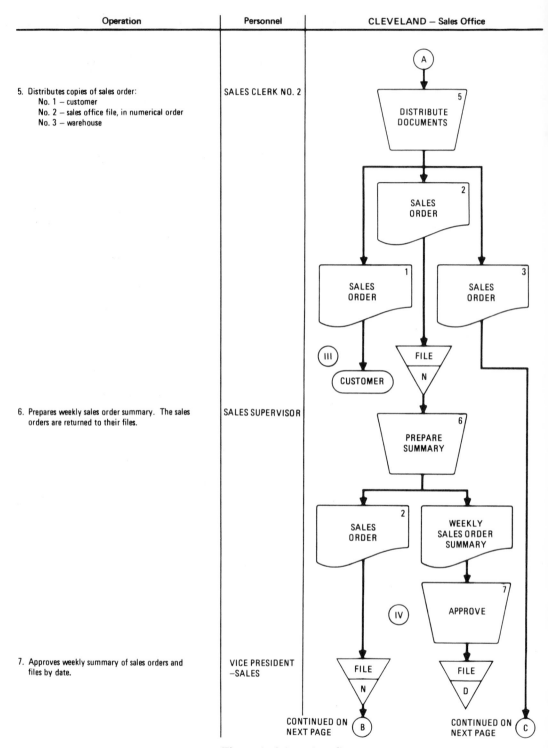

5. Distributes copies of sales order:
   No. 1 — customer
   No. 2 — sales office file, in numerical order
   No. 3 — warehouse

   SALES CLERK NO. 2

6. Prepares weekly sales order summary. The sales orders are returned to their files.

   SALES SUPERVISOR

7. Approves weekly summary of sales orders and files by date.

   VICE PRESIDENT —SALES

Figure 1–6 (*continued*)

possible conditions being built into the program, their design must be reviewed and approved by the user group to be certain they are realistic. Sometimes existing test files will suffice for this purpose. As with programs, test files must bear the proper approvals and codes before keypunching will accept them. All test files are kept by the file librarian and must bear appropriate titles and the required approvals (DeMario and the systems analyst) and project numbers before they are accepted.

Under no circumstances is a programmer permitted to process his own programs, even for debugging purposes. Test programs are submitted to the operators with a job sheet. The job sheet contains proper written approvals, codes and instructions for processing against test files (which the operator gets from the file librarian by submitting the job sheet). After the test run is completed, the program deck and output is sent to the programmer who submitted it; the test file is sent back to the library.

All changes to the program and test file must be keypunched and are subjected to the same controls described above. When programs are completed and approved by the project team, they are cataloged in the appropriate system library by the systems programmers. Controls over program documentation, run manuals, and so on are described under Standards and Documentation below.

Operations.   Werner's data processing department operates on two shifts a day; weekend work is scheduled only when the workload gets too heavy. Although this means the computer they have is presently underutilized, they feel it provides for the expansion that is planned.

Two operators are present during each shift; one is designated as being in charge during that shift. The in-charge operators are more experienced and have some scheduling responsibilities. Under no circumstances are operators permitted to initiate transactions or master file changes or to correct errors. Any errors found in processing are sent back to the user group for correction and processing.

Some of Werner's operators intend to learn programming and transfer to that function. When this happens, they will be transferred to the applications programming area before going to programming school. From a control point of view, Werner feels it is potentially dangerous to have persons with programming knowledge in the operations area, particularly if they are computer operators. For this reason, there is a strictly enforced policy of not permitting transfers from programming to operations.

Werner's concern for the physical security of its computer room is illustrated by the construction of a User Service Area (see ① on Figure 1–4), designed to enable users to submit "non-production jobs" and converse with operators without going into the computer room itself.

Processing which takes place on a regular basis is performed by programs which are cataloged in the system's libraries and which are called into the

Operation	Personnel	CLEVELAND — Sales Office
8. Prepares six–part sales invoice. Files sales orders in numerical sequence.	SALES CLERK NO. 2	
9. Checks extensions and additions on sales invoices.	SALES CLERK NO. 1	
10. Distributes sales invoice copies No. 1 — customer No. 2 — accounts receivable clerk No. 3 — accounting dept. clerk no. 1 No. 4 — filed by date No. 5 — inventory control clerk Nos. 6 & 7 — warehouse	SALES CLERK NO. 1	
11. Picks and ships the ordered items from no. 3 copy of the sales order. Compares with nos. 6 and 7 of sales invoice. No. 6 copy of the sales invoice is sent to the customer with the goods. The no. 3 copy of the sales order is filed by date and the no. 7 copy of the sales invoice is sent to the accounts receivable clerk. NOTE: For out-of-stock items, documents are simply held at warehouse until replenished.	SHIPPING CLERK	

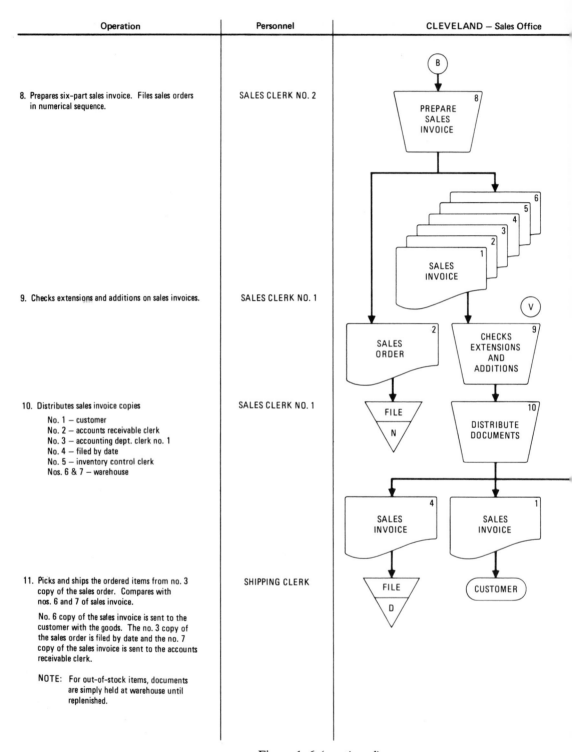

Figure 1–6 (*continued*)

CLEVELAND & REMOTE LOCATIONS — Warehouses

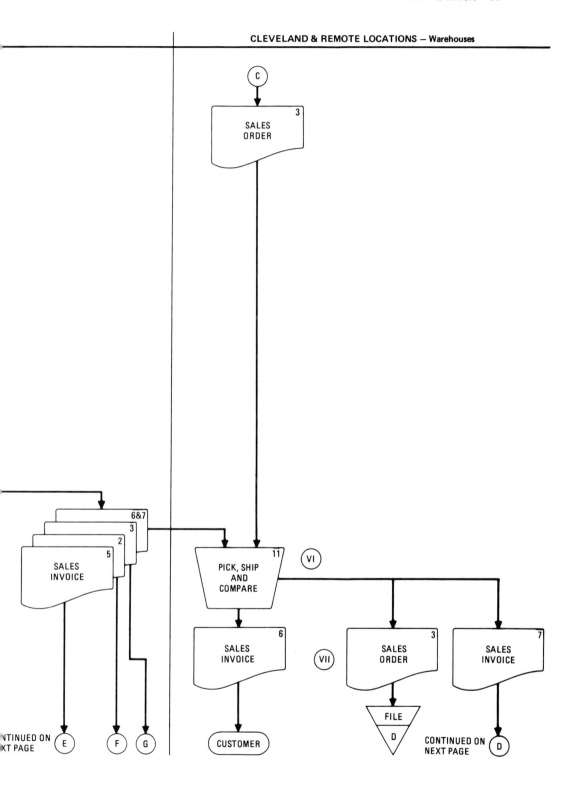

CONTINUED ON NEXT PAGE

CUSTOMER

FILE

D

CONTINUED ON NEXT PAGE

computer's main storage by the appropriate JCL statements. This processing is referred to as *production* (jobs). In contrast, special jobs (many of which are run once or at best sporadically) and test runs of programs under development are processed by the user's completing a job sheet and submitting it with a deck of punched source programs (COBOL, FORTRAN or BAL) and JCL statements. Occasionally, the data for an application will be a punched card file, in which case it too will be submitted with the job sheet and program deck. Generally, however, test files are maintained on magnetic tape or disks and are kept by the tape librarian.

The decks and job sheets are placed in a special drawer built into the glass partition which separates the users' area from the computer room. Completed jobs (e.g., printed output, programs) are placed in a file cabinet in the users' area, so that they can be picked up at any time after processing. Occasionally, a user has to discuss something with one of the operators, such as the status of a job submitted earlier, why a job did not process properly, what JCL to use in a given circumstance, and so on. These discussions are held over telephones placed in the users' area; since the partition is glass, user and operator can see each other while talking.

While the door to the users' area is always open when the computer is in operation (it is locked when the computer room is closed), the door to the computer room itself is locked and may be opened only by a magnetically-coded plastic card issued to authorized persons. At Werner, these authorized persons are:

- K. V. Carson — EDP Manager
- T. K. Knudson — Operations Supervisor
- T. F. McCarthy — File Control Supervisor
- The four operators and the file librarian

When an employee leaves the company, the card is returned and that identification code is cancelled. If a card is not accepted by the sensing device for admission to the computer room, it holds the card and activates an alarm bell.

Since the computer room is a source of pride to Werner, tours are organized from time to time. These are under the close supervision of Carson or Knudsen.

Werner uses a HALON fire extinguisher system in the computer room. This system emits a gas from the computer room ceiling, which extinguishes the fire. It does not, however, harm the personnel or data processing equipment.

File control. The file library (see ② on Figure 1–4) is kept locked whenever the librarians are out of it; no one except the librarians are allowed there. Files are kept under the control of the file librarian, who issues them only upon receiving proper authorization. For production and non-production jobs, the system works as follows:

- Production — The file librarian has a copy of the week's production schedule which shows what files are to be processed, when, and by which operator. This is especially critical when confidential files such as the payroll or personnel master files are to be processed. If an operator requests a file at a time contrary to what is specified on the production schedule, the librarian will demand the written approval of the operations supervisor.
- Non-Production — Files will be accepted and released by the librarian only if a properly approved job sheet is submitted by the operators.

The file library consists of both tapes and disks. Some disk files are issued every morning, for example, the on-line order entry and certain inventory and accounts receivable files. The system residence device (SYSRES) and library disk packs are also kept in the library when not in use. Occasionally, a card file will be kept in the library.

There are two librarians, one of whom is the file control supervisor, McCarthy. Since the computer is only operated on two shifts, it is possible to have a librarian present at all times. Werner expects to go to a third shift in about a year. To avoid having to hire a third librarian, the operations supervisor is considering processing only jobs which do not involve highly sensitive data during the third shift. This will enable the librarian on the second shift to issue all files for third-shift processing at the end of the second shift and then lock the library.

All file activity is recorded in logs by the librarians. At the start of each day's processing, the library and console logs are reviewed by the operations supervisor.

To provide for reconstruction of files, Werner requires that:

- All master files and other critical files are periodically copied onto magnetic tape and stored in specially designed vaults at a private warehouse in Cleveland.
- Whenever possible, tapes of transactions since the last time the file was copied are retained. This enables the data processing area to reconstruct the most recent version of those files, starting with those in the off-premise location.

An exception to this procedure exists in the on-line order entry/sales procedure. This involves updating of back order, customer accounts receivable,

Operation	Personnel	CLEVELAND - Accounting Department

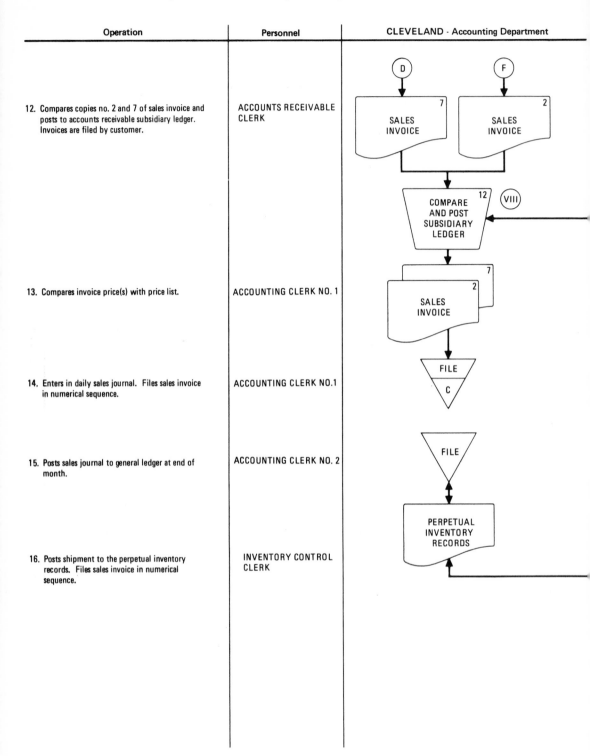

12. Compares copies no. 2 and 7 of sales invoice and posts to accounts receivable subsidiary ledger. Invoices are filed by customer. — ACCOUNTS RECEIVABLE CLERK

13. Compares invoice price(s) with price list. — ACCOUNTING CLERK NO. 1

14. Enters in daily sales journal. Files sales invoice in numerical sequence. — ACCOUNTING CLERK NO.1

15. Posts sales journal to general ledger at end of month. — ACCOUNTING CLERK NO. 2

16. Posts shipment to the perpetual inventory records. Files sales invoice in numerical sequence. — INVENTORY CONTROL CLERK

Figure 1–6 (*continued*)

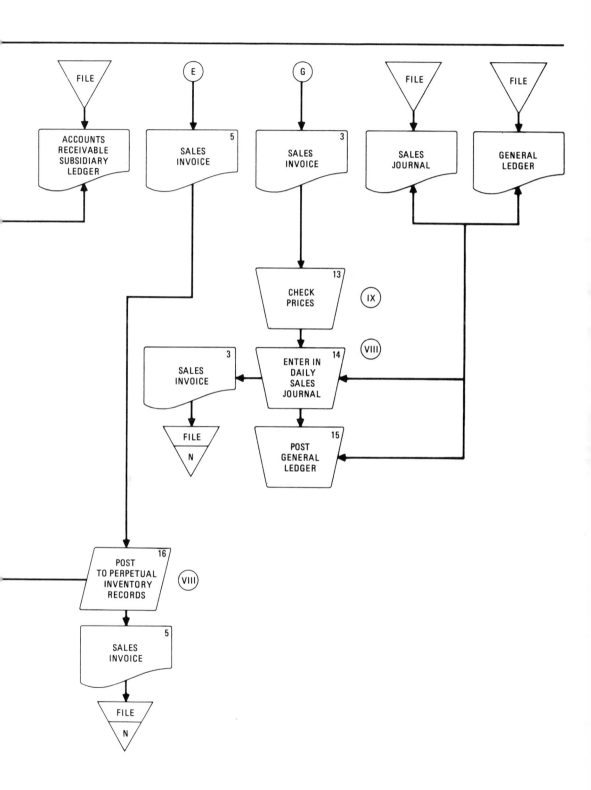

CLEVELAND

Operation	Personnel	Mail Room	

MAIL CLERK

17. Opens mail and prepares three-part listing of checks. (All receipts are by check.)

CUSTOMER

X

17
PREPARES
THREE-PART
LISTING

LISTING   3
LISTING   2
LISTING   1

CHECKS

18. Distributes listings and checks:

No. 1 — cashier with checks
No. 2 — accounts receivable clerk
No. 3 — accounting clerk no. 2

MAIL CLERK

18
DISTRIBUTE
DOCUMENTS
AND
CHECKS

19. Prepares deposit ticket in duplicate. Files no. 1 copy of listing by date. Bank returns validated no. 2 copy of deposit ticket to accounting department.

CASHIER

2
LISTING

20. Compares validated deposit ticket with no. 3 copy of cash receipts listing.

ACCOUNTING CLERK NO. 2

CONTINUED ON
NEXT PAGE   H

Figure 1–6 (*continued*)

Cashier	Accounting Dept.

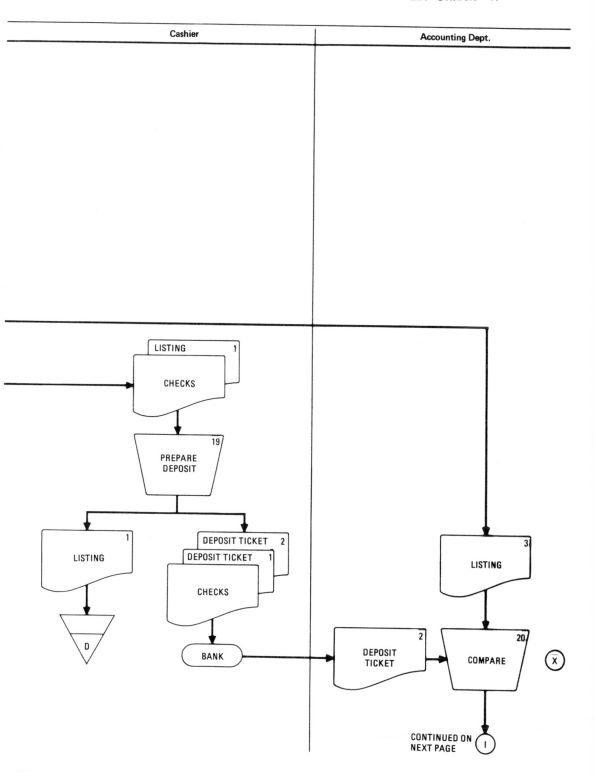

Operation	Personnel	CLEVELAND — Accounting Dept.
21. Posts the accounts receivable subsidiary ledger from no. 2 copy of the cash receipts listing. Files listing by date.	ACCOUNTS RECEIVABLE CLERK	
22. Posts the cash receipts journal. Files no. 3 copy of cash receipts listing and validated deposit ticket by date.	ACCOUNTING CLERK NO. 2	
23. Posts the cash receipts journal to the general ledger at end of month.	ACCOUNTING CLERK NO. 2	
24. At end of month, an aged trial balance is prepared and distributed to: • No. 1 — Vice-president — sales • No. 2 — Credit manager • No. 3 — Controller	ACCOUNTING CLERK NO. 2	

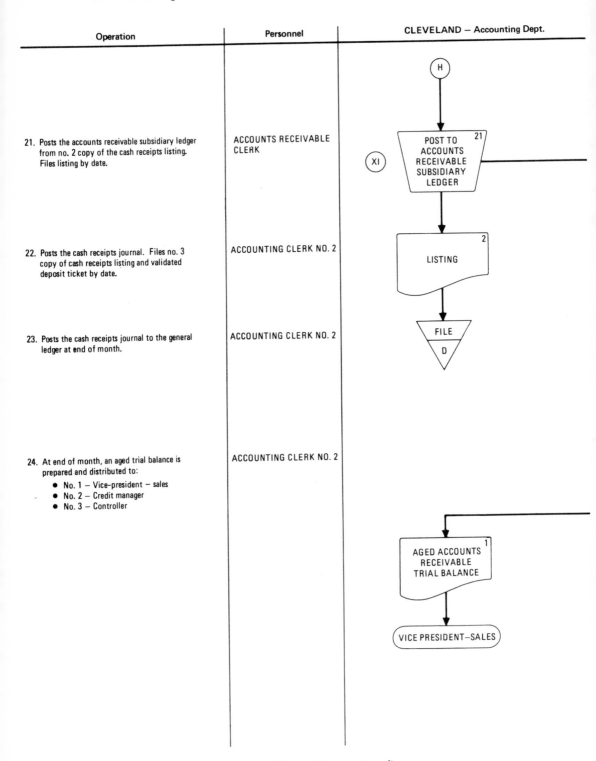

Figure 1–6 (*continued*)

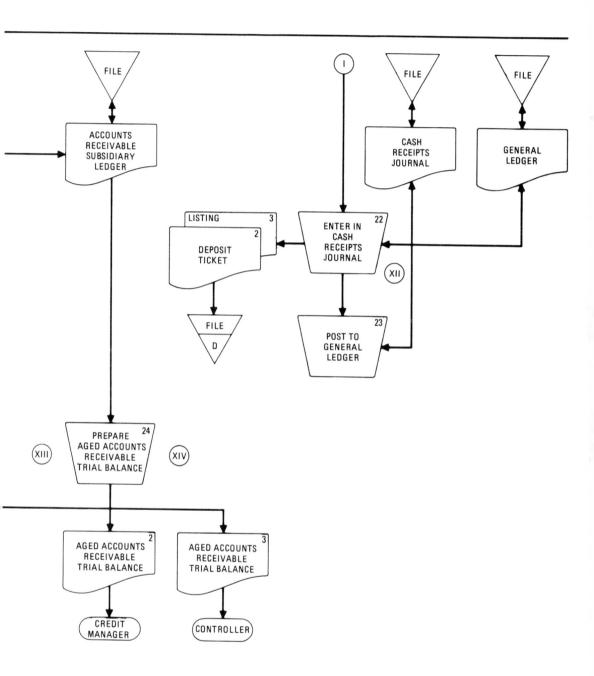

Table 1–4. Sales, Accounts Receivable, Cash Receipts—Computerized—Werner Manufacturing, Inc.

OPERATION	S	W	INTERNAL CONTROL PROCEDURES/IMPLICATIONS	AUDIT IMPLICATIONS
I. Status of the customer's account is determined before any significant processing takes place.	X		Customer accounts are checked before the orders are accepted. Credit review is therefore timely and effective.	Accounts receivable are collectible when recorded.
	X		Terminal operators must have a key to turn the terminal on and must input a valid user number and a password to gain access to the computer.	The users cannot access the central computer at Cleveland unless they possess three access mechanisms: a key to turn the terminal on, an authorized user number, and a password which must coform to passwords in the computer's files. As an additional security measure, the computer could be programmed to match a valid user number to an "answer–back code" which the terminal transmits. Thus, even a valid user number and password would not work unless transmitted by a specific terminal.
	X		Upon accessing the computer, the terminal operator must enter an additional password to use the customer file.	This additional layer of access control enables the company to restrict access to specific files once the terminal operator has "signed on" the system. Once the file has been accessed, the terminal operator is further limited in what can be done with the file, for example, read only, add data only, change data, etc.
	X		The computer maintains a log of valid and invalid access attempts and describes the transactions performed.	Enables the company to review accesses and transactions. The log also provides a hard–copy trail of transactions from each terminal and provides the auditor with a ready means of reviewing activity.

OPERATION	S	W	INTERNAL CONTROL PROCEDURES/IMPLICATIONS	AUDIT IMPLICATIONS
II. Before shipping orders are prepared, the inventory files are queried to determine if there is a sufficient quantity on hand.	X		The order process does not continue unless the order can be completed. Thus, there is no danger a back order will be erroneously treated as a sale because of the creation of sales order listings (see operation 5) and shipping orders.	Accounts receivable and sales are not overstated.
III. A printed list of back orders is given to the sales department. At the same time, the data is kept in computerized files so that a replenishment notice is printed when quantities are restored.	X		In addition to insuring that back orders will not be forgotten, this procedure keeps the shipping decision in the hands of the user (sales department) group. This avoids "automatic" shipments to accounts which may have become delinquent subsequent to the back order date or which may exceed established credit limits.	Accounts receivable and sales are not overstated; sales are not lost through failure to pursue back orders.
IV. Sales orders are sent to the sales department (for accuracy checking) and to the credit manager (for final credit approval) before the goods are shipped.	X		Although the computer is used to check credit when the order is first received, a final opportunity for a manual check is given to the credit manager before shipment. This procedure takes advantage of the exercise of human judgment by responsible company officials. It is the same with the final check performed by the sales department. Most clerical errors will be eliminated because the computer performs many functions previously done manually (e.g., pricing the orders). There is a chance, however, that an error could be made (for example, failure to update the price list in the computer files), and this procedure gives knowledgeable persons a chance to review orders for accuracy and reasonableness.	Accounts receivable and sales are properly stated.

Table 1–4. (continued)

OPERATION	S	W	INTERNAL CONTROL PROCEDURES/IMPLICATIONS	AUDIT IMPLICATIONS
V. Input is sent directly to the data entry operator for entry on key-to-disk equipment and processed.		X	A fundamental input control is missing, as the user department has no input control totals with which to check that (1) all items have been entered, (2) no unauthorized transactions have been entered, (3) transactions have been entered correctly or (4) processing has been performed correctly. Sales should prepare batch totals and match these to totals generated by the computer. This weakness is mitigated to some extent by IX below.	There is no assurance that all items shipped have been recorded, that sales and receivables are properly recorded, or that sales and related costs are properly matched.
VI. Sales orders are not processed until the goods are actually shipped.	X		The data processing department does not update the accounts receivable, open order and inventory files or print the sales documents until the sales transaction has been completed.	Accounts receivable and sales are properly stated and collectible.
VII. Input to the sales/file updating procedure is accepted as long as the sales order number is correct. Processing produces an invoice (three-part) and a sales register (for posting to the general ledger).		X	The computer is not being used to perform accuracy checks. In this case, information such as quantities shipped could be input for comparison with the details in the open order file to verify that no unauthorized changes or errors have occurred.	Accounts receivable, sales and inventory may be distorted and sales and related costs not properly matched.
VIII. Output is distributed to the accounting department by the computer operators.		X	No input/output control group exists (see V above).	Computer-produced data is not verified before being posted to the general ledger, nor is there any assurance that sensitive output is not being sent to unauthorized persons.

OPERATION	s	w	INTERNAL CONTROL PROCEDURES/IMPLICATIONS	AUDIT IMPLICATIONS
IX. Copies of invoices are sent to the originating sales location to review for errors.	X		Computer-produced sales data are sent to knowledgeable persons for review. This procedure does not completely mitigate the weaknesses in V, VII and VIII, however, because human error is still a possibility.	Processing is reviewed to see if it has produced correct results.
X. Checks are restrictively endorsed in the mail room as soon as received.	X		Minimizes the chance for irregularities in cashing checks.	Cash receipts are deposited to company accounts.
XI. Initial control tape is compared with the duplicate deposit slip and cash receipts listing.	X		Insures that all receipts are accounted for and deposited in the bank promptly.	Cash receipts are properly recorded to appropriate accounts.
XII. Input is sent directly to the keypunch operators for conversion to machine-readable format.		X	See V above and XIV, a mitigating strength, below.	Computer processing may take place using incorrect input. This may not be discovered until operation 16. In any case, the entire control procedure over computer processing of cash receipts lies within the data processing department; there is no independent check by the user group until the bank account is reconciled. (See XVI and XVII below.)
XIII. All keypunching is 100% verified by a second person.	X		Minimizes chance of keypunch errors and resulting erroneous accounting information.	Recording of sales results in proper recording of receivables and cash receipts.

63

Table 1-4. (continued)

OPERATION	S	W	INTERNAL CONTROL PROCEDURES/IMPLICATIONS	AUDIT IMPLICATIONS
XIV. A daily listing of transactions is printed and compared with the cash receipts listing.	X		Insures that all cash receipts have been input to the computer. (See, however, XII above.)	Recording of sales results in proper recording of receivables and cash receipts.
XV. Output is distributed by the computer operator.		X	There is no input/output control group. (See XII above.)	Computer-produced data is not verified before being posted to the general ledger, nor is there any assurance that sensitive output is not being sent to unauthorized persons.
XVI. A person independent of the daily recording of cash receipts and disbursements reconciles the bank account. The reconciliation is reviewed and approved by the controller.	X		This enables the controller to detect unauthorized use of company funds and bank and accounting errors.	Cash receipts are deposited to company accounts.
XVII. Trial balances of accounts receivable and inventory and a listing of open orders is sent to responsible persons for review.	X		Gives knowledgeable persons in the user groups an opportunity to review results of a month's processing for reasonableness.	Sales, accounts receivable and inventory are properly recorded; sales and related costs are properly matched.

Note: S = Internal Control Strength
W = Internal Control Weakness.

Table 1-5. Sales, Accounts Receivable, Cash Receipts—Manual—Werner Manufacturing, Inc.

OPERATION	S	W	INTERNAL CONTROL PROCEDURES/IMPLICATIONS	AUDIT IMPLICATIONS
I. After sales orders are prepared and priced, they are not reviewed by the originating salesmen for possible errors.		X	Unauthorized or incorrect sales orders could be processed.	Some sales may not be properly recorded.
II. Sales orders are approved for reasonableness by the sales supervisor and for conformity with credit limits by the credit manager.	X		The risk of incorrect sales orders and bad debt is minimized.	Accounts receivable balances are proper and collectible when recorded.
III. A confirmation of the sales order is sent to the customer.	X		Customers are given an opportunity to correct any errors in the sales order.	Sales result in the proper recording of receivables.
IV. Sales manager reviews the weekly sales summary for reasonableness.	X		A final check is made by a responsible and knowledgeable officer before invoices are prepared.	Sales result in the proper recording of receivables.
V. Sales invoices are checked by someone other than the preparer.	X		The risk of clerical error is minimized.	Sales result in the proper recording of receivables.

Table 1–5. (continued)

OPERATION	S	W	INTERNAL CONTROL PROCEDURES/IMPLICATIONS	AUDIT IMPLICATIONS
VI. Shipping clerk compares items to be shipped with the sales invoice.	X		Minimizes the risk of shipping incorrect quantities.	Sales and related costs are properly matched.
VII. Items selected for shipment are not checked by a second count.		X	Incorrect shipments may not be detected.	All items shipped may not be recorded.
VIII. Sales are not recorded until goods are shipped.	X		The accounts receivable subsidiary ledger, the perpetual inventory records and the sales journal are not posted until the documents from the shipping department are received.	Accounts receivable balances are proper and collectible when recorded; sales and related costs are properly matched.
IX. Prices are checked after sales are posted to the subsidiary ledger.	X		Any errors found must be reversed out of the subsidiary ledger, and the customer must be notified. This is a good internal control procedure, but its timing is wrong. There is the additional danger that the corrections will not be properly made.	Sales and accounts receivable are properly stated, but procedures should take place before posting to the general ledger.
X. The mail clerk prepares a three-part listing of remittances.	X		Copies of the listing are sent to the accounting department to insure that the deposit is correct. Comparison of the listing and validated deposit ticket is made by someone other than the preparer of the deposit.	Cash receipts are deposited to company accounts.

Table 1-5. (continued)

	Control	S	W	Effect
XI.	The accounts receivable subsidiary ledger is posted from the copy of the cash receipts listing which was *not* compared with the validated deposit ticket.		X	If a discrepancy in the bank deposit *is* discovered, the subsidiary ledger posting may be incorrect. This will be discovered only at the end of the month. At that time, the general ledger is posted from the cash receipts journal, created from the copy of the listing which *was* compared with the validated deposit ticket.	The subsidiary accounts receivable ledger may not reflect correct balances.
XII.	The cash receipts journal is prepared from the cash receipts listing after it is compared with the validated deposit ticket.	X		The posting source document reflects cash actually deposited.	Cash receipts are properly recorded.
XIII.	Trial balances of accounts receivable are sent to responsible and knowledgeable company officers for review.	X		Provides for a reasonableness review by persons who may be expected to note discrepancies.	Sales and accounts receivable are properly stated.
XIV.	There is no provision for a monthly review of inventory and open orders.		X	Slow-moving or obsolete items in inventory may not be discovered until it is too late to prevent a loss. Open orders may not be resolved for extended periods without investigation. This may result in cancelled orders.	Inventory may be overstated; old open orders may indicate poor control over the sales function.

Note: S = Internal Control Strength
W = Internal Control Weakness

67

open order and inventory files by terminal or key-to-disk input (see Figure 1–5) and presently produces only hard-copy logs or documentation for a record of daily transactions. When the system was installed, there was no EDP audit function and no thought was given to the timely reconstruction of these important files. The internal auditors were satisfied that the hard copy provided them with an audit trail sufficient to enable them to perform manual auditing procedures. With the hiring of two EDP auditors, however, the security and operational dangers inherent in this procedure were brought to management's attention. Werner is now investigating the possibility of inserting procedures which will generate magnetic tape or disk logs of these transactions to permit file reconstruction.

Standards and Documentation.   Werner has adopted standards for:

- Design of new systems — These require detailed specifications of user's needs, flowcharts, cost justifications, approvals, and state the format in which they are to be prepared.
- Applications   These specify the form and content of the program "run book":
  - Problem definition — general statement regarding objective or purpose of the program
  - System description — flowchart, descriptions of input and output (including reports), file and report layouts
  - Program description —narrative describing what the program does, decision tables, program flowcharts, source listings, and so on
  - Operating instructions — instructions to the computer operator, including restart and recovery, interpretation of error messages, and so on
  - Controls — narrative of controls built into the application: description and purpose

In addition, there is a detailed EDP operations manual which covers personnel policies, operating procedures, security provisions, and job descriptions.

Werner's standards and documentation will be discussed in more detail when systems development procedures are discussed in Chapter 2. At this point, their general structure is outlined above, and the following information is also relevant.

- Computer operators are not allowed to see the entire run manual, or indeed any other documentation that applies to programs. They are only concerned with the operating instructions, which are kept in an open cabinet in the computer room. A complete copy of program documentation is kept in a special file room (see ③ on Figure 1–4), to which the programming supervisors Browne and DeMario, and the senior systems analyst, Greenberg, have keys. A log is kept of all documentation borrowed by programmers and analysts.

- Although Werner's standards are clearly stated in up-to-date manuals, there is no central authority to review systems development and applications documentation to be certain those standards are being followed. It is up to those working on the project, collectively, to understand the standards, enforce them and insure that documentation is proper and complete.

I/O control group.   As points V, VIII, XII and XV on Table 1–4 bring out, the absence of an input/output control group is a recognized weakness in the system of controls. Werner's management realizes it, especially since the EDP internal auditors began stressing it in their reports, and plans to establish such a function with a supervisor and two clerks in about six months.

EDP Internal Auditors.   Eighteen months ago, Werner hired two experienced EDP auditors, one from its firm of independent auditors Brown, Johnson & Co., the other from another company's internal audit department. They report to the chief internal auditor.

The auditor hired from Brown, Johnson & Co. is a CPA who was trained in EDP to function as a computer audit specialist. His primary orientation is auditing. The other auditor is an EDP specialist, an applications programmer, who was given audit training by her former employer; her primary orientation is data processing. By hiring persons from these diverse backgrounds, Werner feels it has acquired a team which is strong in evaluating both EDP internal controls and operations. The chief internal auditor has used them as a team on all assignments to date. Some of their activities and findings are summarized below:

- Terminals located at the remote locations (New York, Houston and Los Angeles) are in a separate room and require a key to operate. Further, the operator needs a user number and password to access the computer and certain files at Cleveland. The auditors found:

  - The terminal rooms were left unlocked and unattended during the day, and the key was frequently left in the terminal.
  - Because of heavy turnover, the user number and passwords were posted on the terminal.

- Keys to the terminal rooms and the terminals themselves were not always returned when employees left the company, nor were locks, user numbers or passwords changed.

- At times, the auditors observed the computer operators at Cleveland to see whether they were following instructions and procedures. They feel the operators are well trained and follow procedures closely.

- Werner uses system management facilities (SMF) to monitor hardware utilization and to keep track of charges to the various user groups. The auditors reviewed the operations supervisor's analyses and comparisons of SMF records with elapsed time on hardware meters. In their opinion, hardware utilization is being effectively monitored; they have not audited either effectiveness or efficiency of utilization, however. They did not find satisfactory written evidence that the console and file library logs were being effectively reviewed by the operations supervisor and have recommended documentation that will provide an effective review record.

- On a surprise basis, one application was selected for processing on the backup facilities in Cleveland. The auditors were accompanied by the operations supervisor and one of the operators. Their findings were as follows:

  - While the backup facility was using almost identical equipment and software when the contract was signed (an IBM 370/145, with OS), it has since converted to a Burroughs 7700. It was impossible to process Werner's application on this computer. Even if the backup facility had not converted, it was learned that Werner instituted its data communications–oriented order entry system after the backup facility was obtained and that the backup facility never had data communications. Werner really has no backup processing capability.

- Restart and recovery operations were tested with the operations supervisor at the Cleveland data center and were found to be working satisfactorily.

- To date, the auditors have not tested whether the operating system is effectively using the available hardware controls.

- An inspection of the data center supply room disclosed that it contains prenumbered payroll and regular disbursement account checks and credit memos. Since the door is unlocked and opens onto the computer room, operators have unrestricted access to them.

- Reviews of specific applications revealed that:

  - Because there is no I/O control group, control totals are not reconciled to computer-generated totals by anyone other than the operators on an informal basis, nor are control totals compared with program-generated trailer labels.

- Header labels are checked to be certain that the correct file is being used. However, file protect rings are frequently kept in tape files which are to be used only as input to jobs.

- Inquiry disclosed there is no formal disaster-recovery plan. The disaster-recovery plan should include, but is not limited to, arrangements for backup processing capabilities.

2
Controls in Systems Design and Development

> Systems analysis and design is the analysis of present methods, applications, objectives, and all pertinent data followed by the design of improved systems using data processing equipment and techniques. The primary aim of this function is to produce the optimum solution for application needs: the most economic solution consistent with management and operating objectives, equipment capabilities, and personnel resources.[1]

The systems design and development process is the critical first step in providing an adequate system of internal control. A poorly designed system will be unable to prevent or detect intentional or unintentional errors or irregularities. A poorly designed system may make it impossible to rely on system controls, and in some cases even to use the output generated by the system.

Provision for error detection and correction procedures should be made at the time an application is designed. These detection and correction procedures may represent a mixture of manual operations and program checks, but efficiency and effectiveness require that these checking features be incorporated as part of the original development work. These procedures should be fully documented with specific instructions about how errors are to be corrected and with specific provision for reintroduction of previously erroneous data once the data has been corrected. In addition, the systems design and development process must provide for adequate user involvement so that the system produced does in fact accomplish the objectives for which it was designed.

The auditor has responsibility for reviewing and evaluating the system of internal control, which consists of a combination of manual and programmed procedures. An additional element in the system of internal control is the process by which these systems are developed, implemented, and maintained. If the development and maintenance process is inadequate, the best designed system will probably prove ineffective. The auditor, therefore, has to be concerned with evaluating this development and maintenance process, as well as evaluating the system in operation.

---

[1] *Organizing the Data Processing Installation,* IBM Manual No. C20–1622 (New York: International Business Machines Corporation, 1965), p. 5.

USER PARTICIPATION AND APPROVALS

The user must clearly define and support the objectives that a system is to accomplish. It is impossible either to develop a system or to evaluate it if the objectives against which that system is to be measured are unknown or the information about input data, required processing, and output data is not clear. Therefore, the appropriate user department personnel should be involved in systems design and testing and final approval of the completed system.

One of the controls in the systems development process that the auditor should expect is appropriate authorization of the plan and evidence of regular appraisal and supervision of the progress of the systems development project. Evidence of close supervision of the development process, such as regular progress reports, planning schedules, and management review reports, can be used by the auditor in making inferences about the effectiveness with which the development procedure was carried out and, more important, the accuracy and adequacy of the resulting system. The auditor must also determine that authorization and approval of the system were obtained not only from the systems development management, but also from the operating or user department for which the data processing system was being designed.

Internal auditors can play an important role in the establishment of good controls. Where a formal internal auditing function exists, internal auditors can help review and test new systems to determine if they include the necessary controls and if they can be audited. The internal auditor's working papers can provide valuable information about the participation of users in the definition of new systems.

In addition, the auditor can interview representatives of management, users, and EDP departments to determine whether appropriate approval procedures were observed and whether the level of user participation was adequate to insure properly defined systems. Written specifications and approvals are also excellent evidence that user departments have reviewed and approved the system and that appropriate authorization has been given.

User review and approval should be an ongoing process throughout the systems design and development activity. Appropriate management and user approval should be required of the initial design. In addition, user personnel should participate in or monitor the test and developmental stages. After a system has been fully developed and before it is placed in operation, it should receive final approval from the appropriate levels of management and user personnel. This should include examination of final test results and review of the documentation and any changes from the original design specifications.

SYSTEMS TESTING AND CONVERSION CONTROLS

The testing procedures performed in the systems development process can have a major impact on the subsequent reliability of that system, including both the manual procedures and the programmed procedures involved in the system. A definite plan should be prepared for testing the system. Testing in an organized and controlled fashion will insure more accurate results and will reduce the amount of time and effort involved. To properly test a new system, it is necessary to keep its objectives and attributes clearly in mind and to design the test procedures accordingly. The entire system should be tested, both manual and computerized portions, to be sure it functions as it was intended. Of critical importance is whether the system is providing users with the information they expected and need, whether controls are working properly, and whether the system is efficient as well as effective.

The programs which comprise the computer processing portion of the system are a prime target of the testing procedures. These may be effectively verified by the use of test data, which should be designed to test every condition (e.g., alternative processing paths, validity checks, limit tests) the programs are designed to handle. It is important to make provision for testing every possible alternative processing path that exists within the system. Furthermore, test data should also include invalid data in order to test the system's ability to recognize and segregate invalid and erroneous data.

When large volumes of data are being handled, erroneous records can slip through the normal verification and other control procedures and reach the processing runs. When constructing test data, the programmer or analyst testing the system should try to include examples of both valid and invalid data conditions. Further tests should be run with essential data missing (fields within records or even whole records) to test whether the programs can detect the absence of needed information. For sequential files, one test should include test data which is out of sequence. For files that need particular activity codes, tests should include data with codes that are incorrect as well as examples of all correct codes. Because testing is such an important part of systems development, it should receive major consideration. A thorough review of the original testing procedure can also be helpful to the auditor when considering preparation of the auditor's own test data to test a processing system.

The system testing process can be divided into phases. Two testing plans, one of two phases, another of three, will be presented. The two-phase approach will be considered first. In the first phase, sometimes called the *acceptance phase,* specially constructed test data are used to test the new programs and operating procedures alone. The special test data can be saved to test a later program revision. In the second phase, the system can be tested with actual data as it is being generated in the installation. This is sometimes called *system integration,* because this test of the new programs is conducted concurrently with continued processing of the total system. In the second phase the files are processed twice, using both the existing and the new or revised programs, and the results are compared. But the second phase should include more than just parallel tests of the new programs. It should actually be an integrated test of the whole system including all related programs and installation procedures.

The purpose of integrated system testing is to test the entire system in an actual operating environment. This can serve two purposes: to insure that the systems description and design accurately reflect the actual environment and to check that the related programs function together as a cohesive system. However, the installation should always be aware of the fact that successful runs do not necessarily guarantee a complete test, since the live data may not contain all possible types of transactions. In most processing environments there are some relatively rare combinations of data conditions that occur infrequently in the normal course of events. Unless the parallel test run should happen to occur when one of these rare combinations exists, the system will not be tested for its ability to handle such a situation. Further, in those new systems which differ substantially from the old, the results from the new system may not be completely comparable to the results of the old or original system without extensive reconciliation. However, parallel operations used in conjunction with carefully prepared test data can be an excellent control.

The three-phase approach performs unit, system and facility testing:

- In *unit testing,* the new or revised program is individually tested with test data. No other programs are involved, except perhaps to input data or receive output. The purpose is solely to determine whether the program being tested processes data as the designers intended it to.
- *System testing* is performed to see how the program performs within its own particular processing system. For example, how an order entry program performs when it is integrated into the sales, accounts receivable and cash receipts processing system. This is also known as *system integration.*
- *Facility testing* involves testing the revised system against the entire processing system, generally in *live mode* (when the system is operating during actual production). For example, the sales, accounts receivable and cash receipts system is placed in contention with all other systems. In this phase, the efficiency as well as the effectiveness of the new system is tested and evaluated.

Regardless of how the testing process is organized, inadequate or careless testing of new systems (both programs and manual procedures) represents a serious control deficiency. The most carefully designed and programmed system may have significant errors in the handling of data. Adequate system testing requires determining that a system operates in conformity with its design specification and that it satisfies the user's requirements. Thus, the auditor should investigate all available evidence to determine the extent of the testing performed. Further, it is desirable that the user department be actively involved in designing the test procedure, and that the user department also be involved in reviewing the results of testing to insure that the system will provide the desired output and that incorrect input, processing, or output will be detected. Evidence of thorough, carefully executed testing and user review and approval of procedures and results are important factors in the auditor's consideration of the adequacy of the client's/auditee's processing system.

After the completed system has been fully tested and is ready for implementation, conversion of the data files from the old media to the new system must take place. Specific responsibility should be assigned to establish the conversion procedures and adequate controls to safeguard against errors in the conversion process. Such procedures as record counts and hash and control totals should be used to reconcile the converted file back to the original file. In particularly sensitive applications, confirmation requests may be sent to third parties to confirm data on the newly converted file.

Inadequately planned conversion procedures and a lack of controls in that conversion process can result in lost or distorted records when the old master files and transaction files are converted to the new storage media. Frequently, the conversion programs are special programs which are not subjected to the same carefully devised testing procedure applied against the new processing system. Because errors in converting the data to the new file storage media can be just as serious as errors introduced by incorrect processing procedures, the auditor should be careful to review the control procedures in effect when a new processing system has been implemented.

CONTROLS OVER SYSTEMS AND PROGRAM CHANGES

Plans should be specified and fully documented as to the way in which individual programs are to be stored and maintained within the installation. This includes plans for control of access to the program libraries as well as specific provision for program modification. One test of a well-controlled installation is the degree to which prior authorization is required for program changes and the degree to which any changes made to computer programs, once those programs are placed in normal operational state, are documented.

Faulty or unauthorized changes to existing systems and programs can completely negate the controls originally built into computer programs. Erroneous changes can eliminate previously developed and tested control procedures. Further, if no clear procedure exists for controlling changes to programs, the auditor cannot rely on any program controls in effect on the review date, because that programmed control could be subsequently eliminated or modified by an unauthorized program change. If controls over changes are poor, there is no assurance that an observed control was in effect before or after the review. Under these circumstances, the auditor can only determine that the control was properly functioning at the date of the review.

One approach to identifying and reviewing authorized program changes is to review program documentation to determine what changes have been made to existing programs and whether the procedures used were proper. This procedure does not guarantee, however, that no unauthorized and undocumented changes were made. Unfortunately, an all too frequent error by installations is to allow changes to programs without adequate correction of the documentation for those programs. Thus, the auditor needs to employ additional procedures to make sure that documentation agrees with the programs actually being used.

Changes to programs and systems should be subject to the same controls as new systems. Program control changes should insure that all proposed changes are previously approved by the user (e.g., financial and EDP management) before programming begins. All changes should be independently tested, and the test results should be reviewed and formally approved by the user department. After program changes have been made, the modified program can usually be tested with the original test data that was used during the initial development of the system. Results of this subsequent testing can be compared and reconciled with the original output.

The problem of controlling changes to programs must be addressed at several levels. First, the systems development process must provide formal procedures for making and documenting authorized changes. Second, appropriate operational controls must be instituted to prevent unauthorized intervention from the computer console once the program is loaded for execution. This type of change could result in an undocumented and therefore possibly undetected change in the program. Operations personnel should never authorize changes. The right to authorize changes should be restricted to the formal procedure for requesting, authorizing and approving all programmed changes.

The operations group should, however, have the responsibility for determining that changes have been approved before placing revised programs in production status. Although this group may request changes for improvements in operational efficiency, the operations group should not have the authority to approve changes. The operations personnel should, however, have the sole authority to put the changed programs into production status, usually by placing the changed program in the program library. By separating the authority to change programs from the authority to place the changed program into service, responsibilities will be properly separated.

SYSTEMS STANDARDS

Standards are the procedures and rules under which the analysts, programmers, operators, and users of a data processing system operate. Standards can provide a dual benefit to an installation. First, they can act as guidelines by which uniform practices and common techniques are established. Second, they can be used as criteria by which the performance of the various computer services functions can be measured. If standards are carefully and thoughtfully established, they can help to improve the productivity of installation activities. Such standards will become the basis for selecting the most efficient procedures for a given installation from a variety of possible alternatives and will provide some formal control over the application development process and subsequent use of that application's design.

A great deal of work has been done in the development of standards for the area of systems and program documentation. To allow others to understand the system and its programs, standard symbols and flowcharting techniques have been established. Within an individual installation, a decision can be made to use a standard form of documentation and, for purposes of installation standards, to specify exactly what kinds of documentation will exist. Thus, an installation could have a standard documentation package in which are specified the various elements that are to be provided, such as a narrative description, a systems flowchart, a program flowchart, record layouts, and operating instructions. All units of the installation should know exactly what information will be available in the documentation package.

Installation standards can be developed in a variety of ways. Some come as a result of external circumstances. The American National Standards Institute (ANSI) is a private, voluntary organization of approximately 150 trade associations, professional societies and companies interested in developing standards. It acts as a national clearinghouse and coordinating agency for voluntary standardization. This agency has worked on standards in a number of areas, such as optical character recognition, input/output standardization, data communication, common programming languages, terminology, problem definition and analysis, and data elements and coded representation. One widely adopted standard of ANSI is that of flowchart symbols. The benefit of using symbols adopted by a national organization such as ANSI is that an installation is saved the necessity of developing its own standards. Further, as the installation hires new programmers who are already familiar with the national standards, the time required to orient those new programmers to standards can be lessened if the installation standards are compatible with industry-wide standards.

In addition, internal standards should be developed that are unique to the needs and operations of the individual installation. In a larger organization, a formal standards committee may be formed. This committee should consist of representatives from user groups as well as the data processing group. It should include representatives from the systems design function, the programming function, the operations function, and the control function. This diverse representation helps to insure that the needs of all segments of the organization are considered when a standard is developed. Standards developed by a consensus of those who will use the information are usually more effective and useful than those dictated by one individual or by a very small group. In addition to determining which languages and which access methods will be used, the standards within an installation or company may also concern themselves with the definition of standard data elements, file structures, file–labelling procedures, and procedures for the design and approval of application development.

Adherence to organization-wide computer systems standards can provide several benefits to an organization. It can help simplify personnel training and increase personnel productivity. It can facilitate communication among the various divisions of an organization (especially communication between the computer staff and non-computer staff) by providing a common vocabulary and method of description, thereby speeding the communication process and eliminating time-consuming and expensive misunderstandings.

The amount of documentation and the number of installation standards developed will vary from installation to installation. The size of the installation and the complexity of the processing it does will influence the degree of formality in the documentation and standardization processing. However, every information system should establish those criteria by which its performance can be evaluated, by which it can effect its objectives, and by which it can document or record its procedures and accomplishments. Even the smallest installation must have some means by which it can guide its operations, communicate with its users, modify its activities, and expand its applications.

DEVELOPMENT, MAINTENANCE AND CONTROL
OF DOCUMENTATION

Documentation is any written record or description of the combination of activities and programs that constitute a data processing activity, including manual operations, computer operations, logic of programs, and contents of data files. It is important that each component be carefully described, and equally important that the interaction or relationship between the components also be fully recorded. Good documentation can prevent expensive misunderstandings and operational errors. It can facilitate the orientation process required for new employees. The continuing tasks of maintenance and changes to existing systems can be aided by clear and precise descriptions of those systems.

An installation should maintain two basic types of documentation. The first type describes the installation and its environment. This is the documentation that describes the hardware and software systems in which all applications development must take place and be executed. The second group—the applications material—describes the data processing information-handling procedures that the installation develops to handle the information needs of the organization.

Quite frequently, the first kind of documentation is ignored or inadequately controlled. It is important, however, that the hardware and programming systems environment in which applications are expected to function are carefully described to all who must use it. The installation has a considerable choice among a wide variety of hardware and software processing options. The process of software selection, generation, and maintenance is frequently an area of some mystery to all but a few specialists. This makes the need for clear documentation, explaining the facilities available and the limitations of the software systems selected, of utmost importance. Precisely because the characteristics of the software are not so physically apparent as the characteristics of the hardware, the documentation of the software system chosen and any subsequent changes to that system is critical.

Application documentation can take several forms. First, there is a certain amount of text or prose material in which descriptions, specifications, objectives, time, and financial constraints are described. In addition, certain fairly standard graphical forms of presentation have been developed. The first of these is a form that is used to describe the format of data files referred to as a *record layout*. The record layout identifies the size and relative location of fields within the records, the location of control codes, and the combination of record types that may be accessed in a given file. Additional information that must be carefully documented is a relationship between the logical record of information and its physical form, the way it is actually stored on an input/output device. The movement toward more complex integrated collections of information that serve multiple applications has created some differences between the form of the logical record and the form of the actual physical record. When the integrated data base is developed, personnel with responsibility for maintenance and control of the data base must provide and use descriptive material that will designate the physical location and relationships among the various elements of the information system. Further, this documentation must also contain information that identifies the paths of legitimate access to each element.

Flowcharts represent a widely used form of documentation. A flowchart is a symbolic or graphic technique for representing the information flow or logic of a problem. A *systems flowchart* attempts to document the overall collection of manual and computer procedures applied to the collection, transcription, manipulation, and reporting of data. It should detail sources of information, procedures executed, the sequence of these procedures, and disposition of reports. The graphic nature of the presentation should make comprehension of the overall system more rapid than the understanding ordinarily accomplished through the use of descriptive prose. The *program flowchart* attempts to show the sequence of logical operations performed within a given program. A program flowchart may be represented on the corresponding systems flowchart as one block in the system.

Another form of graphic presentation that can be used efficiently to describe combinations of data conditions that must be handled and the alternative procedures executed based on those conditions is a *decision table*. A decision table can be used to represent choices among manual operations or it can be used to represent decision points within a given program much in the same way that a flowchart approach can be used to describe a systems design or can be used to describe the logical relationships within a given computer program.

Frequently included in the documentation package for individual programs will be listings of the programs both in *source* (or symbolic) *language* and *object* (or machine) *language*. If the programs are executed under operating systems control from an automated program library, or if they use prewritten subroutines from the program library, the control cards and operating instructions used to control the loading and/or inclusion of subroutines should also be listed.

Documentation for a program should include a list of all potential messages that can be printed to request and control operator intervention as well as complete instructions for any halt or error condition. These instructions should also include specifications detailing the disposition of input data and output (e.g., reports) after completion of each program. Setup information can be provided either in the form of a setup diagram or prose that describes to the operator the files that should be mounted for the execution of a program, their source, the kinds of output files that will be produced, and their distribution. These operating instructions should provide complete descriptions of the various control cards that will be required by the existing operating system to select and load the program and to define the files to be made available to the program.

Carefully developed documentation represents an important working tool to an installation. It also represents a considerable investment of time and expense. Therefore, it should be looked upon as an asset like any other that requires careful management and control. The installation management should assign responsibility for the development of documentation and should exert sufficient supervision to insure the discharge of that responsibility. It is equally important to assign responsibility for the maintenance and control of that documentation. There should be a central collection point or documentation library in which all documentation for the installation is stored as a master copy. By centralizing the storage, control is more easily maintained and expensive duplication can be minimized. It cannot be completely eliminated, however, since it may also be necessary to maintain copies of sections of this documentation, such as copies of the program or operating instructions, within the departments responsible for those functions. This duplication of materials should be kept to a minimum wherever possible.

One of the requirements of adequate internal control is the proper separation of responsibilities. In a data processing installation this translates into controlled access to information about the system. Thus, it is inappropriate to scatter program-logic material throughout the installation so that it is readily available to the operating staff, especially if one of the control procedures employed in the installation is to prevent access to internal program logic by the operations personnel. Carefully centralized records also help to facilitate the maintenance process. Whenever changes are made to an application or program, these changes should be reflected in the documentation. If duplication of documentation exists in many different locations within the installation, the problem of updating each set of documentation provides increased opportunity for error and/or for failure to update one copy or another. This introduces the possibility that erroneous instructions will result from the use of outdated or incorrect documentation, and that confusion will result between different versions of documentation for the same application.

AUDITOR'S ROLE IN SYSTEMS DESIGN AND DEVELOPMENT

There is general agreement on the internal and independent auditor's responsibility to review and evaluate existing systems of internal control. The auditor will look for evidence that there has been adequate user participation in the design of accounting systems, that there is proper authorization of programs and procedures, and that there is adequate attention in the procedures implemented to accomplish the various general and application controls discussed in Chapter 1. In those instances where an application currently under development represents a significant part of the accounting system, the auditor may want to review that application prior to its implementation to help assure adequate accounting control and auditability. The exact extent of the auditor's participation in the systems design process, however, is not as clearly defined as the auditor's responsibility in other areas.

Systems design and development represents a time-consuming and expensive activity. Many of today's systems do not lend themselves well to postinstallation review or modification. It is much more practical and less expensive to include appropriate controls during the development of the system. Thus, it seems sensible to have the auditor review the proposed system at various stages of its development and make recommendations regarding the need for appropriate system control procedures as the system is being developed. In addition, appropriate provision for audit techniques, especially imbedded audit routines, is much more feasible as the system is being implemented rather than after a processing system is in operation. A strong case can be made to support the auditor's involvement in systems design to the extent that the auditor can identify omissions and weaknesses in the system controls and insure that sufficient provision is made for auditability of the system under development. By insuring that systems controls and auditability are accommodated as the system is being designed, the auditor can make certain they are incorporated as integral elements of the new system.

Even though auditors have a very real contribution to make in the design of major systems, many are troubled by the question of their independence when they do in fact participate in systems design. There is some concern that the auditor's participation during the design and implementation process might create a condition in which the auditor could not subsequently review that procedure with complete objectivity. If the auditor participated as an active member of the design team, it could be difficult to subsequently act as an independent evaluator of that design. There appears to be a potential conflict between the desirability of having the auditor identify necessary controls and auditability features in a new system as it is being designed, and the need for the auditor to maintain complete objectivity and independence.

It seems clear that the auditor should not actively develop or install procedures. It does seem entirely appropriate, however, for the auditor to identify standards of control and auditability appropriate to the systems under development and to recommend procedures which will facilitate those standards. Development of the internal audit function is a significant instance of this need to monitor the development process to insure that adequate procedures are being included in the new system, providing for adequate control and auditability.

Evidence of systematic review by internal auditors or some other independent group which reports to management can help the independent auditor in assessing whether the organization is meeting its primary responsibility for designing, implementing, and testing a system in accordance with management's general or specific authorization in a manner that is efficient, leaves an audit trail, and includes adequate control procedures.

WERNER MANUFACTURING, INC.—CASE STUDY

We now continue with the case study to illustrate one approach to the auditor's role in systems design and development.

DEVELOPMENT OF SALES, ACCOUNTS RECEIVABLE AND CASH RECEIPTS SYSTEM

Werner's systems development procedure consists of four phases: *

- *Feasibility study* determines whether computerizing the application is advisable, considering its cost, the technology needed, and the impact of doing so on the present organization.
- *Functional analysis* involves developing project specifications. The user department or group, as part of the development team, specifies what the proposed system should do. Data processing then prepares a set of

---

* Adapted from "Morgan Precision Tool Company," a case study in Peat, Marwick, Mitchell & Co.'s course *Introduction to EDP Auditing.*

specifications which show what the system will look like, how long it will take to develop it, the estimated cost, how it will interface with other (manual and computerized) systems, the cost of operating and maintaining it, and so on. Up to this time, total expenditure on the project should be relatively small. If the company decides to continue beyond this point, costs usually accelerate rapidly. In effect, this is the last chance to cancel the project and escape with little cost.

- *Design* is the preparation of final, detailed specifications for the system. Working with the development team, data processing will produce:
  - A system design that specifies hardware and software components, input and output files, and processing requirements
  - A detailed plan for the implementation phase of the system
  - A plan for converting the user's present system to the new system, which involves computerizing manual files or changing computerized files to properly interface with the new system
  - Updated time and cost estimates

The design specifications include a detailed description of the work to be done during the implementation phase. These specifications furnish detailed information on additions or refinements to data in the functional specifications.

- *Implementation* refers to actually building the system and making it work. It includes all activities, that is, coding the program modules, testing them, combining them into a system, testing the entire system, integrating it into Werner's multiprogramming environment (where it operates in contention with other systems already on the computer), and user acceptance.

The remainder of this chapter will deal with how the computerization of the sales, accounts receivable and cash receipts system progressed through these four phases and how the internal and independent auditors played their respective roles.

COMPUTERIZATION OF SALES, ACCOUNTS RECEIVABLE AND CASH RECEIPTS SYSTEM

Dissatisfaction with manual system.   When Werner computerized its purchasing, accounts payable and cash disbursements system, the benefits immediately became apparent, especially the timely reports the system generated and their role in enabling management to better control inventory levels and cash flow.

Management soon began to question whether computerization of the sales area would not yield the same benefits. In addition to faster reports of sales (e.g., daily sales orders and shipments, sales patterns and projections) and receivables data (e.g., aged trial balances, slow payers, customers placed on a cash basis, orders held up because credit limits were reached), operating benefits were anticipated:

- Upon receipt of customer orders, a four-part sales order was prepared and mailed to the sales office in Cleveland. If it was a rush order, it was telephoned to Cleveland to get the approval before shipment. Considering the delays frequently encountered in the mails, it is not surprising that from several days to a week sometimes passed before the orders were received for processing. Management assumed that by computerizing the order entry process, sales would not only be processed faster, but the danger of lost orders would be virtually eliminated.
- Orders were approved and goods were shipped before the status of inventory was checked to see that the goods ordered were on hand. This often led to situations in which sales were recorded when they should have been backordered. Even when the goods were on hand, the system sometimes resulted in cutoff problems because invoices were sent (see procedure 10 in Figure 1–6) before the goods were actually shipped. Management once again assumed that the situation could be corrected by computerization.

Based on this information, the president, B. T. Summers, ordered the vice president of information systems, J. T. Brown, to begin a feasibility study to determine the advisability of computerizing sales, accounts receivable and cash receipts.

Feasibility Study. After conferring with the various department heads, Brown appointed a project development team including:

- A systems analyst who will be the team leader and prepare the feasibility study report and system proposal. The report will contain the following information:
  - Project identification number
  - Project title
  - Preparation date
  - Estimated completion date for the feasibility and functional analysis phases
  - Estimated completion date for the entire project
  - Costs:
    — Manpower cost to date of feasibility study report
    — Estimated cost for functional analysis phase
    — Estimated cost for design and implementation phases (Note: Estimated costs are accumulated by functional analysis and

later phases because, as was stated above, the functional analysis phase is the last point at which the project may be abandoned without a significant cost being incurred.)
— Total project cost; that is, the total of the foregoing three elements
● Signatures of:
Project team leader
User departments' representatives (accounting and sales departments)
● Dates:
The report is presented to the user departments' representatives for approval
Final approval is granted to extend the project into the functional analysis phase
● The controller and sales supervisor, representing the user groups, who will become the buyers of the proposed system. The controller will also judge the system's cost effectiveness.
● A representative of the internal audit department will monitor the project to determine whether it provides a proper audit trail and internal controls. To keep its organizational independence, the internal audit department does not permit its representative to become identified with the project.

The internal auditor chosen, Steve Blum, is a competent auditor, but is not especially knowledgeable in EDP. He is, however, more knowledgeable in this area than any of the other auditors. Although having the internal auditor monitor the system development process and report on the adequacy of controls and audit trail may somewhat weaken his independence, Werner feels the overall benefits outweigh this disadvantage.

A week after the project development team was assembled (November 4), an organizational change took place at Werner with the formation of the EDP Steering Committee. Members included:

● President   — B. T. Summers, chairman
● Treasurer   — C. R. Borden
● Vice President of
  Information Systems — J. T. Brown
● Chief Internal
  Auditor   — F. L. Bouchard

The first meeting of the project development team took place on November 5. In addition to the team members, the EDP Steering Committee attended. Summers opened the meeting and explained the following points:

- The function of the EDP Steering Committee will be to provide general direction and support to the data processing department in its efforts to use the computer in a cost-effective manner at Werner and to monitor the progress and cost of individual projects.
- A team will be formed for each development project. It will consist of representatives of the controller, the user(s) and a systems analyst. The systems analyst, who will always be the team leader, will prepare a feasibility study report and system proposal (to be collectively referred to as the "report") to the EDP Steering Committee at the end of each phase of the project. A representative of the chief internal auditor will monitor the project for audit trail and controls. In this project, the controller is one of the users, so there is no need to have a representative from his area on the team.
- Each member of the team will sign the report to the EDP Steering Committee, signifying approval with the progress and cost of the project. Approval may be qualified or withheld, but in either case a written explanation must be attached to the report.
- The EDP Steering Committee will have final approval and can terminate a project at any time. It will approve or reject reports within five days; if the committee cannot meet, the president will exercise this authority, subject to his conferring with the other committee members. If the president is unavailable, the treasurer will do this. For sound reasons, any member of the development team may request the committee to terminate or modify a project at any time.

The meeting was then turned over to the systems analyst, Ken Little. He reported that at the time the team's involvement was concentrated on supplying him with the basic objectives of the proposed system in nontechnical language. He said he had studied the present manual system with the controller and sales supervisor, had interviewed the internal auditor who conducted the last examination to learn about the internal control aspect, and was therefore familiar with the present situation.

Little then asked the controller and sales supervisor what they wanted from the computerized version; for example, operational enhancements, reports and controls. He asked the internal auditors and the EDP Steering Committee to interject comments whenever they felt it appropriate to do so. As these persons talked, he took notes. At the end of the meeting, he said (1) he would have the report ready in about five days, that is, on November 12, (2) in the meantime, he would probably contact each person individually to clarify questions as they arose, (3) copies of the report would be sent to each member of the team and the internal auditor and (4) after allowing a couple of days for study and evaluation, another meeting would be held on November 17. The report is reproduced as Exhibit 2–1.

Exhibit 2–1. Feasibility Study Report and System Proposal.

WERNER MANUFACTURING, INC.

Printed in U.S.A.

TO **OFFICE**	Sales, Accounts Receivable, Cash Receipts System Project Development Team	**Date** **Steno**	November 12, 1974
FROM **OFFICE**	K. R. Little	**Enc.**	
CC:		**Contract No.**	

SUBJECT Feasibility Study Report and System Proposal

Your Letter Dated:

Based on the input you gave me at our first meeting on November 5, 1974, I've prepared this report and proposal. Please review it for our meeting on November 17. At that time, if you agree with the facts and the proposal, I'll have a "master copy" ready for the signature of the controller and sales supervisor (as users).

Description of proposed system:

- As sales orders are received, the on-line customer accounts receivable file is queried via remote terminals at the sales offices to determine the customer's credit status. If the customer's credit is not all right, the order is held for clearance by the credit manager; if he refuses, the order is rejected.
- If accepted, the order is matched to the on-line inventory file to see if a sufficient quantity is on hand. If not, the order is placed on a back order file until the inventory is replenished. A back order notice is issued to the customer and sales office. If there is enough inventory on hand, the open order file is updated and shipping orders prepared.
- Items are picked and shipped; an invoice is sent to the customer. The customer accounts receivable, inventory and open order files are updated. A sales register is prepared and is the source of the monthly posting of the general ledger.
- Remittances are keypunched after the deposit is made. Using the cards as input, the customer accounts receivable file is updated. A cash receipts book is produced daily and is the source of the monthly posting to the general ledger.
- At the end of the month, the open order, customer accounts receivable and inventory files are processed and three reports produced:
  - Open Order Listing
  - Aged Customer Accounts Receivable Trial Balance
  - Classified Inventory Trial Balance

Controls:

- On-line access:

  — Terminals are in a locked room and may be turned on only by a key.
  — To access the computer and appropriate on-line files, the terminal operator must enter a user code and passwords.
  — A printed log of terminal accesses is generated to serve as a record of transactions and a means of tracing unauthorized attempts to read critical files.

- Sales processing:

  — Sales orders generated by the computer are sent to the sales department and credit manager for approval before goods are shipped.
  — Sales orders are not processed on the computer until the goods are actually shipped.
  — Copies of invoices generated by the computer are sent to the originating sales office to review for errors.

- Cash receipts procedure:

  — Traditional controls over cash receipts are instituted; for example, restrictive endorsement of checks with preparation of a control tape by the mail opener for comparison with the deposit ticket.
  — All keypunching is keyverified.
  — A daily list of cash receipts is generated by the computer and compared with a list of cash receipts prepared manually from the remittance advices.
  — The bank reconciliation is prepared by someone independent of the cash receipts and disbursements function and reviewed by the controller.

- At the end of the month, the trial balance of customer accounts receivable and listing of open orders is reviewed by responsible persons.

Administrative:

- Project identification number: 001–789–76
- Title: Revenue Cycle
- Estimated completion date for feasibility and functional analysis phases: January 7, 1977
- Estimated completion date for project: June 30, 1977

- Costs:
  — Manpower to date, for feasibility study phase: $ 2,000
  — For functional analysis phase (estimated):   10,000
  — For design and implementation phases (estimated):   200,000
  — Total for project $212,000

- Signatures:
  - Project Leader ———————————— Date ————————
  - User:
  - Controller ———————————— Date ————————
  - Sales Supervisor ———————————— Date ————————

- EDP Steering Committee:
  - ——————————— President Date ————————
  - ——————————— Treasurer Date ————————
  - ——————————— Vice President—Information Systems Date ————————
  - ——————————— Chief Internal Auditor Date ————————

As you read Little's report, note:

- The system and controls are described in very general terms.
- At this point, little or no conscious concern has been given to such details as input/output media, processing characteristics, or specific hardware, certainly not enough to warrant mentioning it in the report.
- Actual and estimated costs illustrate a point made earlier: the functional analysis phase is the cost cutoff point. At that time, approximately $12,000 will have been spent. This is still relatively minor compared with the total estimated cost of $212,000 for the entire project.

Members of the team were satisfied with the proposal and signed it, thereby recommending to the steering committee that the functional analysis phase begin. However, Blum, the internal auditor, had some reservations about controls and audit (or management) trail. His report to the chief internal auditor (see Exhibit 2–2) describes the procedures he followed during the feasibility study and his conclusions and recommendations.

Blum's memo caused Bouchard considerable trouble; not only did it place him in an untenable position regarding his department's ability to perform an important audit function, it also brought instant denials from Little and a charge that his competence and honesty were being questioned. Fortunately, by contacting the senior systems analyst, A. L. Greenberg, further unpleasantness between the internal audit and EDP departments was avoided.

The blame for the situation must fall partially on Bouchard's shoulders, because he tried to accomplish a task with someone who did not have the technical expertise to do it. One cannot effectively review and evaluate EDP internal controls without the proper level of EDP knowledge and expertise. Blum was right in stating he was not technically competent to accomplish the task Bouchard set out for him; he was wrong in assuming that Little was not dealing honestly with him and was deficient in his appreciation of the need for controls because he used computer jargon. Jargon is a legitimate form of communication when all parties agree upon definitions; Little had a right to

Exhibit 2–2.   Report on Project to Computerize Sales, Accounts Receivable, Cash Receipts System.

WERNER MANUFACTURING, INC.

Printed in U.S.A.

TO **OFFICE**	F. L. Bouchard	**Date** November 12, 1974 **Steno**
FROM **OFFICE**	S. G. Blum	**Enc.**
CC:		**Contract No.**

SUBJECT   Report on Project to Computerize the Sales, Accounts Receivable and Cash Receipts System

Your Letter Dated:

As you directed, I am monitoring the development project for computerizing the sales, accounts receivable and cash receipts system. The feasibility study has been completed and has been accepted by the users, that is, the controller and sales supervisor.

I have:

- Reviewed the feasibility study report for internal control weaknesses.
- Discussed the feasibility report with Steve Johnson, who performed the last audit of sales, accounts receivable and cash receipts, and obtained his suggestions for satisfying audit requirements. As part of this work, I reviewed the working papers for that audit to identify any existing internal control weaknesses.

My report is divided into four sections:

- Brief overview of the system
- Control considerations
- Preliminary audit requirements
- Existing control weaknesses

Brief Overview of the System and Control Considerations

See attached copy of K. R. Little's report and system proposal.

Preliminary Audit Requirements

I believe the system as presently outlined will generate an audit trail to enable us to perform proper auditing procedures. Since the description is extremely rudimentary at this point, this has to be a very qualified opinion, especially in view of the tendency during this phase to downplay printed output not directly essential to daily operations. The commitment to audit trail was obtained from Little only after I strongly objected to the direction he was taking.

Existing Control Weaknesses

Once again, the system is rudimentary and difficult to judge. Also, Little does not seem to properly understand the need for adequate control; his stress is on efficiency; that is, processing speed and reduction of paperwork. I am happy to say the users supported me strongly on the need for adequate control.

On this point, I must object to a major weakness in the proposed system:

> Great stress is placed on the review of individual items in computer-generated lists and documents by knowledgeable persons. I feel all input should also be batch controlled by the user groups and that a separate control group should be set up to administer this task. Only cash receipts appears to involve the reconciliation of control totals.

I am also disturbed by the omission of any mention of control (1) over the distribution of output and (2) to insure that changes to the proposed master files have been made properly. Little informs me these will be identified as the system description is refined.

Although Little has assured me that proper consideration will be given to internal control and audit trail "at the proper time," I do not feel comfortable for two reasons:

- He does not appear to have enough knowledge of proper internal control objectives and techniques to build a good system of controls. Indeed, he appears to regard them as unnecessarily expensive frills.
- I do not feel I possess sufficient EDP expertise to recommend all the controls that can be reasonably included. On several occasions I had the distinct impression that Little was making the feasibility of installing such controls sound unnecessarily difficult and expensive. He frequently retreated into jargon that obscured the basic issues.

Recommendations:

- The controls I mentioned above should be put into the system.
- We should obtain the services of a knowledgeable EDP auditor to monitor this project.

I shall be happy to answer any questions you may have on the foregoing report.

expect that Blum would understand certain technical words and phrases without detailed explanation.

To solve his problem, Bouchard got permission to contact Werner's independent auditors (Brown, Johnson & Co.) to ask for their help. They responded by proposing that one of their computer audit specialists, Tom Hanson, monitor the system development project on a consulting basis in conjunction with Steve Johnson, who had performed the last audit of sales, accounts receivable and cash receipts. Hanson and Johnson reviewed the feasibility study report and spoke with Little. Brown, Johnson then issued the letter shown in Exhibit 2–3. Because of the argument caused by Blum's memo,

Exhibit 2–3.   Evaluation of Feasibility Study Report.

BROWN, JOHNSON & CO.
Certified Public Accountants
2730 Lakewood Grove Avenue
Cleveland, Ohio 44114

November 17, 1974

Mr. F. L. Bouchard
Werner Manufacturing, Inc.
27 Oakdale Boulevard
Cleveland, Ohio 44114

Dear Mr. Bouchard

We have reviewed the feasibility study report and discussed its conclusions and recommendations with K. R. Little.

The major control weakness in the proposed system is the lack of a control group. This, however, is an organizational problem which Little fully recognizes but cannot remedy. He recognizes that the system's user controls, as presently proposed, do not compensate for this weakness, but he assured us that during the functional analysis phase he will build such controls into the system.

Although this is not an entirely satisfactory state of affairs, we feel that because the team leader recognizes what has to be done, you are justified in carrying the project into the next phase. We shall closely monitor the functional analysis phase and shall report to you regarding controls and audit trail.

Very truly yours,

BROWN, JOHNSON & CO.

William F. Corbin, Partner

the meeting to consider the next step in the system project was postponed to November 22.

On November 22, based on Brown, Johnson's letter, the users reiterated their approval of the system as it was defined and recommended that the steering committee approve the start of the functional analysis phase.

Functional Analysis.   Based on what had been done so far, Little developed system specifications, and the users more closely defined what the system is to do for them. In contrast to the feasibility study, this means:

- The users specify exactly what and when processing is to be performed, what reports are to be produced, when they are to be ready, and the number of copies.
- Taking this input, Little will:
  - Prepare a preliminary flowchart of the proposed system to show the control points and the processing to be done
  - Specify the general types of data processing hardware and system and application software needed to do the processing, and present a general configuration diagram of the hardware to show what will be needed where
  - Estimate data preparation (input) requirements, transmission speeds and turnaround times
  - Estimate costs to complete the system study (broken down into the design and implementation phases) together with the organizational changes it will impose and the time period needed to make the conversion
  - Estimate the cost to implement and maintain the system

All this information appears in Little's Functional Analysis Report and System Proposal, dated January 10, 1975. Space prohibits its being reproduced here. However, its format would be very similar to the Feasibility Study Report and System Proposal (Exhibit 2–1) and would contain the following information:

- Description of the proposed system:
  - User's specifications concerning output required and expected time frames
  - Input and processing required to produce the needed output and estimated turnaround time
  - Preliminary clerical flowchart to allow the project development team to better understand the system and in particular its data preparation and output features
- Controls:
  Preliminary system flowchart, showing the control points for on-line

access from the sales offices, sales processing and cash receipts. This covers both controls within the data processing portion of the system and external or user controls.

- Administrative:
  - Project number and title
  - Estimated completion date for the design and implementation phases
  - Costs:
    - Actual cost for the feasibility and functional analysis phases
    - Estimated costs for the design and implementation phases
    - Estimated cost to install and maintain the proposed system
  - Signatures:
    - Project leader (K. R. Little)
    - Users (controller and sales supervisor)
    - EDP Steering Committee (president, treasurer, vice president— information systems and chief internal auditor)

On January 17, 1975 the project development team met to discuss Little's Functional Analysis Report. Also attending were Tom Hanson, from Brown, Johnson & Co., and Steve Johnson, internal audit department, who were sent copies of Little's report and have compared their impressions of it.

Rather than issue memos at this stage, they have agreed with Little and Bouchard to wait until the meeting, at which time they will discuss their concerns with the entire project development team.

At the start of the meeting, Little orally summarized the report and asked for comments. The controller had two points to make:

- The projected cost of the system was far more than he had expected, since he thought that much of the work on the accounts payable system would be somehow transferable to this project.
  Little responded by pointing out that this was the case and that the projected cost had taken that into consideration.
- There did not seem to be any provision for reconstructing transactions which originate from the remote locations and the files they update in the event these computerized files are somehow physically damaged or their integrity destroyed through incorrect processing.
  Little pointed out that a printed transaction log would be kept daily and could be used as both an audit trail and as a means of reconstructing master files in the event of destruction. This satisfied the controller.

Discussion then centered upon some of the purely operational aspects of the proposed system, particularly the input requirements that would insure the turnaround and output the users specified. After these were settled, Little turned to Hanson and Johnson and asked for their comments and questions.

Hanson pointed out that Little's plan still did not provide for an input/

output control group and stated that the compensating controls promised after the feasibility phase had not materialized. Johnson agreed and stated that he was also concerned about relying on a printed log of transactions to re-create files built up from transactions transmitted from the remote locations. He felt this would be unwieldy and time-consuming and that some computerized log should be kept.

Little replied that two very valid but quite different considerations were being raised and that he would like to discuss them each in turn. Referring to the lack of a control group and the failure to install compensating controls, he stated that the additional (to those in the feasibility phase) controls he was now proposing would offset the control group weakness. He then inquired what additional controls the auditors wanted. As an aside, he said that he had approached the EDP Steering Committee to propose a control group and had been turned down.

Hanson believed the best way would be to put his recommendations in a letter to Bouchard; Johnson said he would do the same. Hanson also said he wanted to propose two procedures that would enhance the auditability of the system. He would include them in his memo to Bouchard, but first wanted to get the reaction of the project development team by briefly describing them at the meeting.

Each proposal required building auditing procedures into the system during the relatively early stages of its development:

- Imbedded audit routines — Under this system, the internal audit department would design audit-oriented computer programs that would be placed in on-line system libraries. These could be called in to perform their auditing procedures in two ways which could be used separately or in combination with each other.
  - The regular processing programs could contain "call" routines with the names of these programs. This would insure that these programs would be called and executed every time the regular production program was run. Under this plan, the audit program would be used to test and accumulate statistics (in files only the auditors could access) on information created or processed by the production programs. Thus, the traditional audit trail would be redefined to a real-time basis, that is, it would exist as the transactions were being executed; it would be audited at that time and the results would be placed in special files for later access by the auditor. If the audit programs were properly written and used, there might be little or no need to provide for a hard-copy (printed) audit trail, unless the auditors needed one because of special circumstances. This approach would enable the auditor to test whether the computer programs were operating properly.
  - The audit programs could be called (e.g., via a remote terminal)

only when the auditor wanted them, to perform auditing procedures on on-line files. This would enable the auditor to determine the validity of the data produced.

- Integrated test facility (ITF) — This feature would follow transactions as they proceeded through the system to see if the computer programs were working properly. A number of "dummy" (unknown to the operating personnel) transactions would be introduced just as if they were valid ones. They could be for a fictitious department or product and would be subsequently "washed out" of the system by specially designed programs. Under this plan, the auditors would determine in advance how each dummy transaction should be processed if the computer programs were functioning properly. After processing has been completed, the updated files, output, and so on would be examined to ascertain how the transactions were processed, and to compare them with the predetermined results.

Little was open-minded about installing whatever additional controls were needed, but was definitely opposed to the imbedded audit routines and ITF. He felt both would slow down processing and, if not properly handled, would adversely affect the integrity of the system and the data. The users liked both ideas and also seemed to favor the control group. Little thought the computerized log of transactions was a good idea and encouraged Hanson and Johnson to put it in their reports. Once again, the users liked the idea.

Little said the project development team should meet again before the system proposal was submitted to the EDP Steering Committee. He felt there were a number of points still to be settled, not the least of which were those raised by Hanson and Johnson. The date agreed upon was January 24; at Little's suggestion, Hanson and Johnson would send copies of their reports (Exhibits 2–4 and 2–5) to each member of the project development team.

On January 24, the project development team met again. To save time, they were joined by the EDP Steering Committee. The project development team unanimously endorsed the formation of the control group and the provision of a machine-readable transaction tape. By a split vote (users for, K. R. Little opposed), they also endorsed the computer audit routines (imbedded routines and ITF).

The steering committee, which appeared to be increasingly cost conscious, rejected the control group recommendation and directed Little to provide the alternative controls recommended by Hanson. Both Hanson and Little stated the control group might be the least expensive alternative in the long run, but the steering committee held to its decision, agreeing to reconsider it only if an analysis of costs showed the control group to be "definitely the less expensive of the two choices."

Consistent with their cost consciousness, they deferred making a decision about having the machine-readable transaction log and rejected adding im-

Exhibit 2–4. Evaluation of Functional Analysis Study Report.

BROWN, JOHNSON & CO.
Certified Public Accountants
2730 Lakewood Grove Avenue
Cleveland, Ohio 44114

January 18, 1975

Mr. F. L. Bouchard
Werner Manufacturing, Inc.
27 Oakland Boulevard
Cleveland, Ohio 44114

Dear Mr. Bouchard:

We have reviewed the functional analysis study report and discussed its conclusions and recommendations with K. R. Little and the other members of the project development team.

In our letter to you of November 17, 1974 we reported that K. R. Little would build additional controls into the system to compensate for the lack of a control group. Although he has added some controls, they are still not sufficient to compensate for the missing control group. We therefore recommend that a competent control group be established and properly used to insure:

- All input is processed properly.

- Error-correction routines are subjected to the same controls as original data.

- Master file updating is correct and distributed to authorized persons.

If this is not adopted, we recommend the following alternatives:

- For *all* data submitted to data processing, the user groups must keep copies and control totals, to be compared with subsequent output totals and printed copies of especially sensitive master files that were updated by that data.

- All output must be delivered to the user departments for reasonableness review and distribution to authorized recipients.

- The internal auditors must conduct investigations, preferably unannounced, to insure that the above procedures are being carried out.

Should these control procedures not be instituted, the system cannot be relied upon to produce accurate information. This seriously impacts its usefulness as a management tool and would mean extensive substantive testing by us during our annual audit.

To strengthen the above controls, we recommend two auditing procedures which might be adopted, in addition to those recommended by Steven L. Johnson of your staff:

- Imbedded audit routines
- Integrated test facility

If you have any questions, please do not hesitate to contact us.

Very truly yours,

BROWN, JOHNSON & CO.

William F. Corbin, Partner

Exhibit 2–5. Report on Project to Computerize Sales, Accounts Receivable, Cash Receipts System

WERNER MANUFACTURING, INC.

Printed in U.S.A.

TO OFFICE	F. L. Bouchard	**Date**	January 18, 1975
FROM OFFICE	S. L. Johnson	**Enc.**	
CC:		**Contract No.**	

SUBJECT Report on Project to Computerize the Sales, Accounts Receivable and Cash Receipts System

Your Letter Dated:

In conjunction with T. L. Hanson of Brown, Johnson & Co., I have monitored the functional analysis phase of this project. K. R. Little's attached Functional Analysis Report to the project development team, dated January 10, 1975 fully explains the shape of the proposed system, its controls, cost, and target completion dates.

I have also attached T. L. Hanson's report on the recommended controls and computer auditing procedures that should be added to the system. I am in complete agreement with his recommendations.

I have one additional recommendation to make at this time: the system should provide for a computer-readable log of transactions initiated by the terminal operators at the remote locations. The system presently provides only for a printout of such transactions. While this provides for an audit trail, it would be a cumbersome way of reconstructing master files in the event of the current files' destruction due to physical damage or incorrect processing.

During the functional analysis phase, Mr. Hanson and I performed the following auditing procedures:

- We reviewed the documents (including the clerical and system flowcharts) prepared by the project development team to determine whether the controls provided were adequate. We have expressed our opinion on this point above and in Mr. Hanson's letter to you, dated January 18, 1975.
- We prepared some preliminary audit programs for continuing audits of the new system, including the computer audit routines described by Mr. Hanson in his letter to you. These programs (computerized and manual) are attached to this memorandum. [These have not been reproduced in this text.] Note they also cover procedures necessary to verify related systems and master files.
- We prepared a program for the postimplementation audit of the system, to insure the new system has properly converted the manual files as of the implementation date. All programs will be refined as the system is refined and implemented in the next two phases.

I shall be happy to expand upon any of the points covered in this memorandum or related to the project in general.

bedded routines and ITF to the system. Because of Hanson's and Johnson's arguments, however, they did direct Little to refine his present projections on how much it would cost to write these programs and how much it would cost in terms of reduced throughput.

All other aspects of the proposed system were approved by both the project development team and the steering committee; the steering committee therefore authorized the start of the design phase.

Design phase.   During the design phase, Little worked with the controller and sales supervisor to design the programs that would perform the processing outlined in the Functional Analysis Report and System proposal.* This work produced:

- A system design that specified system hardware and software components, input and output files, and processing requirements
- A detailed plan for the implementation phase of the system
- A plan for converting the present system to the new system, computerizing manual files
- Updated time and cost estimates

The design specifications covered:

- File structure
- Programming considerations

* An excellent discussion of the development process is the article "A Methodology for Auditing Project Development," by Thomas H. Fitzgerald which was presented at the Sixth Conference on Computer Audit, Control & Security in San Francisco on March 29, 1976, and which was printed in *EDPACS*, June, 1976, pp. 1–14.

- Hardware configuration requirements
- Internal and external controls
- Security considerations
- Auditing design features
- Backup and restart
- Control totals
- Job control language (JCL)
- System test plan
- Acceptance test plan

The written result of this work was the Design Specification Agreement. In addition to the foregoing information, it contained:

- Estimated completion date for the implementation phase
- Cost to date for the implementation phase
- Signatures

At a meeting of the project development team with Steve Johnson and Tom Hanson on April 18, 1975, Little said the users had signed the Design Specification Agreement and submitted it to the EDP Steering Committee for their approval. He also called particular attention to the following:

- The idea of the control group had been abandoned and the alternative controls advocated by Johnson and Hanson built into into the system.
- Proposals for a computer-readable log of transactions from the remote locations and the computer audit routines had also been withdrawn.

During this phase, Johnson and Hanson closely monitored the progress of the system's development, particularly its controls and audit trail, and reported their findings to Bouchard. In addition they:

- Prepared a system flowchart identifying the programs within the system that have the greatest impact on the master files. This showed those programs which would be subject to a detailed coding review.
- Reviewed file backup and retention requirements to insure compliance with applicable regulations and legal statutes. Checked to insure that source document retention also conformed to legal requirements.
- Determined file layouts to be used by audit programs.
- Prepared functional specifications for audit programs.
- Designed confirmation form(s) as required.
- Prepared test data for audit programs.
- Reviewed preliminary output with the other members of the internal audit department.
- Prepared a final report on design specifications which included:
  - Evaluation of automated controls

- Comments on additional controls needed in clerical procedures
- File backup and retention requirements
- An estimate of when the system would go into production (This would be useful for developing audit deadlines.)
- Reviewed financial audit programs with the other auditors and modified them as needed.
- Proposed EDP audit programs (procedures) for the postcompletion audit.
- Prepared time schedules and manpower resource requirements for the postcompletion audit.

Despite Little's assertion that the alternative controls were sufficient to insure the integrity of the information to be produced by the system, Johnson and Hanson did not agree. They believed the input and output controls were especially weak and said so in their reports to Bouchard and at the April 18 meeting. (See the system flowcharts and explanations in Chapter 1 for an evaluation of the controls.)

At this point in the development of the system, the auditors have some accomplishments to their credit. They have probably influenced the project development team to be more conscious of controls and audit trails than they would have been if the auditors had not been present throughout the project. They have also kept the internal audit department apprised of ongoing developments and have arranged for the development of audit programs that are realistic in terms of what the new system will look like, what it will do, and how it will interact with other systems.

This last point is important to the auditor. Without doing this, the auditors must come in unprepared the first time they audit the new system. That means they must confront an entirely new system, understand it, review and evaluate its internal controls and *then* audit it—if they can. If the audit trail has been destroyed, or if they do not have sufficient computer expertise to audit the system and the computerized files, *they may not be able to do an audit.* Or they *may* be able to do an audit, but at so prohibitively high a price that it would not be cost-effective.

This is not fantasy. It has happened. And as computer systems become more sophisticated, the auditor's involvement in their development becomes more and more necessary. Another thing becomes more and more necessary: computer auditing expertise. You simply cannot audit complicated computer systems if you don't know anything about computers.

With that thought, consider what happened in the final phase of the new system's development.

Implementation phase. The actual production of the system, including programming, acceptance, and system integration is referred to as the implementation phase. We have expanded the definition to include testing and system integration. Some authorities feel this is properly part of the design phase. We do not favor either position. It is important, however, that all involved parties agree on the precise meaning of the terms used.

We described Werner's programming practices and testing procedures in the discussion of general EDP controls in Chapter 1. After the system has been tested successfully by the programmers, the *user* tests it to determine if it does the things that were specified during the first three phases of its development, This is called *acceptance testing* at Werner.

Acceptance testing involves running the programs against test data developed by the project development team. Prior to doing so, the results of such processing were predetermined by the project development team, using the test data as input. If the results were not exactly as predicted by the project development team, the cause was investigated and corrections immediately made.

Acceptance testing was performed with the new system running alone, so that it could not be affected by other systems. When the project development team was satisfied that the programs worked properly, the next testing phase began.

Remember that this was not the first application at Werner to be computerized; the purchases, accounts payable and cash disbursements system was already on the computer. To be sure that the new system, when it was incorporated into the total data processing scheme, did not unnecessarily slow down total processing time or adversely affect the other system's data files, it was necessary to perform system integration testing. This enabled the data processing group to make certain that the new system ran smoothly and was successfully absorbed into the total data processing production mix.

When testing was completed, the system was considered to be operational. At that point, final plans to change over to it were carried out. This involved setting the formal changeover date, completing organiaztional changes, and training user personnel. It also meant that a date had to be set for converting manual files to the new, computerized system.

To document the system's becoming operational, the project development team issued a System Completion Report and all parties signed it. It was then sent to the EDP Steering Committee for final approval. This report contained:

- Project identification number
- Project title
- Dated approval signatures of:
  - Project development team
  - EDP Steering Committee
- Date the present (manual) system was converted
- Total cost for the development of the new system, including explanations of variances
- Estimated annual running cost of the system

During this phase, the two auditors (Johnson and Hanson) finalized the audit programs for the ongoing audit of the new system. In this capacity they worked very closely with the other internal auditors and were careful to fully document their activities. Since they lost on their bid to use imbedded audit routines and ITF, they recommended to Bouchard that a generalized audit software system be purchased, so that the internal auditors could use the computer to perform compliance and substantive auditing procedures.

Bouchard accepted their recommendation and has taken steps to get approval from the president. He has also stated his intention to hire two EDP internal auditors and has requested help from Brown, Johnson & Co. in locating them.

In preparation for the acquisition of an audit software system, they:

- Identified and reviewed the critical programs in the new system to ascertain that all the controls they proposed and which were accepted have survived the final translation into code. They also obtained audit copies of these programs for control purposes and future testing.
- Reviewed procedures manuals and controls external to the new system to ascertain that controls (including separation of duties) are adequate.
- Obtained copies of file layouts to determine the types of computerized audit routines that should be written.

As part of the final acceptance of the system and to determine that the conversion of the manual records was carried out properly, they conducted a postimplementation audit of the computerized files as of the conversion date. Their examination disclosed that the conversion was performed properly and that the new (computerized) files contain the same information as the manual records did at the conversion date.

By closely monitoring the development of the new system, the internal auditors (with the assistance of their independent auditors) were able to insure their ability to audit it upon implementation and to satisfy themselves that the conversion did not cause any distortion of financial data. They were not successful in getting all the controls and enhancements they felt were desirable, but they did:

- Keep the necessity for adequate controls and audit trails in the minds of the members of the project development team
- Accumulate the necessary information to produce effective programs for the ongoing audit of the system
- Train the other members of the internal audit department in the procedures necessary to properly audit the new system
- Lay the groundwork for the use of computerized audit programs by a suitable generalized audit software system

- Convince the chief internal auditor of the necessity for EDP audit expertise in his department, so that he:
    - Endorsed the necessity of obtaining a generalized audit software system.
    - Determined for himself that he needed an experienced and competent EDP audit group. (As we saw in Chapter 1, he was successful in obtaining two persons to fill this need.)

3
Auditing in a Computerized Environment

The American Institute of Certified Public Accountants has stated that:

> The objective of the ordinary examination of financial statements by the independent auditor is the expression of an opinion on the fairness with which they present financial position and results of the operations.[1]

The auditor's task in a financial audit usually consists of an analysis of the accounting data and systems and of the resulting financial statements. The auditor must be thoroughly conversant with the client's/auditee's accounting system and must pay particular attention to the capture and verification of the original data input to the system; to the processing procedures applied to this data, consisting of summarization, classification, allocation, and combination; and to the accuracy and completeness of the reports and other output generated by the processing of this data.

An operational or management audit does not focus on evaluating the fairness of the financial statements. Instead, the operational or management audit deals primarily with such matters as efficiency, cost control, profit maximization, and general adherence to managerial policy. Although the objectives of financial and operational audits may differ, the methodology is often the same.

Extensive use of computer-based systems to produce the financial statements and operating data of a firm does not change the basic goal of auditing, which is to verify the reliability of those statements and records and the degree to which they represent the true status of the firm. Extensive use of computers, however, does mean that the auditor must be adequately trained and sufficiently familiar with EDP techniques to adapt new approaches to the audit procedures.

Computers have changed the form of many records and the techniques by which they are processed. In many cases, transactions can now be recorded without ever producing any written copy. Audit trails have changed and often will no longer provide convenient signposts unless they have been care-

---

[1] Committee on Auditing Procedures, *Statement on Auditing Standards No. 1* (New York: American Institute of Certified Public Accountants, 1973), par. 110.01.

fully designed for that purpose. The auditor's evidential matter will now frequently include newer forms of documentation such as flowcharts, decision tables, program listings, record layouts, and operator log books. In some instances, the auditor can use the computer itself to perform some auditing tasks, such as selection and analysis of items for closer examination.

AUDIT PLAN

Evaluating the internal control of an organization is essentially a multi-stage operation. First, the auditor must become acquainted with the installation, including its organization, hardware, and software systems. If the auditor decides to rely on the system, he must acquire a firm understanding of the flow of transactions through the accounting system and the processing objectives of the organization against which the installation's performance can subsequently be evaluated. The applications implemented by the EDP department must be studied to acquire a thorough understanding of the procedures, programs, data files, and controls employed by the installation. If the auditor does not decide to rely on the system, he need only obtain a general understanding of it.

After completing this preliminary review of the system of internal control, the auditor must carefully evaluate those procedures and controls to determine whether the specified operations can accomplish the objectives designated and whether the controls can provide adequate assurance as to the accuracy of the data and the reliability of the resulting financial and operating records. If the auditor decides that the internal control system is reliable, substantive testing may be reduced.

If the auditor decides to rely on the system of internal control, sufficient tests of compliance must be performed to establish a reasonable degree of assurance that the prescribed procedures are in use and operating as planned. Tests of compliance may be applied on a subjective or statistical basis. The extent of testing done and the level of assurance deemed acceptable or reasonable are a matter of auditing judgment. The degree of assurance achieved is a function of the results obtained from the tests. It is the auditor's responsibility to judge what control procedures are appropriate to the system, to test that they operate as intended, and to assess any weaknesses resulting from the absence of a needed control or the failure of prescribed procedures to function as intended.

The purpose of compliance testing is to verify the existence and effective operation of controls in a processing system. Compliance testing is performed by both external and internal auditors, often using the same techniques. However, the results of compliance tests are often used for different purposes. In an internal audit, the evaluation of internal control and the verification of compliance with controls is frequently the primary function—whether these are financial (accounting) controls or managerial (administrative) controls.[2] The primary concern of the internal auditor in evaluating controls and verifying their implementation is to provide appropriate information to management for its operational use. An effective internal audit function is often itself an internal control which may be taken into consideration by the external auditor.

For the external auditor conducting a financial audit, the evaluation and subsequent compliance testing of controls serves a different purpose. The external auditor evaluates internal control (and performs compliance tests) as a basis for forming an opinion on the reliability of the financial records and for determining the extent to which substantive tests of the records may be restricted.

The Second Standard of Field Work, specified by the American Institute of Certified Public Accountants, states that:

> There is to be a proper study and evaluation of the existing internal control as a basis of reliance thereon and for the determination of the resultant extent of the tests to which auditing procedures are to be restricted.[3]

The second field work standard does not suggest elimination of substantive tests of the financial data. Indeed, regardless of how strong internal control may be, the auditor must still do some substantive testing. These are represented by various tests of details of transactions and balances and by analytic review of significant ratios and trends and unusual fluctuations shown as a result of the analysis. The review and evaluation of internal control is intended to help the auditor develop the plan of substantive testing.

> A function of internal control, from the viewpoint of the independent auditor, is to provide assurance that errors and irregularities may be discovered with reasonable promptness, thus assuring the reliability and integrity of the financial records. The independent auditor's review of the

---

[2] The American Institute of Certified Public Accountants has defined administrative and accounting controls in *SAS No. 1* (pars. 320.27 and 320.28) as follows:
Administrative control includes, but is not limited to, the plan or organization and the procedures and records that are concerned with the decision processes that lead to management's authorization of transactions. Such authorization is a management function directly associated with the responsibility for achieving the objectives of the organization and is the starting point for establishing accounting control of transactions.

Accounting control comprises the plan of organization and the procedures and records that are concerned with the safeguarding of assets and the reliability of financial records and consequently are designed to provide reasonable assurance that:
   a) Transactions are executed in accordance with management's general or specific authorization.
   b) Transactions are recorded as necessary (1) to permit preparation of financial statements in conformity with generally accepted accounting principles or any other criteria applicable to such statements and (2) to maintain accountability for assets.
   c) Access to the assets is permitted only in accordance with management's authorization.
   d) The recorded accountability for assets is compared with the existing assets at reasonable intervals and appropriate action is taken with respect to any differences.
[3] *SAS No. 1,* par. 150.02.

system of internal control assists him in determining other auditing procedures appropriate to the formulation of an opinion on the fairness of the financial statements.[4]

The relationship between the evaluation of internal control (supported by the results of compliance tests) and the need for substantive tests of the data is expressed in the following statement:

> The ultimate risk against which the auditor and those who rely on his opinion require reasonable protection is a combination of two separate risks. The first of these is that material errors will occur in the accounting process by which the financial statements are developed. The second is that any material errors that occur will not be detected in the auditor's examination.
>
> The auditor relies on internal control to reduce the first risk, and on his tests of details and his other auditing procedures to reduce the second. The relative weight to be given to the respective sources of reliance . . . are matters for the auditor's judgment in the circumstances.
>
> The Second Standard of Field Work recognizes that the extent of tests required to constitute sufficient evidential matter under the third standard should vary inversely with the auditor's reliance on internal control. These standards taken together imply that the combination of the auditor's reliance on internal control and on his auditing procedures should provide a reasonable basis for his opinion in all cases, although the portion of reliance derived from the respective sources may properly vary between cases.[5]

The sequence of procedures involved in the study and evaluation of EDP-based applications in a financial audit is outlined in Figure 3–1.

COMPLIANCE TESTING

Statement on Auditing Standards No. 1 says that "the purpose of tests of compliance is to provide reasonable assurance that the accounting control procedures are being applied as prescribed," and that tests of compliance "are concerned primarily with these questions: Were the necessary procedures performed, how were they performed, and by whom were they performed?" [6] *SAS No. 3* goes on to say that:

> The review may be done manually if conditions permit, or the auditor may be able or find it necessary to use EDP to detect unacceptable condi-

---

[4] *SAS No. 1,* par. 320.64.
[5] *SAS No. 1,* pars. 320A.14–15, 320A.19.
[6] *SAS No. 1,* pars. 320.55 and 320.57.

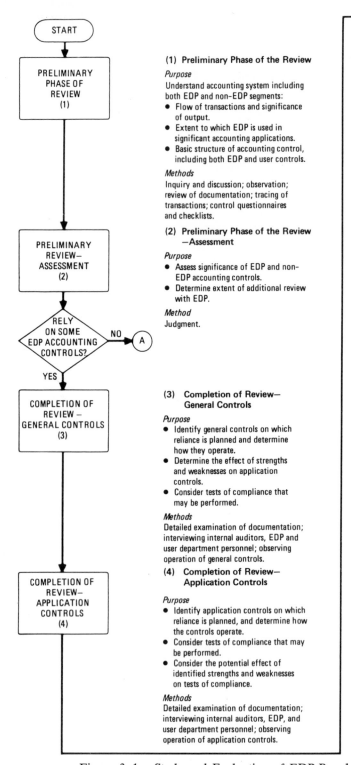

START

PRELIMINARY PHASE OF REVIEW (1)

(1) Preliminary Phase of the Review

Purpose
Understand accounting system including both EDP and non-EDP segments:
- Flow of transactions and significance of output.
- Extent to which EDP is used in significant accounting applications.
- Basic structure of accounting control, including both EDP and user controls.

Methods
Inquiry and discussion; observation; review of documentation; tracing of transactions; control questionnaires and checklists.

PRELIMINARY REVIEW— ASSESSMENT (2)

(2) Preliminary Phase of the Review —Assessment

Purpose
- Assess significance of EDP and non-EDP accounting controls.
- Determine extent of additional review with EDP.

Method
Judgment.

RELY ON SOME EDP ACCOUNTING CONTROLS? — NO → **A**

YES

COMPLETION OF REVIEW – GENERAL CONTROLS (3)

(3) Completion of Review— General Controls

Purpose
- Identify general controls on which reliance is planned and determine how they operate.
- Determine the effect of strengths and weaknesses on application controls.
- Consider tests of compliance that may be performed.

Methods
Detailed examination of documentation; interviewing internal auditors, EDP and user department personnel; observing operation of general controls.

COMPLETION OF REVIEW— APPLICATION CONTROLS (4)

(4) Completion of Review— Application Controls

Purpose
- Identify application controls on which reliance is planned, and determine how the controls operate.
- Consider tests of compliance that may be performed.
- Consider the potential effect of identified strengths and weaknesses on tests of compliance.

Methods
Detailed examination of documentation; interviewing internal auditors, EDP, and user department personnel; observing operation of application controls.

Figure 3–1. Study and Evaluation of EDP-Based Applications.

Reprinted by permission from: *The Auditor's Study and Evaluation of Internal Control in EDP Systems*, © 1977 The American Institute of Certified Public Accountants, pp. 21–24.

NOTE: At any point after the preliminary phase of the review, the auditor may decide not to rely on EDP accounting controls for all or some applications (see *SAS No. 3*, par. 26). The

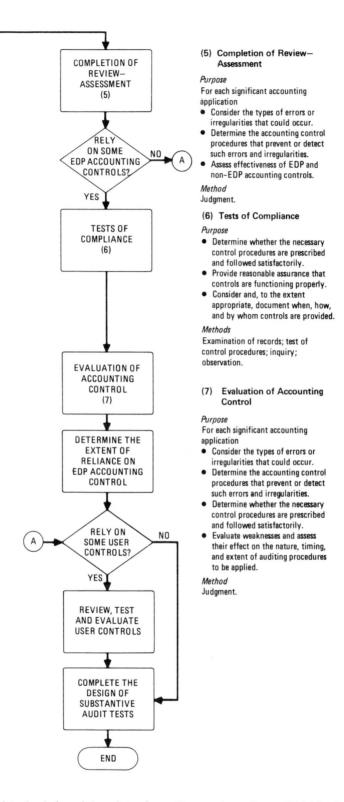

(5) Completion of Review—Assessment

Purpose

For each significant accounting application

- Consider the types of errors or irregularities that could occur.
- Determine the accounting control procedures that prevent or detect such errors and irregularities.
- Assess effectiveness of EDP and non-EDP accounting controls.

Method

Judgment.

(6) Tests of Compliance

Purpose

- Determine whether the necessary control procedures are prescribed and followed satisfactorily.
- Provide reasonable assurance that controls are functioning properly.
- Consider and, to the extent appropriate, document when, how, and by whom controls are provided.

Methods

Examination of records; test of control procedures; inquiry; observation.

(7) Evaluation of Accounting Control

Purpose

For each significant accounting application

- Consider the types of errors or irregularities that could occur.
- Determine the accounting control procedures that prevent or detect such errors and irregularities.
- Determine whether the necessary control procedures are prescribed and followed satisfactorily.
- Evaluate weaknesses and assess their effect on the nature, timing, and extent of auditing procedures to be applied.

Method

Judgment.

auditor would then complete the design of the substantive audit tests. According to *SAS No. 1*, Section 320.70, substantive tests consist of the following classes of audit procedures: (1) tests of details of transactions and balances and (2) analytical review of significant ratios and trends and resulting investigation of unusual fluctuations and questionable items.

tions, either by using his own independent programs or by using copies of the client's programs that the auditor has independently determined to be adequate for his purposes. An alternative approach to testing compliance with accounting control procedures in computer programs is to review and test the programs and then to perform tests to provide assurance that the tested programs actually were used for processing. However, the auditor should be aware that this approach can be used only when effective controls exist over access and changes to programs used for processing.[7]

Some control procedures leave an audit trail of documentary evidence. For these procedures, tests of compliance involve inspection of the supporting documents for signatures, initials, audit stamps, or similar evidence to determine who performed the procedures and to evaluate whether such performance was properly authorized. Other control procedures, such as those that depend upon segregation of duties or many EDP procedures, may leave no audit trails. These procedures must be tested by direct observation, inquiry of installation or user personnel, or other reconciliations, confirmations, or audit tests which may substantiate the accuracy of the underlying records.

Direct observation of installation operations by the auditor can be most useful. Visits to the machine room and file libraries can show whether access to these facilities is limited to authorized operating personnel, whether the file libraries are properly controlled, and whether the documentation library is conveniently organized and properly safeguarded. Interviews with operating personnel, programming personnel within the installation, and personnel of the user departments that either receive reports from the computer installation or provide data to it can be a good source of information as to how the operations actually do take place and the extent to which data controls are implemented.

Other evidence of compliance with controls can be obtained by examination of authorization forms for proper signatures. Review of console logs can provide insight into the typical operating procedures for the computer and the extent of unusual operator interventions. Depending upon his objectives, the auditor may also observe the way in which the console log sheets are used in the installation. Installation management should review those logs, and evidence that they are being used and reviewed by management (such as a complete file of a log sheet and initials by supervisors indicating examination) is useful in helping the auditor formulate an opinion about the supervisory control exercised in the installation.

Most operating systems also provide a rich source of information about the operation of the computer, including data such as the jobs being run on the computer and the system resources they require. This data is usually

---

[7] Auditing Standards Executive Committee, *Statement on Auditing Standards No. 3: The Effects of EDP on the Auditor's Study & Evaluation of Internal Control* (New York: American Institute of Certified Public Accountants, 1974), par. 29.

provided automatically by the operating system and includes copies of input information such as project code, job name, and input file. Other statistics produced automatically by many operating systems document the operations of the systems, such as run time and system utilization. The auditor can use these automatic reports and operating system printouts to review the work performed by data processing to determine that only authorized applications are being executed and unauthorized intervention is prohibited.

Examining the file records maintained in the file library and tracing actual files to specific tape reels or disk packs from the file library records helps establish evidence as to the actual operation of the data library procedures. Reviewing the error listings from selected edit runs and tracing the activities performed in correcting those errors and their subsequent reentry into the system is another way in which the auditor can verify compliance with internal control.

The maintenance records kept by an installation can also be an important source of information. Evidence such as complete performance and maintenance records and a regular schedule of preventative maintenance is an indication that the installation is maintaining its hardware in a reliable condition. Examination of the backup or contingency plans for hardware and files, as well as restart provisions, gives an indication of the degree to which the installation has made provisions for major breakdowns. Included with contingency plans may be provision for insurance, and an examination of the policies showing the degree of coverage is also useful.

The auditor can interview user department personnel to determine if they do in fact understand the processing performed for their departments and did authorize the EDP procedures involved. Testing standards, original test data, and the output of original program tests should be reviewed to determine that the testing process for the programs and EDP systems in effect were comprehensive. The auditor should examine all evidence of authorizations for changes to programming systems and should review all existing processing systems for evidence of changes to the operating system since the last review. Changes should be fully documented, and any discrepancy between the documentation and the actual state of affairs should be fully explored.

The computer can be used to facilitate this review. Compilation of source decks in the documentation library can produce object copies of programs for the auditor. These can then be compared instruction by instruction with working copies of those programs in the program libraries to determine whether there are any undocumented changes. Another technique which can be used is an automatic flowcharting program to produce an independent flowchart of a working program in the program library to be compared with the installation's documentation.

Before we discuss automatic flowcharting, we should bear in mind that it is not a technique intended primarily for auditing. It is a systems development technique which auditors, especially internal auditors, have adapted to their needs. Nevertheless, it deserves coverage in this discussion of computer-assisted techniques available to auditors.

With the availability of a number of commercial packages that automatically flowchart the logic of computer programs, the auditor can use the computer to diagram existing programs so that the program logic, including exception routines, calculations, and other functions, can be verified independently of the installation's documentation. The auditor can use this automatically produced flowchart to become acquainted with the logic of the program, to identify any changes in the program, and to compare it with the installation's documentation, thus providing insight into its accuracy and dependability.

By comparing the automatically produced flowcharts with the installation's documentation, the auditor can note any changes made in the existing programs that have not been reflected in corrections or adjustments of the documentation. This is especially helpful in those instances where the auditor examines the installation's documentation but does not want to take the time to go through the program listings in detail, checking for changes. It also helps the auditor in evaluating the installation's procedures for controlling changes and updating the client's programs.

Automatic flowcharting programs do have disadvantages. Some, especially for long, complex programs, produce very large printouts that are difficult to follow. The flowchart does not in itself point out control strengths and weaknesses; it is only an early step in the auditor's search for those strengths and weaknesses.

Actual distribution of computer-generated reports should be checked to verify that they are distributed as indicated in the systems plan and that they are providing the user with the processing results needed. Similarly, source documents should be examined to verify that the information is as described and to determine whether they are properly verified as they move into the installation. Examination of sample error listings, batch control records, and authorization records all help to determine the flow of information as it actually occurs within the installation.

A great deal of the auditor's time in an EDP environment is spent in verifying that the programs of the installation perform as intended, that there are no undetected program errors, and that there have been no unauthorized changes. One technique which can be employed is that of actually reviewing the program code to validate the processing taking place. This technique, however, requires a high degree of technical data processing expertise, is extremely time-consuming, and must be repeated each year to check any changes which may have been made to the program. An alternative to the actual detailed review of program code can be a procedure in which a sample of representative transactions is traced from the recording of source documents, through whatever intermediate records exist, to the output. Thus, the auditor determines in advance what results a given source transaction should produce when processed by a given program and then compares it with the results produced by that program. This approach has some popularity because of its simplicity and because it requires little direct or detailed knowledge of computer processes by the auditor. It can be justified in those systems characterized by fairly complete printouts of all transactions and intermediate results and in which the transactions are originally recorded manually before being transcribed to machine-readable form.

Tracing actual transactions through the processing system becomes less desirable in those instances where the volume of information is large, the transactions are not originally recorded in manual form, or the processing is such that the machine-produced result cannot be easily traced back to the manual record. When these conditions exist, the use of the computer to test itself and the data processing system is a more realistic and reliable way of evaluating the system. One process in which the system can be used to test itself is that of *system* or *parallel simulation*.

In system simulation, the auditor develops an independent processing system designed to accomplish the same processing as the application being tested. This "independent auditor system" can be developed by specially written audit programs, or can be assembled through the use of vendor-provided utility packages or the proper processing modules from a generalized audit software package. The simulated system processes the same live input as that which went through the actual system. The resulting outputs can be compared and exceptions noted and fully investigated. If all the exceptions are satisfactorily explained, the application program can be considered correct. Another procedure for using the computer to test the processing system is the use of test data which can be used to "exercise" the processing system and programs. The test data should include samples of all conditions critical to the audit objectives, including both valid data which the system should handle, and invalid data which the system should be able to detect and reject.

In using test data to test the system, it is frequently difficult for the auditor to process the test data in the actual processing environment (or as close to that actual environment as possible) and at the same time avoid the potential problem of creating distortions in the live master file. Auditors therefore prepare duplicates of the files in which they are interested and process test data against them in separate runs. This not only requires separate processing but also forces the auditor to be sure the programs used for the test are the same as those used to process live data during the period being audited.

The integrated test facility (ITF) is a variation of the test data technique designed to overcome these problems. In an ITF, a number of dummy (or audit) records are built into the current master file. Test transactions can be run along with live transactions in the normal processing routine; the test transactions will update only the dummy records. The dummy records are called the *facility*. This eliminates the concern of impacting actual master records with test data and, further, the dummy master records will have no effect during those live processing runs in which test transactions are not processed. During systems tests using these facilities, dummy or audit records should not be so identified. The audit crew introduces the fictitious entities to the installation's staff. These are added to master files and can have transactions processed against them using normal company processing procedures. The advantage of this technique is that it allows the test of the actual operating facility without any unnecessary disruption or the need for subsequent reversing activities. This approach requires, however, attention to the proper limitation and control of the power of the audit group to generate the records for these fictitious entities.

The auditor's tests of compliance should also include review and observation of procedures for original entry of data and for performance of the verification procedures for that data. Batch totals should be traced to the control logs on a test basis and input transactions should be traced to the original source documents on a test basis. The auditor should observe the movement of data from one processing station to another and should verify that users do in fact examine output and balance results with original input controls. The auditor also ought to verify that distribution of output from EDP operations is in accordance with authorized procedures.

SUBSTANTIVE TESTS

SAS No. 1 defines substantive tests as "those audit procedures which provide tests of details of transactions and balances and analytical review of significant ratios and trends and resulting investigation of unusual fluctuations and questionable items." [8] The purpose of these procedures is to obtain evidence as to the validity and propriety of accounting treatment of transactions and balances or of errors or irregularities within these accounting data.

The extent of the substantive tests performed will be determined in part by the results of the auditor's evaluation of internal control. A system of internal control which is judged to be adequate and for which tests of compliance support that judgment can provide the basis by which the auditor will reduce the amount of substantive testing performed. Tests of compliance are often closely interrelated with substantive tests. In many cases, specific auditing procedures concurrently provide evidence of compliance with accounting control procedures as well as substantive evidence of accurate financial records.

The computerization of accounting records can change the audit trail substantially. However, in a well-designed system the audit trail continues to exist. Legally, installations are required to provide (at least for the Internal Revenue Service) the opportunity to trace any transaction back to the original source or forward to a final total. If the auditor has sufficient technical proficiency

[8] *SAS No. 1,* par. 320.70.

to take advantage of existing new audit trails, the computer can be used to test the transactions and balances of the client's/auditee's records.

The use of the computer can provide two potential benefits to the auditor. First, it can enable the auditor to minimize the amount of time spent on the routine clerical and nonjudgmental aspects of auditing. Second, it can help the auditor gain greater assurance about the reliability of the financial statements by allowing an extension of the scope of the examination and an increase in the number of items tested by substituting the computer's speed in information retrieval and calculation for the more expensive and scarce time of audit personnel. Thus, by applying computer techniques, the auditor not only gains access to a great deal more information than would be economically feasible under traditional manual techniques, but the computer also frees a much larger percentage of auditor time for evaluative and judgmental activities than was previously possible.

One of the major uses to which the computer can be put is to search and retrieve records from the existing files. The computer can search huge volumes of records or transactions in a relatively short time, identifying and selecting items that may have a particular audit significance. As long as the characteristic by which the selection is to be made can be described in an objective manner (e.g., costs exceeding a particular limit, items with a particular characteristic, or just every nth item of so many items), a computer can be programmed to recognize this characteristic and select the record for further attention by the auditor.

Using the computer in this way gives an additional advantage to the auditor, for every item in a file can be reviewed. Selecting for further detailed examination only those items with the particular criteria specified, but at the same time scanning all records within the file for internal consistency, completeness, and validity, and calculating totals within the file, provides a broader base for an opinion than examination of a limited sample of items. While the file is being passed for selection of the test items, every record can be examined for internal consistency and completeness, and any records that do not pass one of the completeness or consistency tests can also be selected for attention by the auditor. An example of this ability of the computer to search the computer files and retrieve certain records is the use of the computer in selecting and printing confirmation requests.

The computer can be used to select audit samples on the basis of any objectively defined characteristic or condition. In addition, however, the computer can be used to formulate and select random samples. Generation of random numbers can be a time-consuming manual procedure, but on the computer it can be done rapidly. Furthermore, the auditor can be aided in determining sample sizes needed to satisfy certain statistical confidence levels and to sort and print out lists in numerical sequence of records, documents, or other forms to be audited.

Another area in which the computer can be of great use to the auditor is in facilitating the many mathematical computations that must be made. Verifying the extensions, additions, and calculations of the records selected for audit can be performed on all records rather than just the sample being selected. Further, the auditor can use the computer for the auditor's own calculations. Because of the efficiency of the computer, the auditor can develop a much greater variety of ratios and averages from the financial and operating data. These figures can be used to identify deviations within the current year's results or to provide better comparisons with the prior year's results.

Procedures such as the aging of accounts receivable, preparation of inventory usage requirements, and analysis of inventory for obsolescence can all be facilitated by computerization. The computer represents a great advantage in handling data files, because large-volume machine-readable files can be easily summarized and used to provide reports to the auditor in whatever detail or level of summarization may be most useful.

The ability of the computer to read rapidly through large volumes of information can also make it convenient for the auditor to use the computer to make comparisons between two or more files of data. Comparison of two generations of a file (e.g., payroll) can provide a change log against which to verify all transactions affecting a change in the master records (such as terminations and additions to the employee rolls). The computer can also be used to compare independently collected data with installation records. For example, the auditor can compare the results of test counts of selected items of a physical inventory with the inventory records and very quickly identify any discrepancy. During the comparison the computer can be calculating costs and price extensions and comparing those, as well as the quantity counts, with the installation's records. Discrepancies can immediately be brought to the auditor's attention. Similarly, the auditor can compare the previous year's expense records with the current year's expense records, selecting for further detailed examination items that show unusual variation or change.

If the auditor has the means of transcribing the confirmation replies into machine-readable data, the computer can be used to compare the results of the audit tests with the client records, generate second requests, and calculate confirmation statistics. As the auditor develops techniques to input audit data as well as to use the live data, the computer can be used to analyze investment portfolios, income, depreciation schedules for both tax and financial statement purposes, and to calculate or verify projections of income, expense, and liability.

COMPETENT EVIDENTIAL MATTER

The Third Standard of Field Work requires that "sufficient competent evidential matter . . . be obtained through inspection, observation, inquiries, and confirmations to afford a reasonable basis for an opinion regarding the financial statements under examination." [9]

Physical evidence supplied by inspection or count of certain types of assets is highly desirable. Procedures such as verifying the amount of cash on hand by counting; examining and counting notes receivable, marketable securities, and inventories; and physically inspecting property and equipment are all sources of important evidence for the auditor. Evidence provided by external sources, such as confirmation of accounts receivable by customers or confirmation of cash balances by the bank, is very desirable. The auditor can use the computer to prepare the original requests, but the value of the activity as evidence comes from the action of the independent agencies outside the organization.

Ledgers and journals or other forms of intermediate records, such as transaction listings generated when the accounting records are computerized, can also be evidence that is potentially useful to the auditor. If the accounting records agree with the original documents supporting the initiation of transactions, and if any other records of transactions affecting the particular assets or liabilities involved also agree with the accounting records, they can be considered evidence that the transactions being examined were legitimate and properly recorded.

The auditor can collect much data from the client's files. For example, listings of the employees from the payroll master files can be used to verify pay rates, and the year-to-date earnings shown in the master files can be reconciled to the printed payroll registers. At the same time, the payroll register can be compared with cancelled payroll checks for agreement of check numbers, dates, payees, and amounts. Further, the payroll register can be traced to the labor distribution reports to reconcile dollar amounts. Time reports can be used to verify gross earnings calculated for each employee. The computer can be used to perform arithmetic checks on the calculations or to compare employee's accumulated earnings for two consecutive pay periods to verify the intervening payroll reports.

Evidential matter in a system that depends upon computerized controls and processing procedures draws heavily on the documentation of the system's processing procedures and programs. This documentation frequently consists of record layouts, program listings, flowcharts, decision tables, and run manuals. The documents represent the installation's formal description of the system, and an understanding of these materials can help the auditor to design the computer audit program.

Also important are the listings and calculations assembled by the auditor as the system and data are examined and evaluated. Since much data is in machine-readable form, the auditor may be required to use computer-assisted

---

[9] *SAS No. 1,* par. 150.22.

audit techniques to test those machine records in order to verify their accuracy as part of the compliance test of internal controls or the substantive tests of the accounting records.

WERNER MANUFACTURING, INC.—CASE STUDY

The next section of the continuing case study shows how general control strengths are verified by compliance tests and how application control strengths and weaknesses determine the nature and extent of compliance and substantive tests.

AUDITING PROCEDURES: GENERAL

In Chapter 1 we evaluated the internal controls in the system by identifying them as either strengths or weaknesses. We stated that these controls should be evaluated on a total system basis; that is, the entire network of controls (computerized and manual) should be evaluated as they interact. In this approach, weaknesses in computerized controls may be ameliorated or completely offset by manual strengths in the user departments. Conversely, weaknesses in user controls may be ameliorated or offset by strengths in the computerized area of the system. And, overlying the whole system of application controls are the general controls.

This section will relate the evaluation of internal controls to auditing procedures in two stages by:

1. Identifying auditing procedures for testing compliance with the *general* control strengths identified in Chapter 1.
2. Preparing a working paper to relate *application* control strengths and weaknesses to detailed auditing procedures.

Instead of just performing auditing procedures because they are traditional, this approach will relate them directly to the evaluation of internal control by auditing both the system and the amounts generated by the system.

We will assume that the auditor has performed the "preliminary review" in accordance with *SAS No. 3*.

TESTS OF COMPLIANCE WITH GENERAL CONTROL STRENGTHS

Assume that the EDP internal auditors are established and are performing their regular auditing procedures. The sales, accounts receivable and cash receipts computerization project has been successfully completed and is fully operational. Tables 3–1 and 3–2 describe the auditing procedures they pres-

Table 3–1. General Control Compliance Tests—Werner Manufacturing, Inc.

DESCRIPTION OF GENERAL CONTROL STRENGTH	AUDITING PROCEDURE TO TEST FOR COMPLIANCE
1. The EDP department is organizationally independent of the user departments.	Werner's EDP internal auditors: • Reviewed the organization charts and job descriptions for the entire company and for the EDP organization to satisfy themselves that Werner's policies and procedures require this independence. • Interviewed EDP and user department personnel to find out whether the procedures designed to insure organizational independence are: — Clearly understood by those most directly affected by them — Adhered to by those charged with carrying them out • Observed data center operations on a surprise basis as a further test of adherence to company policies and procedures. They were particularly interested in the actions of management personnel to determine the effectiveness of supervision. • Reviewed available management reports (including the independent auditors' management letter) to determine whether control over information to be processed was being maintained by the EDP department or whether EDP was initiating transactions and/or correcting any but keypunch or other EDP-generated errors.
2. All transactions are initiated and/or authorized by the user departments.	• Reviewed user department approvals on output sent to them for verification. • Examined the reconciliations to control totals prepared by the EDP department's operations personnel on an informal basis. Note: Since, as the application controls in the system flowcharts clearly show, there is no I/O control group, little audit reliance can be placed on this strength. The auditors cannot satisfy themselves that this control is being complied with. Audit reliance would therefore have to depend on the user departments' review of output and/or the effectiveness of programmed controls (if any). Werner's auditors concluded no reliance should be placed on these controls and decided to expand the scope of their substantive auditing procedures.

Note: Unless explicitly stated otherwise, assume the auditing procedures have shown that the general controls are effective and are being complied with.

Table 3–1.   (continued)

DESCRIPTION OF GENERAL CONTROL STRENGTH	AUDITING PROCEDURE TO TEST FOR COMPLIANCE
3. There is a good segregation of duties within the EDP department.	• Observed EDP operations personnel on a surprise basis. (See item 1.) They noted that the computer room is a "closed shop"; that is, access can be gained only by the use of a magnetically-coded plastic card (to open a locked door) issued to authorized persons. Systems and programming personnel do not have such cards and therefore do not have access to the computer room. • Reviewed the file library and the control log maintained by the librarian. Observed that operators are not allowed in the library and that files are issued only to authorized operators for specific jobs. • Observed that programs under development are submitted to operators for test processing. • Examined time and job logs to ascertain that operators' responsibilities are rotated, that vacations must be taken, and that vacationing operators' duties are performed by other operators.
4. Systems design procedures require the formation of a project development team which includes representatives of the user departments (including the accounting department) and the active involvement of the internal auditors.	• Reviewed documentation prepared to support the computerization of the sales, accounts receivable and cash receipts system. (See Chapter 2 for the details of this project and the involvement of the user departments and the internal auditors.) • Interviewed user department personnel to ascertain whether they were truly involved in the system's development, particularly whether they felt the system was designed to meet their departments' needs.
5. Written specifications for computerized systems are adequate and show that they have been reviewed and approved by user departments, the internal auditors and management (as represented by the EDP Steering Committee).	• See item 4 above.
6. Systems testing is a joint effort of the user departments, EDP personnel and the internal auditors. Further, it encompasses both the manual and computerized portions of the system.	• Reviewed the documentation supporting the implementation phase of the sales, accounts receivable and cash receipts system computerization project, including the procedure for reconciling output produced during parallel testing. • Interviewed user and EDP personnel to determine if the implementation phase test procedures were adequate. • Designed their own test data and ran production programs in the sales, accounts receivable and cash receipts system against it. The results

Table 3-1. (continued)

DESCRIPTION OF GENERAL CONTROL STRENGTH	AUDITING PROCEDURE TO TEST FOR COMPLIANCE
	were then compared with those predetermined by the internal auditors.
7. New systems are not placed into operation until written final approvals have been obtained.	• See items, 4, 5 and 6 above.
8. Master and transaction file conversions are properly controlled to prevent unauthorized changes and to insure accurate and complete results.	• Reviewed the conversion from manual to computerized files during the implementation phase of the sales, accounts receivable and cash receipts computerization project. • Tested the conversion by tracing detailed records from the old, manual files to the new, computerized ones. • During selected periods after the conversion, tested the master file updating procedure by using computer programs to trace the old balances to the new ones.
9. All program changes are subject to the same effective controls as are new ones.	• Interviewed operations and systems personnel to ascertain that program changes are in fact subjected to the same controls as are new ones. • Reviewed documentation supporting program changes to determine if procedures are being followed. • Selected several revised programs and compared them with their audit control copies to isolate the changes. Then they traced these changes to the required approvals. • Reviewed the EDP department's documentation to determine whether the changes to the programs selected for the review were properly tested to verify their correctness.
10. EDP applications are well documented at all levels.	• Reviewed EDP documentation standards to insure they are adequate. • Examined documentation for the sales, accounts receivable and cash receipts system to insure standards are being complied with. • See Chapter 2 for procedures followed in the implementation phase of the computerization of sales, accounts receivable and cash receipts.
11. Control features inherent in computer hardware, the operating system and supporting software are utilized to provide control over operations and to detect and report hardware malfunctions.	• Reviewed vendor's literature and systems documentation to determine what control capabilities are present. • Evaluated the operation of the identified controls by reviewing the EDP department's documentation (e.g., SMF reports, logs of usage and down time, console logs, etc.). Their review disclosed that console logs were not being regularly reviewed, and they reported this weakness to management.

Table 3–1. (continued)

DESCRIPTION OF GENERAL CONTROL STRENGTH	AUDITING PROCEDURE TO TEST FOR COMPLIANCE
	• Performed simulated malfunctions to determine whether the hardware and software controls did in fact detect and report them. Their tests did not disclose any weaknesses in this area.
12. Systems software changes are well controlled.	• Reviewed the EDP department's control procedures for changes to the system software. • Reviewed documentation supporting changes to system software. Note: See Chapter 1 for a discussion of the controls Werner has installed, for example, the approvals required before any changes may be made. • Selected several software changes, including the most recent SYSGEN and those made to accommodate the computerization of the sales, acounts receivable and cash receipts system, and: — Determined that there were valid reasons for the changes. — Reviewed the documentation to insure it accurately reflected those changes and contained proper approvals. — Reviewed preimplementation tests to insure the authorized changes were made correctly.
13. Access to program documentation is restricted to those who require it in the performance of their duties.	• Reviewed procedures for controlling access to documentation. • Interviewed the systems personnel, including the supervisor (Browne), to ascertain whether the stated procedures were being followed. • Tested the adequacy of the controls by attempting to gain access to the documentation for the purchases, accounts payable and cash disbursements system.
14. Access to data files and programs is limited to those authorized to process or maintain those systems.	• Reviewed the librarian function to ascertain that the librarians have been given explicit instructions as to which operators may have which files and programs. • Reviewed the file librarian's log to determine that these instructions were being complied with and that files and programs have been issued only at those times when the production schedule called for those particular applications to be processed. (See item 3 above.)
15. Access to computer hardware is limited to authorized persons.	• Reviewed procedures for collecting and analyzing utilization data, including logs and SMF reports. Identified questionable entries and statistics and obtained satisfactory explanations from operating personnel.

Table 3–1.   (continued)

DESCRIPTION OF GENERAL CONTROL STRENGTH	AUDITING PROCEDURE TO TEST FOR COMPLIANCE
	• See procedures performed in connection with items 3 and 14.
16. Written manuals of systems and authorized procedures are prepared and maintained for all computer operations. These constitute general and specific management authorization to process transactions by computer.	• Reviewed computer operators' manuals to determine if they provide operators with a clear understanding of processing. • Observed operations to insure that they are in fact being carried out as specified in the manuals. • See procedures performed in connection with items 1 and 3.
17. Internal auditors review and evaluate proposed systems at critical development stages.	• See Chapter 2 for a description of the EDP internal auditors' participation in the computerization of the sales, accounts receivable and cash receipts system.
18. Internal auditors review and test computer processing activities on a continuing basis.	• See procedures performed in connection with items 1–17. The independent auditors, Brown, Johnson & Co., performed the following procedures in accordance with *SAS No. 9* as part of their annual audit: — Reviewed the internal auditors' scope, procedures and working papers and found them to be adequate. — Test-checked selected auditing procedures performed by the internal auditors and found no exceptions.

ently use, after familiarizing themselves with the computerized systems and reviewing and evaluating the internal controls in them. As you read the chart, keep in mind that it does *not* list control *weaknesses,* as no compliance tests would be performed on them.

Since these auditing procedures involve interaction between the internal and independent auditors, provisions of *SAS No. 9* must be considered. *SAS No. 9* says that:

- The independent auditor is to review the internal auditor's scope and auditing procedures as part of his review and evaluation of internal control. If he concludes the internal auditor's work represents an internal control strength and decides to rely on it, the independent auditor must perform compliance tests on the internal auditor's procedures.
- Regardless of his evaluation of the internal auditor's work as an element of internal control, the independent auditor may use the internal auditor to perform certain independent auditing procedures. If he does so, the

Table 3-2. Substantive and Compliance Tests—Werner Manufacturing, Inc.

DESCRIPTION OF APPLICATION CONTROL STRENGTH OR WEAKNESS SALES AND ACCOUNTS RECEIVABLE	AUDITING PROCEDURES—SUBSTANTIVE AND COMPLIANCE		REMARKS
	INTERNAL AUDITOR	INDEPENDENT AUDITOR	
I. Status of the customer's account is determined before any significant processing takes place.	1, 2, 3 and 4	1 and 2	Note that the independent auditor's scope depends on whether the internal auditor has performed his work adequately.
II. Before shipping orders are prepared, the inventory files are queried to determine if there is a sufficient quantity on hand.	5 and 6	1 and 2	Same as above.
III. A printed list of backorders is given to the sales department. At the same time, the data is kept in computerized files so that a replenishment notice is printed when quantities are restored.	7, 8 and 9	1 and 2	Same as above.
IV. Sales orders are sent to the sales department (for accuracy checking) and to the credit manager (for final credit approval) before the goods are shipped.	10	3a–b and 4	Same as above.
V. Input is sent directly to the computer operator for entry on key-to-disk equipment and processed.	—	4, 5 and 6	Since this is a weakness, there is no point in performing a compliance test. The scope of the cutoff test (step 4) and confirmation of balances (step 5c) were increased to compensate for this weakness. Note that here the independent auditors are *not* relying on the internal auditor's work.
VI. Sales orders are not processed until the goods are actually shipped.	10	3a–b and 4	Note that the independent auditor's scope depends on whether the internal auditor has performed his work adequately.

VII. Input to the sales/file updating procedure is accepted as long as the sales order number is correct. Processing produces an invoice (three-part) and a sales register (for posting to the general ledger).	—	4, 5, 6 and 7	See comment for V.
VIII. Output is distributed to the accounting department by the computer operators.	—	4, 5, 6 and 7	See comment for V.
IX. Copies of invoices are sent to the originating sales location to review for errors.	11	—	Although this is a strength, the independent auditors are not going to rely on it in setting their audit scope. They feel the reviews performed in IV are more effective. Since they are not going to rely on the strength, they have not tested compliance with it. Since the internal auditor's work is more procedural in scope, he *does* have an audit procedure for testing compliance.
CASH RECEIPTS			
X. Checks are restrictively endorsed in the mail room as soon as received.	13	8	See comment for I.
XI. Initial control tape is compared with the duplicate deposit slip and cash receipts listing.	12	8	See comment for I.
XII. Input is sent directly to the keypunch operators for conversion to machine–readable format.	—	5, 8, 9 and 10	See comment for V.
XIII. All keypunching is 100% verified by a second person.	15	—	Although this is a strength, the independent auditors will not rely on it. They consider the procedures described in XI, XII and XIV to be more significant for their purposes.

Table 3-2. (continued)

DESCRIPTION OF APPLICATION CONTROL STRENGTH OR WEAKNESS CASH RECEIPTS	AUDITING PROCEDURES— SUBSTANTIVE AND COMPLIANCE		REMARKS
	INTERNAL AUDITOR	INDEPENDENT AUDITOR	
XIV. A daily listing of transactions is printed and compared with the cash receipts listing.	12	8	See comment for I.
XV. Output is distributed by the computer operator.	—	5, 8, 9 and 10	See comment for V.
XVI. A person independent of the daily recording of cash receipts and disbursements reconciles the bank account. The reconciliation is reviewed and approved by the controller.	—	—	Auditing procedures to compliance-test this strength would normally be found in the audit program for bank accounts, which is not covered in this case study.
XVII. Trial balances of accounts receivable and inventory and a listing of open orders are sent to responsible persons for review.	14	5, 8, 9 and 10	See comment for I.

Note: Roman numerals refer to the flowcharts and accompanying schedules in Chapter 1. Arabic numerals refer to the auditing procedures on pages 131–133 (Internal Auditor) and 129–131 (Independent Auditor). For our purposes, we are not considering sales returns and allowances.

independent auditor must insure that the internal auditor operates under his supervision and control.

Assume that in this case, Brown, Johnson, the independent auditors, concluded that the internal auditors' work represents an internal control strength and test-checked (compliance-tested) their work. If they were not able to rely on the internal auditors' work, the independent auditors would probably have performed these procedures themselves. Read Table 3–1 and return here.

SUBSTANTIVE AND COMPLIANCE AUDITING PROCEDURES

Werner's general controls are strong with the exception of two aspects:

1. They do not have an I/O control group.
2. The terminals at remote locations do not have adequate security.

Consider the following compliance and substantive tests (see Table 3–2) performed in connection with application control strengths and weaknesses in the sales, accounts receivable and cash receipts system with those factors in mind. In doing so, assume (as we did with the general controls) that the internal auditors concentrate their work on compliance auditing procedures. Consequently, most of the substantive test work will be performed by the independent auditors. This approach requires that there be very close and effective coordination between the internal and independent auditors and that the requirements of SAS No. 9 are carefully adhered to. Read Table 3–2 and return here.

INDEPENDENT AUDITORS' PROCEDURES—SALES, ACCOUNTS RECEIVABLE AND CASH RECEIPTS SYSTEM *

1. Review and document (system flowcharts, narratives, questionnaires, checklists, and so on) the system and determine the adequacy of internal control, including the internal auditors' procedures and working papers. (See items 2, 3 and 8 in this audit program.)
2. Determine whether the internal auditors are properly testing compliance with the following order entry control procedures:
   a. Determining the status of customers' accounts before sales orders are entered.
   b. Establishing that inventory quantities are sufficient to satisfy an accepted sales order.
   c. Updating back order files and querying them when stock is replenished. If the internal auditors' procedures are adequate, select

---

* Paragraph numbers refer to the auditing procedures—independent auditor—column of Table 3–2.

a sample of their tests, review them for adequacy, and perform them again to see if they were performed properly. If procedures are inadequate or improperly performed, expand your scope to test a sufficient number of transactions to enable you to decide whether the control procedures are being complied with.

3. Obtain and check or prepare a monthly summary of sales, check it against the general ledger, and compare it with prior years. Investigate and explain any material changes and:

   a. Determine whether the internal auditors' sales auditing procedures are adequate to enable them to decide whether control procedures are being complied with. If their procedures are adequate, select a sample of the following tests (see item 10 in their audit program) and perform them again to see if they were performed properly:

      i. Obtain a sample of sales orders from the entire year and examine them for evidence that they were checked for arithmetical accuracy and correct pricing by the sales department and for final credit approval by the credit manager *before* the goods were shipped.

      ii. Trace the sales orders to related shipping orders, the sales register and the customer receivables file and recheck them for arithmetical accuracy and pricing. Trace the sales register to the general ledger posting.

   b. If the internal auditors' procedures are inadequate or improperly performed, expand your scope to test a sufficient number of transactions to enable you to decide whether the control procedures are being complied with.

4. For fifteen days before and after the audit date, perform a sales cutoff by comparing sales invoices with shipping reports and the sales register.

5. Obtain and check or prepare an aged trial balance of customer receivables as of an interim date and:

   a. Foot the totals and crossfoot selected accounts.

   b. Compare the total receivable balance with the general ledger.

   c. Confirm selected accounts: all $10,000 and over; 10% of the rest

   d. Prepare a schedule to reconcile the balance as of the interim date to the balance on the audit date; vouch the accuracy of the reconciling amounts (sales, cash receipts, adjusting journal entries, and so on).

6. For customers who do not respond to the request for confirmation, trace the balance outstanding to subsequent cash receipts. Check for fictitious debtors by reference to telephone directories and credit services.

7. Review the client's aging policy; verify the adequacy of the allowance for doubtful accounts by:

   a. Comparing the aging with prior periods and investigating any material changes

    b. Reviewing and vouching material write-offs during the period

    c. Reviewing subsequent periods for credit memos or write-offs on accounts with large balances

    d. Reviewing individual, large accounts for collectibility with a responsible official of the client

8. Determine whether the internal auditors' cash receipts auditing procedures are adequate to enable them to decide whether control procedures are being complied with. If their procedures are adequate, select a sample of their tests (see items 12, 13 and 14 in their audit program) and perform them again to see if they were performed properly. If the internal auditors' procedures are inadequate or improperly performed, expand your scope to test a sufficient number of transactions to enable you to decide whether the control procedures are being complied with.

9. For selected periods during the entire year, vouch entries in the general ledger cash accounts from sources other than the cash receipts or disbursements book.

10. For the period following the audit date, scan the cash receipts book and credits on the bank statements for unusual items.

Note: Items 8–10 refer only to cash receipts. Cash disbursements would be covered by the audit program for the purchases, accounts payable and cash disbursements system. Bank accounts would be covered in another program.

INTERNAL AUDITORS' PROCEDURES—SALES, ACCOUNTS RECEIVABLE AND CASH RECEIPTS SYSTEM *

1. On a surprise basis at Cleveland and each of the remote locations, attempt to turn on the terminal. If you are successful:

    a. Dial the computer and input a random user number and password, using the correct format as described in the operator's manual, to access the customer, order entry and back order files. If you are successful, do the next procedure.

    b. For each of the online files, enter a random password, using the correct format as described in the operator's manual, and attempt to:

        i. Read selected records.

        ii. Add data to the file.

        iii. Change records in the file.

2. Rent a terminal identical to the models used at Cleveland and the remote locations and attempt to do the same things in step 1 above. This is to test whether the answer-back codes are working correctly.

3. At the Cleveland data center:

    a. Obtain the log of valid and invalid access attempts and trace the attempts in steps 1 and 2 above.

* Paragraph numbers refer to the auditing procedures—internal auditor—column of Table 3–2.

    b. If you were successful in adding or changing records, you should first tell the manager of the data center to see if he can access those files from a terminal in the EDP department and reverse the transactions. If the manager cannot do this, tell the user departments so that they can carry out the reversals.

4. Prepare dummy transactions and attempt to enter them via the internal audit department's user number and terminal. These should attempt to enter a credit sale for:

    a. A fictitious customer

    b. A valid customer whose credit limit will be exceeded by a sale of that size

    c. A valid customer who is on a cash-only basis

    d. Products that Werner does not sell

5. Enter a dummy transaction representing an order from a valid customer which exceeds the available quantity of the item ordered. Check to see if the transaction was processed to the point where a shipping order was issued.

6. Check the log of terminal accesses to determine whether the inventory file was queried for the dummy transaction in 5 above.

7. For the same transaction in 5 above: check the status of the back order file to determine whether it reflects a back order for the item ordered.

8. Ascertain when that item is to be replenished and check to see that the replenishment has triggered a replenishment notice.

9. When steps 5–8 have been completed, advise the manager of the data center of the dummy transaction and observe whether he is able to reverse it from the EDP department. If he cannot, notify the user department so it may make the reversal.

10. For selected dates throughout the year:

    a. Review sales orders to determine that they were checked for (1) arithmetical accuracy by the sales department and (2) credit approval by the credit manager *before* the goods were shipped.

    b. Trace those sales orders to related shipping orders, to the sales register and to the customer receivables file, and check them for arithmetical accuracy and pricing. Trace sales register to general ledger posting.

11. For selected periods throughout the year, examine invoices for evidence they were reviewed and approved by the originating sales location.

12. For selected dates throughout the year:

    a. Foot and crossfoot the cash receipts book.

    b. Check the posting from the cash receipts book to the general ledger.

    c. Trace selected cash receipts to the daily listing of transactions; trace the daily listing to the cash receipts listing and to selected customer accounts.

    d. Trace initial control tape to the duplicate deposit ticket and the cash receipts listing.

    e. Trace cash receipts listing total to the bank statement.

    f. Compare dates and amounts of daily deposits as shown on the bank statements with the cash receipts book.

13. Observe the mail room to see if remittance checks are restrictively endorsed.

14. Check for approvals on selected copies of accounts receivable, inventory and open orders trial balances.

15. Observe the keypunching function to be sure that input is being key-verified.

Note that even though Werner Manufacturing has a computerized accounting system, all the auditing procedures (both internal and independent) are manual. This is not wrong: one does not *have* to audit "through" or "with" the computer (we will define these terms in Chapter 4). One *does,* however, have to understand the entire system before he reviews and evaluates internal control.

Using the computer to perform auditing procedures is frequently more desirable than doing so manually. Chapter 4 will show how this can be so, what these procedures are, and how some of them could be used for Werner Manufacturing.

4
Computer-Assisted Audit Techniques

Computers have changed the audit environment but not the professional responsibilities of the auditor. The principles of auditing remain unchanged: the independent auditor must still exercise professional judgment to render an opinion on the fairness of the financial statements, and the internal auditor must do the same to be able to report on the area he is examining. Proper attention to professional responsibilities, however, requires new skills, including the ability to handle, understand, and use data processing facilities.

While integrated data processing may require that the auditor become more involved in understanding an organization's computer operation in addition to its financial and accounting activities, this involvement can be used to enhance the auditor's ability to provide an increased service to the organization. If the auditor masters the capabilities as well as the complexities of the computer, it can be used to accomplish traditional investigations more quickly and to extend the auditor's investigation to areas that are extremely helpful to the examination but may have previously been impractical because of cost and time limitations. The computer represents a very powerful tool for the auditor, one that can be used to enhance his judgment and decision-making abilities. Kept in proper perspective, the computer can be used to explore and develop new opportunities to increase the professional service provided.

Those areas in which the computer is potentially useful occur where there are fairly large volumes of data or fairly complex calculations or analyses. Other potentially advantageous applications of the computer occur when there is a great deal of summarization to be performed or when the criteria by which the selection is to be made or a task to be performed can be specifically and objectively defined.

Another advantage that should not be underestimated is the improved knowledge and understanding that an auditor can gain of the organization's system of procedures and controls when the auditor must actively use some of those procedures and controls and/or use the data produced by them. In deciding how to apply the computer to auditing tasks, the auditor must analyze the tasks to be performed and identify those areas in which the computer can help to do the job better or at lower cost.

Frequently, the speed and accuracy of computers can lower the cost of the examination sufficiently so that the auditor can use the computer to extend the scope of the review and increase the level of confidence without substantially increasing the amount of time or expense required to do the work. The speed and accuracy of computers make the accumulation of additional information both practical and economical. At a minimum, the computer should certainly remove the restrictions previously imposed by the amount of clerical work provided—but even further, the computer should open up additional analytical opportunities.

RELATIONSHIP OF COMPUTER-ASSISTED COMPLIANCE AND SUBSTANTIVE TESTS

The computer can be used in two ways: to test the information processing system or to test the data. Techniques to test the system are compliance tests. Techniques to test the data may be either compliance or substantive tests, depending upon the use to which they are put. For example, testing data to determine the incidence or rate of certain errors or the predictability of results is a compliance test. Using the same client data to verify the financial values represented by that data is substantive testing.

Frequently, tests of compliance are closely interrelated with substantive tests. Specific auditing procedures may concurrently provide evidence of compliance with accounting control procedures as well as substantive evidence of accurate records. In some cases, actual data may be used as the auditor samples the results of processing for the existence of conditions that should have been detected by programmed controls. While some of the compliance testing procedures may use actual data, others may introduce simulated or test data for purposes of tracing the way in which the system handles the simulated data. Whatever procedures are used, the primary purpose of *compliance testing* is to test the system, not the data. The primary purpose of *substantive testing* is to verify the accuracy of the data.

Systems testing procedures include the following computer-assisted techniques: program code review using computerized tools such as automatic flowcharting programs; the use of copy utilities which allow the auditor to make copies of program code for subsequently controlled use or comparison; the introduction of test data to test the organization's existing processing system; the use of integrated test facilities (ITF); system or parallel simulation; and several sophisticated procedures for analyzing program code, including the use of cross-reference systems and optimizer packages. Computer-assisted techniques which test data always involve the use of some program—either one prepared by or controlled by the auditor—to access and analyze the data. These programs which are used to test the data may be generalized computer audit packages or generalized computer software, the latter frequently provided by the vendor of the client's processing system. Occasionally the auditor will write special programs for particular audit problems or the auditor may use built-in audit routines which have been imbedded in the organization's computer system.

Another use that the auditor may make of the computer is to analyze data that the auditor has generated or collected as a part of the audit procedures. These analytical processes can include such functions as the aging of accounts receivable, preparation of usage reports, analysis of inventory, analysis of the organization's investment portfolio, and analysis of depreciation schedules.

INTEGRATED TEST FACILITY

The integrated test facility (ITF) technique was originally developed in internal auditing and continues to have considerable potential for internal auditors. It is also applicable as a useful tool for the independent auditor. This approach integrates permanent test data into regular master files in a way that permits the auditor to process test transactions during the normal processing of live data. The principal objective is to allow the auditor to continuously monitor the performance of the system.

Continuous monitoring is facilitated because the auditor can enter the data processing system during the normal processing cycle. It has the operational advantage of allowing the auditor to gain greater assurance that the actual production system is being tested. Further, the ITF facility provides the means by which auditors who do not have extensive understanding of computer technology can effectively use the computer. While the ITF technique does not require great EDP technical expertise by the auditor using the ITF system, it does, however, require such expertise during the development of the integrated test facility. The ITF can also represent a potential degradation of the system's performance if the test data inserted into the files are too voluminous or improperly placed.

The ITF is an extension of the test deck concept. It involves the establishment of a fictitious entity in the organization's data files against which test data can be processed. This fictitious entity can be a division, a customer, an employee, or an account. Once this entity has been established, transactions can be processed against it using company procedures for normal transactions. Thus the need for special knowledge of computer formats or for special computer runs is eliminated. By being able to intermix test data along with normal transactions, the auditor does not have to be concerned with separate runs or controlled access to the computer system.

In an ITF procedure, test transactions need not be provided in machine-readable form but can go through the normal data collection and recording procedures. In addition, the auditor need not be concerned with the continued maintenance of artificial test decks or the possibility that the programs being tested by specially constructed test data are not those being used to process live data. Further, this approach can test all of the organization's procedures, manual as well as programmed. By using the ITF approach, the auditor can test the system over a period of time, allowing the test accounts to accumulate statistics or data for several weeks, a month, or the full year. This ability to allow the results of test transactions to accumulate over a period of time is one that is ordinarily not possible under the more traditional test data approach.

In order to use the ITF method successfully, the auditor must make some provision for insuring that the results of the test transactions and the test records contained in the files do not ultimately materially distort the accounting records and financial statements resulting from normal company business. One approach to preventing such distortion is to modify the programs to insure that they segregate the test transactions prior to combining the test data with other legitimate accounting data. This is less desirable than allowing the results of test data to be included in the normal operations and to reverse the results of the test transactions at predetermined points via journal entries. Particular care should be taken in constructing and making these reversing entries in order to prevent misstatement of the financial statements. A third alternative is to create test transactions of small dollar amounts, so that the need for reversing entries is eliminated.

The ITF method seems to have potentially large benefits for those organizations in which continual testing is desirable. This is particularly true for real-time on-line systems, where files are being continually updated and for which interruption of the system for more traditional techniques should be minimized. As a safeguard against unauthorized manipulation of the built-in test records, these records should be regularly reviewed and analyzed. The identity of these test records should be kept secret, and both the initial introduction of the test entity into the master files and subsequent transactions to be processed against it should be executed through the normal authorization and recording procedures. This helps to protect the identity of the test records and prevents unauthorized personnel from generating their own test records for personal manipulation.

USE OF TEST DATA TO TEST PROCESSING SYSTEM

The use of test data for evaluating the processing system requires that the auditor calculate the results that would be produced by the test data, execute the program (or systems procedures) using the test data under properly controlled conditions, and compare the results obtained from the test execution with those results calculated prior to the test. The auditor must spend some time in advance determining what the calculated results should be and planning how and when the test data will be introduced. Provision must be made for obtaining the contents of the master records that will be affected by the test transactions so that the net impact of test data on the records can be calculated. In the batch mode, information about the contents of the master files may be obtained from the last normal processing run—that is, status reports printed as a by-product of the updating run, or dumping the contents of the latest generation of the file. In a real-time system, the auditor can make an inquiry to the master record to obtain its contents, enter the transaction, and then make a subsequent inquiry to the master record to verify the updated results.

The auditor should remember that test data can be used to evaluate more than computer programs alone. Test data can be used to test the transcription or data entry procedure, the editing procedure, and the manual correction procedure in use by the installation. After determining which conditions are to be tested, the auditor must decide at which point and in which form the test data are to be introduced. If the auditor wishes to introduce machine-readable test data, provision must be made for the transcription of that test data into machine-readable form.

The test data approach does have some disadvantages. This approach requires computer time that may be difficult to obtain. Further, in a real-time system it is rarely possible to have controlled access to the system while the test is being run. If the programs change frequently, the maintenance of the test data may be costly and time-consuming. Further, the use of test data does not guarantee that the program being tested is that actually in use by the organization, and it must therefore be used in conjunction with other evaluation techniques.

The auditor must obtain assurance that the program processing the test data is the program actually in use. In those instances where the test data are simply intermixed with live transaction data and run during the normal processing cycle (ITF), the auditor does have assurance that the program being tested is the actual operating program normally in use. In addition to determining that the program used by the computer during the test run is the same as that used by the installation for live processing at the time the test was made, it is also necessary to establish whether the program currently in use was the same program in use throughout the audit period under consideration. This means that the auditor must be able to establish which program was used throughout the period. To the extent that the organization has a good system of control over the programs and program changes, the auditor can place some reliance on the installation's documentation. Whenever possible, the auditor should conduct tests periodically throughout the audit period.

The test data should be developed by preparing simulated transactions for all significant audit conditions, including those that the system should handle and those that the system is not designed to handle. It is important that any data processing system has the ability to recognize not only valid transactions, but also transactions that should not be included. Thus, properly controlled programs recognize data that do not belong in the processing run and will identify and reject that data. The test data should include invalid information (such as out-of-sequence data, amounts that exceed reasonable limits, invalid codes, and missing fields) to test whether the processing system can identify and reject those conditions as well as every possible type of valid routine to test all the processing activities.

Test data may be introduced at any of a number of places within the processing system. If the auditor feels sufficiently assured of the adequacy of the data collection procedure, the test data may be developed to test only the processing programs. The auditor may wish to test the data collection procedure itself, however, in which case the test transactions or test data should be introduced into the system in the form of simulated source documents to test the transcription or original recording procedure and the editing routines as well as the processing routines.

In generating test data, the auditor may choose to use selected transactions from the organization's actual data, may select test data used by the original programmer to check out or test programs, or may generate the test data specifically for the audit. Selections from the input data for the programmer's original test data may not contain or include all possible variables, and therefore additional transactions may have to be created. Care should be taken to document the conditions chosen for testing and the process employed so that the auditor can collect sufficient evidential matter to support subsequent conclusions. Frequently, the testing is documented by a simple listing of the test transactions in the output from the test runs.

TEST DATA GENERATORS

Test data that are used to evaluate a processing system must contain examples of all of the processing options provided within that system that are critical to the auditor's objectives as well as examples of invalid data and errors within the processing system to test fully how the system handles legitimate and erroneous data. As processing systems become more sophisticated, the construction of test data becomes more complicated and more time-consuming. The additional complexity in the systems, the many alternative processing paths, and the need to have either tape or disk data make the construction of valid test data commensurately more difficult. Further, the auditor needs to review the test data for each audit and to update it to make sure that in each subsequent audit it does in fact check the processing system currently in use and recognize and account for any changes that may have been made within that processing system since the preceding audit.

As the task of constructing appropriate test data becomes more time-consuming and more complex, a need has arisen to facilitate its generation. In the last several years programming packages, called *test data generators,* have been developed. These accept definitions of the processing system and the data conditions that that system is designed to handle and generate large volume test data files that will test all of those conditions. Data containing a wide range of error conditions as well as valid data can be created for use in testing the system. Frequently, the test data generator packages succeed in creating test transactions that might have been overlooked by the auditor, since the generator packages systematically generate data for all of the specifications named.

In addition to providing a more encompassing test file, test data generator programs can also make the generation of test data, and therefore its use, more efficient. The test data generator packages can produce test data in card, tape, or disk form. The test data can be generated in response to constants or ranges of values defined by the auditor. The data can be generated at random within a range defined by the auditor and can be designed deliberately to violate specifications of predefined valid data. Test data generator packages vary as to the hardware and software requirements for the package and in the kinds of processing procedures that the user may request.

PARALLEL SIMULATION

Parallel simulation is basically a compliance test technique in which the auditor develops an independent processing system or model to simulate the application processing system being tested. The same data is processed through the auditor's simulated system as is processed through the live application system. The results of the test and live processing are compared and all differences are investigated. If there are no unexplained differences in results, then the live or actual processing system is considered to be processing accurately and as expected.

The parallel simulation can be developed through several alternatives. Theoretically, the auditor could write independent programs to simulate the installation's processing procedures, but this is rarely practical. More often, standard utility programs or other generalized software will be used to duplicate the processing logic of the application being tested. The generalized audit software packages are probably the most popular means of implementing parallel simulation.

In order to successfully use parallel simulation, the auditor must develop a thorough understanding of the processing flow of the application. It is not necessary to simulate all functions of the application, but rather, the auditor can concentrate on those functions which have been determined to have audit significance. The use of parallel simulation can facilitate verification of complex processing systems efficiently and objectively.

COMPUTERIZED AIDS TO PROGRAM AND SYSTEMS REVIEW

There are a number of computerized aids which help the auditor in reviewing and analyzing programs and other systems procedures. One tool which can be helpful to the auditor is an automatic flowcharting program. Automatic flowcharting programs are used primarily to aid the installation in documenting its programs and subsequently maintaining that documentation as changes are made to the programs. Application programs are used as input to the flowcharting programs, and the flowchart is automatically printed. Computerized flowcharting can save time and avoid errors, since the flowchart comes directly from the program and eliminates the possibility of the documentation writer either omitting a function from the flowchart that exists in the program or incorrectly flowcharting instructions from a program. Further, when a change is made to a program, that program can simply be run through the flowcharting program to produce an automated and updated version of the flowchart.

Auditors can also make use of automatic flowcharting programs. When an auditor is interested in analyzing a particular program, he can make use of the automatic flowcharting program to provide a flowchart whose logic might be easier to follow than the source listing. Of course, the auditor must make certain that the program being interpreted by the automatic flowcharting technique is in fact the program currently being used by the client for processing financial data.

Most systems of any size utilize an operating system which includes program libraries. These program libraries are maintained by standardized librarian programs. These librarian programs produce "audit trails" in which additions to the library, deletions of programs from the library, and changes to programs in the library are automatically documented. The auditor can make excellent use of this audit trail produced by the librarian program to review those changes which have been made to the existing client program libraries.

Programs which provide cross-references within individual programs or within program libraries are also useful to an auditor in those instances where the auditor must make detailed analyses of the logic of particular programs. These cross-reference systems allow the auditor to trace all occurrences of a particular data name within a program or library. This can save a great deal of time when reviewing that program, since such a search is difficult to perform from a source code listing. In those instances where the cross-reference tool pertains to an entire program library, the auditor then can find cross-references between the program under study and other programs within the library.

Frequently, operating systems provide, as a by-product, a log of all activities taking place within the operating system for a given period of time. This "job accounting data" can be helpful to the auditor in such activities as: verifying computer users' billings; checking that authorized personnel use particular programs, data files, or computer resources; verifying that production programs were run at the correct time and for the correct number of times according to the schedule set up in the control procedure; determining whether unauthorized use or attempts to use remote terminals have occurred; verifying that only authorized programs were run.

GENERALIZED COMPUTER AUDIT PROGRAMS

A *generalized computer audit program* is a prewritten program designed to perform certain audit procedures on a computer through provision of a group of optional routines that can be selected by the auditor as the requirements of a particular audit situation dictate. A number of these generalized computer audit programs or packages are available. Some have been written by software vendors who hope to sell them for a profit, and others have been written by auditing firms for their own purposes. They have all been designed to make it easier for the auditor to use the computer in the performance of an audit. While it is not necessary to write the programs to perform the procedures desired, the auditor must still communicate with the generalized audit program in order to identify the processing to be done and to describe the data files of the organization. This is necessary because the generalized audit programs must be designed to handle many different forms of data with many different types of organizations and fields—otherwise they would not be generalized programs.

Among the many generalized audit programs there are basically two approaches to the way in which the auditor communicates with the generalized audit program. The first approach is to have the audit program available in source form and then have the auditor complete the program coding, using a subset of the coding language of the basic package. The other approach is to have the audit programs in object or executable form and have the auditor complete specification sheets which are keypunched and read by the program.

The generalized computer audit programs are usually stored on some machine-readable medium (usually tape or disk) and brought by the auditor to the computer site at which the processing is to be executed. These generalized packages can be run on the client's/auditee's computer system, the auditor's own system, or at a third-party installation such as a service center. In some cases they must be run on a stand-alone basis, but in others the generalized package is so designed that it can or must be loaded into the normal object program library of the client's/auditee's operating system, so that it can be used in a multiprogramming environment. Whenever any of these generalized packages are executed under the control of the installation's operating system, particularly in a multiprogramming environment, the auditor must take precautions to insure that none of the installation's personnel or programming systems interferes with the operations of the audit package.

When the auditor is concerned with testing existing data for either compliance or substantive purposes, there are usually certain basic functions which are performed on that data. These functions are to search large computerized files and retrieve items that have audit significance; to select samples from computerized files using systematic random sampling techniques or to calculate a sample size necessary to satisfy desired statistical confidence levels; to perform basic mathematical operations of addition, subtraction, multiplication, and division; to perform file comparisons, merges, and sorts; to summarize large volumes of data and report the results; and to output the result of these operations in some suitable form—usually printed reports. All of the generalized audit packages are designed to perform these functions.

Generalized computer audit software can be expensive to develop, test, and place into use. Further, the firm developing these generalized packages must select those hardware systems on which the package will run. It is generally not economically feasible to provide a package to run on every conceivable hardware system. Therefore, these packages are usually designed to run on those systems which are installed in sufficient numbers to make development of the package practical; frequently, they can be modified to run on other systems. Since the computer audit packages are user-oriented, they make it possible for staff auditors to use the computer efficiently without having to become skilled EDP technicians.

GENERALIZED COMPUTER SOFTWARE

As discussed in the preceding sections, there are certain common functions frequently performed in the audit of data (retrieval, sample selection, file manipulation, calculation, and printing). These same functions are also frequently performed for installation operations, and therefore these standard functions are often included in the *general software support systems* provided by the vendor to customers. Usually these take the form of utility programs within the vendor-provided operating systems. Where these facilities exist in the installation's standard software, and the auditor has enough knowledge to use them effectively, these generalized computer packages themselves may be used to perform certain audit functions.

Generalized computer software frequently has great flexibility in handling files. However, these generalized computer software packages usually require greater user expertise than generalized computer audit software, since they are designed for use by EDP personnel. This means that the auditor must have a higher level of technical knowledge and understand the functioning of that particular computer software package in order to successfully use it. When the auditor does have this expertise, however, use of generalized computer software to perform certain audit functions on client data provides access to a wider variety of systems than would be the case with generalized audit packages alone. Also, these generalized audit packages are usually developed for those systems sufficiently numerous to justify the developmental expense.

Thus, for the variety of computing systems for which no generalized audit package has been developed, use of the generalized computer software provides a handy tool for the auditor.

BUILT-IN OR IMBEDDED AUDIT MODULES

Built-in audit modules are incorporated within processing programs. These modules are sections of program code that produce special by-product information on the files or functioning of the program as the program is executed. Usually the audit module is executed only on a selective basis when activated within the program by special instruction or control message. An example of an audit routine could be an automatic logging procedure for accesses to selected and confidential files or a module which would extend the accounts receivable aging program to concurrently produce confirmation requests for the auditor.

Another use of built-in audit modules would be the implementation of the technique of "tagging." In tagging, certain transactions are identified (either through a sampling procedure or because of certain attributes in the transaction) and subsequently traced through the computer processing. A systems control and review file (SCARF) is created by logging all of the processing performed on these tagged transactions. This SCARF file can then subsequently be reviewed by the auditor. Tagging and the use of built-in audit modules are particularly effective in large integrated processing systems where files are updated on-line and subsequent auditing of the transactions would be difficult.

Developing and incorporating built-in audit modules require careful advanced planning to prepare the modules and insert them in the processing programs. Further, much attention must be given to the procedures by which the modules will be controlled to prevent unauthorized tampering or modification.

In summary, computerized audit procedures make it possible to expand the scope of audit activities and to perform the necessary audit procedures more efficiently. As an audit tool, the computer provides excellent opportunities for testing and verifying internal controls, assessing the effectiveness of the data processing operations, and verifying the accuracy of financial and operating data. The speed and accuracy of the computer allows the auditor to reduce the clerical work load, thus reducing audit test time and eliminating the source of many human errors. The same speed of the computer allows the auditor to perform a greater number of tests without unduly increasing the cost of the audit. In addition, using the computer may provide the auditor with much better insight into the processes employed within the data processing department.

WERNER MANUFACTURING, INC.—CASE STUDY

Part four of the case study illustrates how the auditing procedures designed in part three can be performed with computer-assisted audit procedures.

COMPUTER-ASSISTED AUDITING TECHNIQUES

Having related internal control strengths and weaknesses to auditing procedures, we are now going to see how those procedures may be performed by auditing "through" and "with" the computer. In doing so, we will consider procedures performed by both the independent and internal auditors.

In order to demonstrate the use of the greatest number of techniques, we will use a somewhat contrived situation, one in which the independent and internal auditors use five techniques:

1. Test decks
2. Specially written programs
3. Generalized audit software
4. Parallel simulation
5. Integrated test facility (ITF)

There will be a certain amount of overlap in presenting these procedures, as both specially written programs and generalized audit software will be used to perform both substantive and compliance tests (parallel simulation). Our approach will be to cover the internal auditors' procedures first, then those of the independent auditors.

The internal auditors decided to use the test deck approach in connection with their audit procedure 12. To properly understand how Werner will use this approach, we have to go back to the flowchart of the system (Chapter 1: Figure 1–5) which describes the computer processing applied to cash receipts.

Note that this is a batch processing system, as opposed to that for sales and accounts receivable which is on-line real-time. We are especially concerned with procedures 16 and 17, which cover inputting the punched cards (each of which is a cash receipt on an outstanding balance) to produce the cash receipts book and associated listings and to update the customer accounts receivable file.

Comparing these operating procedures with audit procedure 12, we see that using the computer via the test deck approach really applies to procedures 12a, c and d. Procedures 12b, e and f must, given Werner's system, be performed manually. With this in mind, we can see how the internal auditors set up the test.

Reviewing procedures and controls. Reviewing internal controls and processing, particularly the preparation of input for computer processing and the procedures performed by the computer programs, is the first step in preparing for the test. In reviewing the computer programs, it is sufficient to become familiar with what they are doing by interviewing data processing personnel, reviewing system documentation, and examining output to determine which files they update, what printed reports they produce, what tests they perform, and so on. It is not generally necessary, unless the documentation is poor, to perform a detailed review of the program code. For our purposes, we will assume Werner's internal auditors have done these things and are ready to set up the test.

Setting up the test—test deck. The internal auditors establish their audit objectives and the scope of their test work at the outset. To be certain there is no misunderstanding, they state these explicitly in their working papers (see Exhibit 4–1). Their working papers also contain the following information: [1]

• Test data control	describes the conditions to be tested, shows the expected results and reports the actual results of the test. See Exhibit 4–2.
• Transaction data and solutions	lists valid and invalid transactions to be processed; shows solutions for test transactions. See Exhibit 4–3.
• Master file data	describes the format and content of the master file (customer accounts receivable) to be used in the test. See Exhibit 4–4.

Exhibit 4–1. Test Deck Audit Objectives.

WERNER MANUFACTURING, INC.
4/30/77
Test Deck Audit Objectives

General — to insure that the recording of sales results in the proper recording of receivables and cash receipts

Specific — to determine whether the programs in operations 16 and 17:
- properly list the cash receipts cards on the transaction listing report and obtain a dollar total for comparison with the cash receipts listing (prepared manually)
- edit the cards and flag errors for follow-up
- process the edited receipts cards to properly update the customer accounts receivable file and print a daily cash receipts book

[1] Gordon B. Davis, *Auditing & EDP* (New York: American Institute of Certified Public Accountants, 1968), pp. 170–173.

Exhibit 4–2. Test Data Control.

WERNER MANUFACTURING, INC.
4/30/77

INPUT TEST TRANSACTION NUMBER	DESCRIPTION OF TEST [a]	RESULTS EXPECTED	ACTUAL RESULTS
1	Invalid customer number	Rejected—error report	Rejected—error report [b]
2	Invalid invoice number	Rejected—error report	Rejected—error report [b]
3	Invalid transaction date, that is, other than the date it is processed	Accepted—appears on special report for follow-up. Appears on daily cash receipts book and transaction listing.	Accepted—appears on special report for follow-up.[c] Appears on daily cash receipts book and transaction listing.
4	Remittance amount different from amount in customer receivables file	Accepted—appears on special report for follow-up. Appears on daily cash receipts book and transaction listing.	Accepted—appears on special report for follow-up.[c] Customer receivables file contains debit and credit (remittance) for open invoices. Appears on daily cash receipts book and transaction listing.
5	All input correct— remittance amount matches customer balance for that invoice	Accepted—open invoice deleted from customer receivable file. Appears on daily cash receipts book and transaction listing.	Accepted—open invoice deleted from customer receivables file. Appears on daily cash receipts book and transaction listing.

[a] See Exhibit 4–2.1 for layout of cash receipts input card.
[b] See output report produced by computer—Exhibit 4–7.
[c] See output report produced by computer—Exhibit 4–8.

Exhibit 4–2.1. Record Layout for Cash Receipts.

Exhibit 4–3. Transaction Data and Solutions.

WERNER MANUFACTURING, INC.
4/30/77

INPUT TEST TRANSACTION NUMBER	CUSTOMER NUMBER	INVOICE NUMBER	TRANSACTION DATE	INVOICE (REMITTANCE) AMOUNT	MASTER (CUSTOMER RECEIVABLES) FILE BALANCE AFTER PROCESSING [a]
1	137425	65746	4-14-77	437.25	Rejected—no change in master file
2	235814	70047	4-14-77	8,481.27	Rejected—no change in master file
3	187659	70132	4-15-77	385.10	4,781.59 (open invoice)
4	143729	69784	4-14-77	2,789.15	10,781.59 (open invoice) (2,789.15) (unapplied remittance)
5	139984	70042	4-14-77	9,489.27	–0–

[a] This is the "solution" or end result of processing, as predetermined by the auditors. The output reports in Exhibits 4–6, 4–7 and 4–8 confirm this result.

Figure 4–4. Master File Data.

WERNER MANUFACTURING, INC.
4/30/77

CUSTOMER NUMBER	CREDIT LIMIT	T/C	TRANSACTION DATE	REFERENCE– INVOICE NUMBER	AMOUNT TRANSACTION
137426	50,000	1	3-25-77	58928	340.29
		1	3-31-77	68543	14,721,29
		1	4-10-77	74401	210.96
139984	15,000	1	4-8-77	70042	9,489.27
143729	6,000	1	4-2-77	69784	10,781.59
187659	18,000	1	4-9-77	70132	385.10
		1	4-12-77	70325	4,781.59
233625	4,000	1	2-28-77	54375	314.44
		1	3-1-77	54407	2,754.81
		2	3-2-77	54375	(14.44)
		1	4-10-77	70581	301.87
235814	25,000	1	3-4-77	54509	810.76
		1	4-8-77	70048	8,481.27
		1	4-11-77	70635	105.66
		3	4-12-77	J4035	(27.67)

Note: Transaction code (T/C): 1 = Sale
2 = Cash receipt unapplied—pending investigation.
3 = Adjustment—pending investigation.

| • Decision table | puts the conditions to be tested and actions to be taken by the computer in an easy-to-read format. See Exhibit 4–5. |
| • Computer printouts | contains results of the test, showing the error reports and the cash receipts book obtained from processing the test transactions. See Exhibits 4–6, 4–7 and 4–8. These are cross-referenced to Exhibits 4–2 and 4–3. |

To carry out the test deck approach for this application, one additional step must be performed—obtaining a copy of the master file for customer accounts receivable. The internal auditors will keep control of this copy and use it in their test deck processing. A description of the master file, showing the contents of the records contained in it, appears in Exhibit 4–4. The information in Exhibit 4–4 was obtained by computer-printing (dumping) the records in the master file.

To make our example easy to follow, we will assume the internal auditors' test deck consists of five transactions, each of which is a punched card (Exhibit 4–2.1) representing a cash remittance on an outstanding invoice. Similarly, the master file contains only six records. In reality, both the test deck and the master file would consist of many more transactions and records.

Exhibit 4–2 describes the test to be performed by each transaction card and the expected and actual results of the processing in narrative form, based on the assumption that the programs being tested are properly processing data. Exhibit 4–3 describes those results in terms of actual processing. Note

Exhibit 4–5. Decision Table.

WERNER MANUFACTURING, INC.
4/30/77

			RULES		
CONDITIONS	1	2	3	4	5
Customer number invalid	Y	N	N	N	N
Invoice number invalid		Y	N	N	N
Transaction date invalid			Y	N	N
Remittance amount not equal to open balance for invoice				Y	N
ACTIONS					
Reject transactions—print on error report	X	X			
Accept transactions—print on special report			X	X	
Accept transactions					X

Note: Y = Yes
    N = No
    X = Action to be taken, based on the above conditions

Exhibit 4–6. Cash Receipts Book.

WERNER MANUFACTURING, INC.

CASH RECEIPTS BOOK

APRIL 14, 1977

CUSTOMER NUMBER	INVOICE NUMBER	REMITTANCE AMOUNT	
187659	70132	385.10	
143729	69784	2,789.15	See Exhibits 4-2 and 4-3.
139984	70042	9,489.27	
		12,663.52	

that each of the first four cards contains an error condition, while the fifth is an errorless transaction.

Performing the test. To be certain the conditions of the test and the results are clearly understood, the internal auditors prepared a decision table (Exhibit 4–5). This decision table shows in tabular format the results one may expect from each of the five conditions described in Exhibits 4–2 and 4–3, provided the programs to be tested are processing data properly.

Before we describe the results obtained by processing the five test trans-

Exhibit 4–7. Error Report—Rejected Transactions.

WERNER MANUFACTURING, INC.

ERROR REPORT - REJECTED TRANSACTIONS

APRIL 14, 1977

	CUSTOMER NUMBER	INVOICE NUMBER	REMITTANCE AMOUNT	DESCRIPTION
See Exhibits 4-2 and 4-3.	137425	65746	437.25	INVALID CUST NO
	235814	70047	8,481.27	INVALID INV NO

Exhibit 4–8. Special Report.

WERNER MANUFACTURING, INC.

SPECIAL REPORT

APRIL 14, 1977

CUSTOMER NUMBER	INVOICE NUMBER	REMITTANCE AMOUNT	DESCRIPTION
187659	70132	385.10	INVALID TRANS DATE
143729	69784	2,789.15	UNAPP REMITTANCE

e Exhibits 4-2, 4-3, and 4-6.

actions, let us look again at the system flowchart for the cash receipts operations in which we are interested (Chapter 1: Figure 1–5). Note that, in
addition to updating the master file (customer accounts receivable), these
operations produce several output documents, including a cash receipts book.
Although not shown, we will now assume that the system also produces an
error report and a special report, both of which are referred to in the right-
most columns of Exhibit 4–2.

Our example will concentrate on the cash receipts book and the error and
special reports, as the internal auditors have decided they are the most critical
to proper processing. Since the test deck will produce the same output as
regular processing, these reports will be available to the auditors to enable
them to evaluate the results of the test. See Exhibits 4–6, 4–7 and 4–8 for
examples.

We can now trace each of the test transactions:

• Transaction 1 has an invalid customer number. A transaction such as
this should not be permitted to update the master file, as doing so would
create an error. To permit investigation and yet not interrupt processing,
Werner's system provides for such a transaction's being rejected and
listed on an error report. When the situation has been corrected, the
transaction will be processed in a subsequent run.
We see from Exhibit 4–6 that the system does *not* allow the transaction
to enter the cash receipts book and from Exhibit 4–7 that it *is* printed on
the error report.

• Transaction 2 involves an invalid invoice number which prevents the
remittance from being matched with an open invoice. It is handled in
much the same way as a transaction with an invalid customer number.
We can see from Exhibits 4–6 and 4–7 that it is *not* part of the cash
receipts book and *is* on the error report.

It probably has occurred to you that by not booking remittances which involve errors of this type, there will be a discrepancy between the bank accounts and the cash ledger balance until the error is corrected, since the remittance check must be deposited. This is true. Werner's system provides that an adjusting entry must be made at the end of the month for remittance errors being investigated. The credit is to a suspense account which will be a clearly identified item in reconciling the bank and general ledger accounts at the end of the month.

- Transaction 3 involves a date different from the current one. This is a minor item, since it probably involves an undetected keypunch error. It is printed on a special report (Exhibit 4–8) and is investigated; it also appears in the cash receipts book (Exhibit 4–6).

  Note that it has properly updated the master file. As Exhibit 4–4 shows for customer number 187659, there were two outstanding invoices before the test transactions were processed: 70132 and 70325. After the test transactions were processed, only invoice 70325 is outstanding (Exhibit 4–3).

  The internal auditors verify the ending balances in the master file by using the computer to list the contents, as they did to obtain the beginning balances for preparing the right-hand column of Exhibit 4–4).

- Transaction 4 appears in both the cash receipts book and the special report, as it involves an apparently correct transaction in which the customer has not remitted the full amount of the open balance. If investigation shows that the transaction *is* correct, the two amounts for the same invoice (a debit and a credit) will be carried in the master file until either the customer remits the remaining balance or an adjustment is posted. Note from Exhibits 4–3 and 4–4 that the master file *does* in fact show both balances as the result of the addition of the unapplied remittance.

- Transaction 5 contains no errors or cause for investigation; it is valid in all respects. Consequently, it should not (and does not) appear on Exhibits 4–7 or 4–8, but *does* appear in the cash receipts book (Exhibit 4–6). Note from Exhibits 4–3 and 4–4 that it has also correctly updated the master file: the only open invoice has been deleted and the balance is now zero.

As a result of the test deck auditing procedures, Werner's internal auditors are satisfied that the cash receipts computer programs are providing for proper processing. Keep in mind that the test deck approach does not cover *all* auditing procedures, just 12a, c and d; procedures 12b, e and f must be performed manually.

Before we proceed to ITF, note that each test transaction tested *one* factor. It is possible to have a single transaction test more than one factor, but doing so might confuse the situation and possibly lead to either incorrect conclusions and/or the expenditure of unnecessary audit time.

The internal auditors will use the integrated test facility (ITF) technique to perform their auditing procedures 4, 5, 7, 8, 9 and 10. However, computer-assisted auditing techniques are not always directly equivalent to manual techniques on a one-to-one basis, and this is a case where they are not. To better understand how ITF will be used here, you should refer back to the system flowchart (Chapter 1: Figure 1–5).

We are interested in operations 1 through 8, which cover the order entry and sales procedures. The internal auditors want to design a test which will tell them if those procedures are working as they should. As the preceding text described ITF, they will first define their facility and then show how the test transactions of which it is comprised are integrated into the regular processing streams to carry out the audit objectives.

Before proceeding to the test itself, we will reiterate some important points which were made previously but which tend to be forgotten as one gets into the details of auditing procedures and the techniques by which they are performed:

- To use ITF or any auditing technique effectively, there must have been a review and evaluation of internal control.
- As the tables in Chapter 3 show, there must be an audit plan based on a clear understanding of the total system. Each auditing procedure, regardless of the technique used to perform it, must fit into the plan to insure that the objectives of the audit are met; see Exhibit 4–9.
- Auditors perform compliance tests on strengths not weaknesses. An internal auditor may perform auditing procedures on a weakness to determine its total effect on his company's affairs, but he will not audit for compliance once he knows the control is weak or nonexistent.

This last point is important to Werner's internal auditors. Turn to Table 3–2 in Chapter 3 which deals with application controls. Read items I through VII. Items V and VII are weaknesses. The internal auditors did not design manual compliance tests for these weaknesses, although they will probably do further testing to determine their total financial effect. In using ITF, however, the internal auditors *are* going to run their test transactions through these operations (1–8 on the system flowchart). To do otherwise would be to make an artificial and probably time-consuming distinction between the operations in which they are and are not interested. Once the processing starts, ITF can just as (or more) easily carry the test through all computer processing phases as it can only some of them.

In Chapter 2 we noted that the auditors' proposal to get imbedded audit routines and ITF was refused by the EDP Steering Committee. Their refusal was based on data processing's argument that to do so would (1) delay the

Exhibit 4–9.   ITF Audit Objectives.

WERNER MANUFACTURING, INC.
4/30/77

ITF Audit Objectives:

General — to insure that the recording of sales results in the proper recording of receivables and matching of revenue and expense

Specific — to determine whether the computer programs in operations 1 through 8:

- properly compare sales orders with the customer accounts receivable file and determine credit status
- are able to determine if inventory quantities are sufficient to cover sales orders and:
  - If quantities are not sufficient, to backorder them, print back order advices and print replenishment advices when quantities are restored
  - If quantities are sufficient, to update the open order file and print shipping orders and lists of accepted sales orders
- are, upon shipment of the ordered items, able to:
  - update the order entry, customer accounts receivable and inventory files
  - print a three-part invoice and a daily sales register

sales, accounts receivable and cash receipts computerization project, (2) seriously interfere with regular production processing, and (3) cost too much to implement. With the hiring of the two EDP internal auditors, however, the proposal to use ITF was reopened and finally adopted. The EDP auditors showed that the benefits of ITF far outweigh its cost and that its use would involve so few transactions as to have a negligible effect on daily processing.

The question of how to relieve the accounts and reports of the effects of the test transactions was satisfactorily resolved. However, since this topic is related to the explanation of their integration with live transactions, it will be deferred for the present.

Setting up the test—ITF.   The internal auditors have decided that the facility will be several fictitious customers whose customer numbers (see record layouts for the customer receivables master file and sales transactions in Exhibit 4–10.1) are similar to valid ones. Thus, it is not possible for operating personnel to tell if a transaction is live or test from its customer number.

To accommodate ITF, master file records for the fictitious customers have been set up. Each test transaction will involve only one test variable, as was done in the test deck technique. Also, there will be both valid and invalid transactions, so that the system's ability to test all conditions critical to the audit can be determined. Note that, for illustrative purposes, the master file layout for customer receivables has been expanded from that used in the test deck illustration to include four more fields:

- Item number
- Quantity
- Unit price
- Quantity backordered

In addition, "transaction amount" is now called "extended cost." This will be the layout used in the remainder of the case study.

Look at Exhibit 4–10. The internal auditors decided to use seven test transactions: five are sales orders, two are shipping advices. Keep this distinction in mind as we proceed through the test.

Transactions one through five are entered in the processing sequence at operation 1 (Chapter 1: Figure 1–5). Transactions six and seven enter the processing sequence at operation 7. We will assume that the preceding sales orders for transactions six and seven were entered at the proper time and were properly reflected in the open order master file.

In setting up ITF, the internal auditors and data processing personnel discussed how to relieve the accounts of the effect of the test transactions. They decided to do so by an adjusting journal entry, leaving the test transactions and records in the computerized files. Data processing felt that to develop programs to delete such a small number of items was not worth the effort.

Performing the test.   As shown in Exhibit 4–10, transaction 1 tests the system's ability to reject a transaction with an invalid customer number. The master file (Exhibit 4–12) shows a record with customer number 148228; the test transaction (Exhibit 4–11) shows number 148229. To simplify our example we have limited the master files to a few items, generally those affected by the test transactions.

As we see from Exhibit 4–14, this transaction was rejected and printed on a special report. Keep in mind that neither this nor the reports in Exhibits 4–15 through 4–17 are specially generated by the auditors: they are reports that are printed in the ordinary processing of sales transactions. This is in direct contrast to the test deck method in which the auditors made a special "run" through the computer to determine if the programs were processing data properly.

Transaction 2 tests the system's ability to reject sales which if accepted would exceed the established credit limit. Note on Exhibit 4–12 that customer 143201 has a balance of $70,000 before test transaction 2 is processed. If test transaction 2 were accepted, the balance would increase to $151,728.97, $1,728.97 over the credit limit. The system did not permit this to happen: it rejected the transaction and printed it on the pending sales report (Exhibit 4–15) for review by the credit manager.

Exhibit 4–10. Test Data Control.

WERNER MANUFACTURING, INC.
4/30/77

INPUT TEST TRANSACTION NUMBER	DESCRIPTION OF TEST [a]	RESULTS EXPECTED	ACTUAL RESULTS	REMARKS
SALES ORDERS:				
1	Invalid customer number	Rejected—error report	Rejected—error report [b]	
2	Total of sales order and existing balance exceeds the credit limit	Rejected—pending sales report	Rejected—pending sales report [c]	
3	Customer has been put on a cash-only basis	Rejected—pending sales report	Rejected—pending sales report [c]	
4	Quantity of two of the items ordered is not sufficient to fill the order	Rejected—pending sales report and back order advice (the ability to print replenishment advices will be tested in the purchases and inventory audit work)	Rejected—pending sales report [c]	
5	All input correct—credit limit is not exceeded, quantities are sufficient, etc.	Accepted: • Accepted order added to the order entry file • Reports printed: — Shipping orders — Accepted sales orders	Accepted—order entry file updated and shipping orders printed. Appears on list of accepted sales orders (See Exhibit 4–16.)	

Shipping Advice—After Actual Shipment:

6	Invalid sales order number	Rejected—error report	Rejected—error report [b]	Input here is the no. 1 copy of the shipping order (See operation 8 on the system flowchart, Chapter 1: Figure 1–5.)
7	All input correct	Accepted: • Order entry file relieved of the shipped order (sale) • Sale added to the customer receivable file • Inventory file relieved of the shipped items • Sales register and three-part invoice printed	Accepted—order entry file, customer receivables and inventory files updated. Invoices and sales register printed (See Exhibit 4–17.)	As the flowchart and accompanying schedule of strengths and weaknesses state, no. 1 copies of shipping orders are accepted as valid key-to-disk input as long as the sales order number is valid, per the open order file.

[a] See Exhibit 4–10.1 for layouts of customer receivables master file and sales transaction input records.
[b] See output report produced by computer—Exhibit 4–14.
[c] See output report produced by computer—Exhibit 4–15.

Exhibit 4–10.1.   Record Layout for Customer Receivables Master File and Sales Transactions.

WERNER MANUFACTURING, INC.
4/30/77

DATA NAME	RECORD LENGTH IN BYTES	CHARAC- TERISTIC		REMARKS
Customer Number	6	Numeric	(2)	This information will be
Credit Limit	7	Numeric		present for all active
Transaction Code	1	Numeric		customers
Transaction Date	6	Numeric		
Invoice Number	5	Numeric	(1) (2)	
Item Number	6	Numeric		
Quantity	7	Numeric		
Unit Price	7	Numeric		
Extended Cost	9	Numeric		
Quantity Backordered	6	Numeric		

Note: (1) = Receivables master file, which designates customers by customer number. There is also a name and address file, which is used for billing, monthly statements, etc. This file is not shown in connection with ITF because it has no audit significance. It will, however, be used in connection with the auditor's confirmation work.

(2) = Sales record fields.

Transaction 3 is similar to 2 in that it involves testing the sale amount against the established credit limit. In this case, the limit of zero (Exhibit 4–12) means customer 152005 is not allowed credit; that is, it is cash only. As with transaction 2, it is rejected and printed on the pending sales report (Exhibit 4–15), for review by the credit manager.

Customer 100037 ordered two items which had to be backordered, since they were not in stock. Note on Exhibit 4–12 that before this transaction (4) was processed to this point, item L652 was already backordered (customer 128341). This sale was entered on the pending sales report (Exhibit 4–15).

Transaction 5 does not contain any errors, consequently it was accepted and the appropriate master files updated. For example, note that Exhibit 4–11 shows a balance after processing of $51,498.10 in the open order file. This is the extended value of transaction 5 ($41,498.10) plus the existing balance of $10,000 (Exhibit 4–13) for customer 128341. Note that it appears on the accepted sales order listing (Exhibit 4–16).

Transaction 6 is a shipping advice. The warehouse reported that open sales order 70007 (Exhibit 4–13) was shipped on 4/14/77. However, since it was erroneously enterd as B0007, the system rejected it, and the master file was not updated. It consequently was printed on the rejected transactions report (Exhibit 4–14) for follow-up and correction.

Exhibit 4–11. Transaction Data and Solutions.

WERNER MANUFACTURING, INC.
4/30/77

INPUT TEST TRANSACTION NUMBER	NUMBER	TRANSACTION DATE	CUSTOMER	SALES ORDER NUMBER	ITEM NUMBER	QUANTITY	UNIT PRICE	FILE BALANCES AFTER PROCESSING [a]
1	148229	4-14-77		66241	J3201	100	147.2946	Rejected—no change in master file
2	143201	4-14-77		65143	K12747	1000	81.72897	Rejected—no change in master file
3	152005	4-14-77		66789	Z43287	2	990.52	Rejected—no change in master file
4	100037	4-14-77		70041	J14327 L652	23 10	1000.00 7.652	Rejected—back order file updated for items J14327 and L652
5	128341	4-14-77		65139	B2174	1000	41.4981	$51,498.10 Order Entry
6	136809	4-14-77		B0007	Q128	50	N/A	Rejected—no change in master file
7	102973	4-14-77		60327	L217	100	N/A	-0- —Order Entry $2,171.76—Customer Accounts Receivable

[a] This is the "solution" or end result of processing as predetermined by the auditors. The output reports in Exhibits 4–14, 4–15, 4–16 and 14–7 confirm this result.

Exhibit 4–12. Master File Data—Customer Receivables.

WERNER MANUFACTURING, INC.
4/30/77

CUSTOMER NUMBER	CREDIT LIMIT	TRANSACTION DATE	T/C	INVOICE NUMBER	ITEM NUMBER	QUANTITY	UNIT PRICE	EXTENDED COST	QUANTITY BACK-ORDERED
148228	$ 37,500	3-29-77	1	65807	J4971	100	50	5,000.00	—
		4-01-77	1	65989	L207	5000	3	15,000.00	—
143201	$150,000	3-28-77	1	66001	D69741	200	100	20,000.00	—
		4-04-77	1	66003	L1099	50	1000	50,000.00	—
152005	-0-	—		—	—	—	—	—	—
100037	$ 25,000	4-11-77	1	68729	G89727	1000	27	27,000.00	—
128341	$100,000	4-08-77	1	67999	L652	100	7.652	765.20	50
136809	$ 20,000	—		—	—	—	—	—	—
102973	$ 50,000	—		—	—	—	—	—	—

Note: Transaction code (T/C): 1 = Sale
2 = Cash receipt unapplied—pending investigation
3 = Adjustment—pending investigation

Exhibit 4–13. Master File Data—Open Orders.

WERNER MANUFACTURING, INC.
4/30/77

CUSTOMER NUMBER	TRANSACTION DATE	SALES ORDER NUMBER	ITEM NUMBER	QUANTITY	UNIT PRICE
148228	4-06-77	66175	V37427	500	10.05
143201	4-08-77	66310	C435	10	367.50
152005	4-07-77	66297	Z9105	100	34.17
128341	4-12-77	67507	T40873	1000	10.00
102973	4-13-77	60327	L217	100	21.7176
136809	4-12-77	70007	Q128	50	10.00

Transaction 7 is also a shipping advice. It contains no errors; therefore, the master files were updated:

- Open order file (Exhibit 4–13) had a balance of $2,171.76 and after processing had a zero balance (Exhibit 4–11), as that was the only open order for customer 102973.
- Customer receivables file (Exhibit 4–12) showed the previous balance for customer 102973 was zero; it shows a balance of $2,171.76 (Exhibit 4–11) after processing transaction 7.

Exhibit 4–14. Error Report—Rejected Transactions.

WERNER MANUFACTURING, INC.

ERROR REPORT - REJECTED TRANSACTIONS

APRIL 14, 1977

CODE NO	CUSTOMER NUMBER	SALES ORDER NO	AMOUNT OF SALE	DESCRIPTION	
01	148229	66241	14,729.46	INVALID CUST NO	See Exhibits
02	136809	70007	4,897.23	INV SALES ORD NO	4-10 and 4-11.

LEGEND:

01 - SALES ORDER

02 - SHIPPING ADVICE

Exhibit 4–15.   Pending Sales Report.

WERNER MANUFACTURING, INC.

PENDING SALES REPORT

APRIL 14, 1977

CUSTOMER NUMBER	SALES ORDER NO	AMOUNT OF SALE	DESCRIPTION OF ITEM
143201	65143	81,728.97	EXC CR LIMIT
152005	66789	1,981.04	CASH BASIS CUST
100037	70041	23,076.52	BACKORDERED:
			J14327 23 PCS.
			L652 10 PCS.

See Exhibits 4-10 and 4-11.

Exhibit 4–16.   Accepted Sales Order.

WERNER MANUFACTURING, INC.

ACCEPTED SALES ORDERS

APRIL 14, 1977

SALES ORDER NO	CUSTOMER NUMBER	AMOUNT OF SALE	
65139	128341	41,498.10[a]	Test transaction
65140	304007	3,641.75	
65141	235231	10,001.78	
65142	107654	135,724.87	
65144	009727	345.65	
65145	100400	3,757.80	Live transactions
•	•	•	
•	•	•	
•	•	•	
70042	211789	45,650.94	
		783,459.63	

[a]See Exhibits 4-10 and 4-11.

Finally, to show that sales are recorded after the goods are shipped (proper matching of revenue and cost), we see on Exhibit 4–17 that this transaction now appears on the sales register.

After reviewing the results of the ITF audit procedures, the internal auditors concluded that this portion of the sales processing system is working properly.

At this time, we want to emphasize an important point. In Chapter 3 we prepared auditing procedures that would be performed manually. In this chapter, we are computerizing some of them. But in doing so, we have changed the method of performing the procedure to best use computer technology and still achieve our audit objectives.

For example in Chapter 3, the internal auditors' procedure 12a calls for footing the cash receipts book. Procedure 12c calls for tracing selected cash receipts to the related customer account in the subsidiary accounts receivable ledger—two separate actions. In using the test deck to perform these procedures, both were carried out in one pass through the computer. Further, instead of looking for an entry in a ledger account, the internal auditors in

Exhibit 4–17. Sales Register.

WERNER MANUFACTURING, INC.

SALES REGISTER

APRIL 14, 1977

SALES ORDER NO	CUSTOMER NUMBER	AMOUNT OF SALE	
60 327	102973	2,171.76 [a]	} Test transaction
60 328	125789	37,499.81	
60 329	110431	42,627.30	
60 330	119173	3,070.51	
60 331	120001	2,797.80	
60 332	130654	32,581.94	} Live transactions
•	•	•	
•	•	•	
•	•	•	
63 895	18177	2,191.20	
		696,989.24	

[a]See Exhibits 4-10 and 4-11.

fact re-created that account after having predetermined what it should look like.

The distinction may not seem important, especially since the same audit objectives were attained. The point is that the performance of auditing procedures by computer may sometimes look radically different from those same procedures when performed manually. The important thing is not to let one's judgment be impaired by confusing methods and objectives. By keeping the objective firmly in mind, the appropriate method, whether manual or computerized, can more easily be identified and performed.

Refer back to Chapter 3: the independent auditors' (Brown, Johnson & Co.) program, step 3aii. They too have decided to use computerized audit techniques, in this case parallel simulation. As described in the text, parallel simulation is the reprocessing of live data, using the auditors' specially prepared programs. This is the direct opposite of the test deck and ITF approaches in which the auditor processes test transactions against client programs used to process data on a regular or "production" basis.

Audit program step 3aii covers processing operations 5 and 8 (Chapter 1: Figure 1–5). Since these do not involve continuous processing by computer, the auditors will use two separate programs, one for each processing operation. The programs will be written in COBOL, a very commonly used computer programming language for business applications.

Brown, Johnson & Co. uses computer audit specialists. These are auditors who have been given enough computer training to enable them to work with the audit team to review and evaluate EDP-related internal controls, plan the auditing procedures and execute computer-assisted auditing techniques. The system flowcharts, review and evaluation of internal controls, and the auditing procedures we have been considering were prepared/performed by the audit team, working with the computer audit specialist.

Operation 5:

- Updates the open order file
- Produces the listing of accepted sales orders and shipping orders

Operation 8:

- Updates the open order, customer accounts receivable and finished goods inventory files
- Produces the sales register and invoices

Brown, Johnson's audit objectives are explicitly stated in Exhibit 4–18. We will not list the COBOL programs the independent auditors wrote, but concentrate on auditing in a computer environment. We will therefore go directly to the test data schedules and the projected results. This follows the same pattern established in the sections on the test deck and integrated test facility approaches.

Exhibit 4–18. Parallel Simulation Audit Objectives.

WERNER MANUFACTURING, INC.
4/30/77

General — to insure that the recording of sales results in the proper recording of receivables and matching of revenue and expense

Specific — to determine whether the computer programs in operations 5 and 8:

- properly update the open order, customer accounts receivable file and finished goods inventory files.
- produce accurate:
  - accepted sales order lists
  - shipping orders
  - sales registers
  - invoices

In addition to Exhibit 4–18 in which Brown, Johnson explicitly stated their audit objectives, they use the following working papers:

- Test data control—Exhibit 4–19 shows the conditions to be tested and how the results are expected to appear, that is, how the files will look after processing and the information that will appear on the output reports.
- Transaction data and solutions—Exhibit 4–20 lists the valid and invalid transactions to be processed. Note in operations 5 and 8 that the input comes not from cards or a magnetic medium, but from a key-to-disk device. This is direct keyboard input, and it is how the auditor must input his test transactions. We will see later what audit control considerations this involves for the auditor.
- Master file data—Exhibit 4–21 shows the format and content of the customer accounts receivable, open order and inventory files.
- Computer printouts—The following exhibits show how the audit output is used to achieve objectives:
  - Exhibit 4–22—Error report
  - Exhibit 4–23—Accepted sales order report
  - Exhibit 4–24—Shipping order
  - Exhibit 4–25—Invoice
  - Exhibit 4–26—Sales register

Before we go through the independent auditors' procedures, bear in mind that there are two separate programs being processed. There are, in effect, two separate simulations.

Exhibit 4-19. Test Data Control.

WERNER MANUFACTURING, INC.
4/30/77

INPUT TEST TRANSACTION NUMBER	DESCRIPTION OF TEST	RESULTS EXPECTED	ACTUAL RESULTS	REMARKS
OPERATION 5:				
1	Invalid customer number	Rejected—error report	Rejected—error report	See Exhibits 4–22 through 4–24.

2–5	All input correct, followed by last transaction record	Accepted:
		• Accepted order added to the open order file
		• End-of-job routine performed:
		  • Reports printed:
		    — Errors
		    — Accepted sales orders
		    — Shipping orders
		  • Open order file dumped
			Accepted—open order file updated and end-of-job routine performed	

OPERATION 8:

6	Invalid customer number	Rejected—error report	

7–10	All input correct, followed by last transaction record	Accepted:
		• Sale recorded on the customer accounts receivable file
		• Open order deleted from open order file
		• Inventory file relieved of items shipped
		• End-of-job routine performed:
		  • Reports printed:
		   — Errors
		   — Sales register
		   — Invoices
		  • Open order, customer accounts receivable and inventory files dumped
			Rejected—error report
			
			Accepted—order entry, customer accounts receivable and inventory files updated and dumped
			Error report, sales register and invoices printed
				See Exhibits 4–22, 4–25 and 4–26.

Exhibit 4–20.   Transaction Data and Solutions.

WERNER MANUFACTURING, INC.
4/30/77

INPUT TEST TRANSACTION NUMBER [a]	TEST PERIOD [a]	NUMBER OF TRANSACTIONS PROCESSED	RESULTS OF PROCESSING [b]
OPERATION 5:			
1	May, 1976	2306	One transaction had an invalid customer number. See Exhibit 4–22. The other 2305 transactions were processed and produced output reports: • Accepted Sales Orders (Exhibit 4–23) • Shipping Orders (Exhibit 4–24)
2	July, 1976	1937	All transactions processed properly.
3	October, 1976	2145	All transactions processed properly.
4	December, 1976	1874	All transactions processed properly.
5	February, 1977	2411	All transactions processed properly.
OPERATION 8:			
6	June, 1976	1837	One transaction had an invalid customer number. See Exhibit 4–22. The other 1836 transactions were processed and produced outputs reports. • Invoices (Exhibit 4–25) • Sales Register (Exhibit 4–26)
7	August, 1976	2104	All transactions processed properly.
8	November, 1976	2007	All transactions processed properly.
9	January, 1977	1731	All transactions processed properly
10	April, 1977	2214	All transactions processed properly.

[a] Since parallel simulation involves reprocessing client data, "transactions" here denotes a month's processing.

[b] This is the "solution" or end result of processing as predetermined by the auditors. The output reports in Exhibits 4–22 through 4–26 confirm this result.

Setting up the test—parallel simulation.   Since the parallel simulation method involves the reprocessing of live client data, there is no guarantee that all conditions (e.g., errors) will be tested. The auditor is limited to the data with which he is dealing. How does he, then, insure that he will test all the conditions that are critical to his audit objectives?

He must review the client's output *before* deciding on the transactions to be reprocessed. In this example, we will assume that the auditor has done this and selected transactions which will enable his programs to give him the information in which he is interested. Keep in mind that the independent auditor

Exhibit 4–21.   Master File Data—Layouts.

WERNER MANUFACTURING, INC.
4/30/77

Operation 5:

Open Order File—See Exhibit 4–13.

Operation 8:

Customer Accounts Receivable—See Exhibit 4–12.

Open Order File—See Exhibit 4–13.

Finished Goods Inventory File (Perpetual):

ITEM NUMBER	DATE	RECEIPTS QUANTITY	UNIT COST	DATE	SHIPMENTS QUANTITY	UNIT COST	BALANCE QUANTITY	UNIT COST

is prohibited *in any case* from selecting all of his test transactions from one single period, that is, from performing a "block test" (*SAS No. 1*). He must test transactions from the entire period being audited.

After selecting the transactions to be tested, the auditor is ready to run his programs against the live data. In preparation for this, he has accumulated copies of output and has calculated how the files should look after the reprocessing. He will compare these with the actual reprocessing results.

Before reviewing Exhibits 4–19 through 4–26, which represent these calculations and results as they may appear in the auditors' working papers, we should consider how the auditor will perform the simulations (reprocessing). To do this, review the flowcharts (Figures 4–1 and 4–2) the auditor prepared for the two simulations. For ease of presentation and consistency, we will assume that two programs were developed, one each for operations 5 and 8, since this is how Brown, Johnson defined its audit objectives (Exhibit 4–18).

Since we are dealing with live client data, consisting of many transactions from the entire period being audited, it is not feasible to check the outcome of every transaction individually. Doing so would make the parallel simulation method too expensive for the auditor and is unnecessary in light of his audit objectives. Instead, the auditor will be able to accomplish his objectives by:

• Comparing control totals (e.g., footings, record counts) with those generated by the client's results

Exhibit 4-22.   Error Report—Rejected Transactions—Operations 5 and 8.

WERNER MANUFACTURING, INC.

ERROR REPORT - REJECTED TRANSACTIONS

MAY 5, 1976

CODE NO	CUSTOMER NUMBER	SALES ORDER NO	AMOUNT OF SALE	DESCRIPTION
01	151407	43471	15,487.01	INVALID CUST NO[a]

LEGEND:

01 - SALES ORDER

02 - SHIPPING ADVICE

[a]See Exhibits 4-19 and 4-20.

WERNER MANUFACTURING, INC.

ERROR REPORT - REJECTED TRANSACTIONS

JUNE 10, 1976

CODE NO	CUSTOMER NUMBER	SALES ORDER NO	AMOUNT OF SALE	DESCRIPTION
02	158070	43042	28,349.17	INVALID CUST NO[a]

LEGEND:

01 - SALES ORDER

02 - SHIPPING ADVICE

[a]See Exhibits 4-19 and 4-20.

Exhibit 4–23. Accepted Sales Orders—Operation 5.

WERNER MANUFACTURING, INC.

ACCEPTED SALES ORDERS

MAY 5, 1976

SALES ORDER NO	CUSTOMER NUMBER	AMOUNT OF SALE	
40470	127842	435.07	
40472	167009	6,731.21	
40473	195803	4,897.69	
40474	007527	10,897.69	
40475	159034	779.27	
•	•	•	See Exhibits 4-19 and 4-20.
•	•	•	
40687	204791	11,507.20	
40688	057892	135,742.91	
40689	122905	4,007.01	
40690	057998	321.87	
		947,607.95	

Exhibit 4–24. Shipping Order—Operation 5.

WERNER MANUFACTURING, INC.

MAY 5, 1976

ORDER NO.   40499

CUSTOMER NO.   134271

        NAME   AJAX INDUSTRIES, INC.

     ADDRESS   127 WARRENTON STREET

                 HOLTSVILLE, NEW YORK 11742

ITEM NO	UNIT	QUANTITY	
A402	EACH	30	
S20784	DOZEN	10	See Exhibits 4-19 and 4-20.
X8009	EACH	25	
T537	POUNDS	25	

Exhibit 4–25.   Invoice—Operation 8.

```
WERNER MANUFACTURING, INC.


           INVOICE

SOLD TO:                     ORDER NO. 43040

ACME INDUSTRIES, INC.        DATE:   JUNE 10, 1976
134 WAINRIGHT STREET
HICKSVILLE, NEW YORK 11801


  ITEM          QUANTITY       PRICE       TOTAL
 ------        ---------      -----      -----------


 J347           57            10.00        570.00  )
                                                   |
 S20784         10 DOZ.        3.00         30.00   |
                                                    } See Exhibits 4-19, 4-20, and 4-26.
 A5401          50            34.00       1,700.00  |
                                                   |
 T537           25 LBS.        5.00        125.00  )


                                          -----------
                                          2,425.00
                                          -----------
```

Exhibit 4–26.   Sales Register—Operation 8.

```
WERNER MANUFACTURING, INC.

           SALES REGISTER

           JUNE 10, 1976



     SALES            CUSTOMER          AMOUNT OF
   ORDER NO            NUMBER              SALE
  ---------          ---------         -----------


   43040             100207            2,425.00[a] )
                                                   |
   43041             013789           37,581.50    |
                                                   |
   43043             191782           52,004.29    |
                                                    } See Exhibits 4-19 and 4-20.
   43044             100045              321.94    |
                                                   |
   43045             121114               10.81    |
     •                 •                   •       |
     •                 •                   •       |
   43090             107574            3,209.10    |
                                                   |
   43091             125555              100.74   )


                                       -----------
                                       247,670.81
                                       -----------
```

[a]See Exhibit 4–25.

Annotation

The transactions are entered via keyboard CRT terminal.
This is the result of the "quantity sufficient" branch,
which updates the open order file.

After the last transaction has been entered and processed, a
specially coded record is entered. The system reads it and
begins the end-of-job routine.

The rejected order file will be printed on the error report as part
of the end-of-job routine.

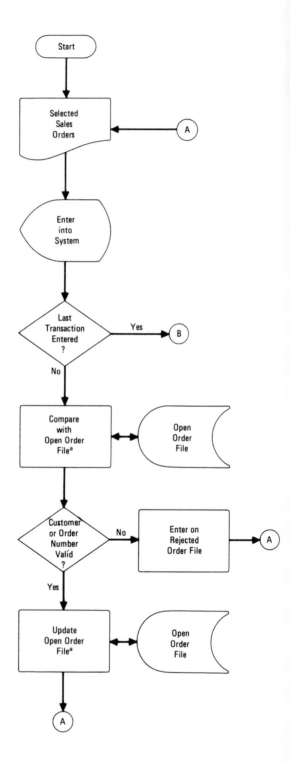

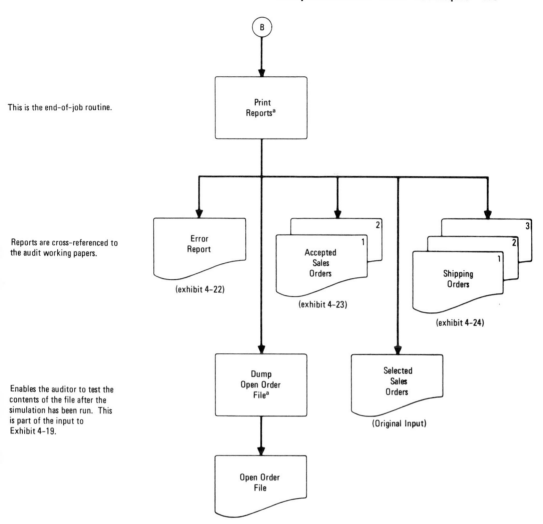

This is the end-of-job routine.

Reports are cross-referenced to the audit working papers.

Enables the auditor to test the contents of the file after the simulation has been run. This is part of the input to Exhibit 4-19.

ᵃUsing auditor-written program.

Figure 4–1. Flowchart Worksheet for Test of Operation 5.

• Inspecting selected transactions (involving the conditions in which the auditor is interested) and comparing how they are processed in the simulation with how they were processed in the client's regular operations

Exhibit 4–19 reflects this approach. Note also that all the exhibits reflect the fact that this is really two separate but related simulations, for operations 5 and 8.

In using the parallel simulation approach, Brown, Johnson worked very closely with the internal auditors, particularly the EDP internal auditors, to help insure that:

Annotation

Shipping orders received from the warehouse. Represent goods actually shipped.

After the last transaction has been entered and processed, a specially coded record is entered.

The system reads it and begins the end-of-job routine.

The rejected order file will be printed on the error report as part of the end-of-job routine.

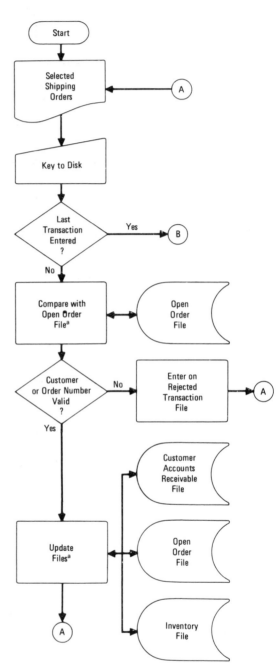

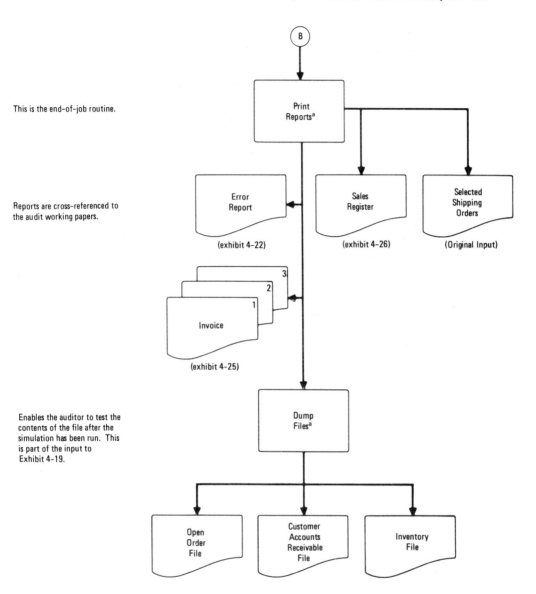

This is the end-of-job routine.

Reports are cross-referenced to the audit working papers.

Enables the auditor to test the contents of the file after the simulation has been run. This is part of the input to Exhibit 4-19.

[a] Using auditor-written program.

Figure 4–2. Flowchart Worksheet for Test of Operation 8.

• The programs they wrote properly tested for the conditions of greatest audit significance in Werner's system and therefore satisfied their stated audit objectives (Exhibit 4–18). This required a full understanding of what the client's programs do and a thorough testing of the simulation programs they wrote. Indeed, when auditors write computer programs for audit purposes, they should be documented and tested (debugged) as rigorously as any production programs. If any question should arise as to the adequacy of the auditor's procedures, the computer programs he uses must meet the same professional standards as any other auditing procedure.

● The simulation processed the correct files. During the development of the system, Brown, Johnson and the internal auditors developed their auditing procedures to test the system once it became operational. As part of that process, the internal auditors agreed to make control copies of certain live files on magnetic tape as they were created and keep them for use by the independent auditors.

● The actual processing was performed under properly controlled conditions. This was relatively easy, since Werner's data center is generally closed on weekends. Brown, Johnson and the internal auditors, with one of the regular operators, took over the entire computer installation on a weekend and processed the test files themselves, thereby controlling the input, the processing and the output. If this had not been possible, they would have to:

● ● Process the test data at an outside data center, for example, a service bureau

● ● Devise controls to insure that processing the test data by Werner's data center as part of the daily processing stream did not cause a loss of audit control

As was the case with the test deck and ITF approaches used by the internal auditors, parallel simulation follows a review and evaluation of internal control.

Performing the test.   Which procedures the auditor uses depends on the nature of the system being audited and the objectives he is trying to accomplish. In this case, we are performing a compliance test of a strength that was identified in the review and evaluation of internal control. (See Chapter 1: Figure 1–5 and the explanation of strength IV.) Chapter 3 relates strength IV to several auditing procedures. One of these is procedure 3aii, which we are performing *in part* by parallel simulation. Let's reiterate auditing procedure 3aii and relate it to the objectives of the parallel simulation as they are stated in Exhibit 4–18.

Trace the sales orders to the related shipping orders, the sales register and the customer receivables file and recheck them for arithmetical accuracy and pricing. Trace the sales register to the general ledger posting.

As Exhibit 4–18 states, the parallel simulation will tell us if sales orders result in a proper sales register and customer receivables file. It will *also* tell us whether the output (the sales register, invoices, updated customer receivables file, and so on) is arithmetically accurate. It will *not* perform a pricing test, nor will it trace the sales register to the general ledger; these procedures must be performed manually.

Because of the nature of Werner's computer system, performing a parallel simulation on operations 5 and 8 will also tell us something about the inventory files. Ostensibly this is not in our scope, because this case study is concerned only with sales, accounts receivable and cash receipts. In actual practice, however, these audit procedures would be related to our audit objectives for inventories.

Exhibit 4–20 shows which periods in the year being audited (May 1, 1976 through April 30, 1977) were selected for processing in the simulation and the expected results of that processing. For illustrative purposes, we will show only the computer output for a day's activity in May, 1976 (operation 5) and June, 1976 (operation 8).

Assume that the auditors reviewed the printouts (dumps) of the key files as shown in Figures 4–1 and 4–2 and ascertained that they were updated as expected.

Refer to Exhibit 4–19. Input test transaction 1 (May, 1976 as Exhibit 4–20 tells us) had one erroneous record and should produce an error report; the other records are correct and should produce correct output. Exhibit 4–22 shows us that an error report was produced for sales order 40471 on May 5, 1976. Similarly, Exhibit 4–23 shows that an accepted sales order report was produced. Note that sales order 40471 does not appear on it. The auditors traced the total, $947,607.95, and selected lines in the report to the output the client produced as a result of its regular daily processing. Exhibit 4–24 shows an example of a shipping order produced on May 5, 1976. It and the others were also test-traced to the client's output. No differences were found. Output is shown for only one day in May, 1976, as that for all other periods is identical to the reports shown in Exhibits 4–23 and 4–24.

Look at the second part of Exhibit 4–22. It shows the error report predicted in Exhibits 4–19 and 4–20 for operation 8. There is only one substantial difference between it and the error report for operation 5: it is a code 02 transaction rather than code 01. As Figures 4–1 and 4–2 show, the input to operation 5 consists of sales orders, while the input to operation 8 consists of shipping orders.

Input test transaction 6 (June, 1976 according to Exhibit 4–20) is the first period selected for operation 8, and from that month we have selected June 10 for illustrative purposes. Exhibit 4–25 shows an example of the invoices generated. It and a number of others were compared with the invoices produced by regular daily processing. No differences were noted.

Exhibit 4–26 shows the sales register for June 10. Note it does *not* show sales order 43042, which had an error and is listed on the second part of Exhibit 4–22. This is correct processing. Brown, Johnson traced the total, $247,670.81, and selected lines in the sales register to the output produced by regular daily processing.

Although not a computer auditing procedure, it is appropriate to mention here that some follow-up procedures would be performed by Brown, Johnson in regard to the error reports in Exhibit 4–22: how errors are corrected and reentered in the processing stream. Basically, the auditors would be interested in satisfying themselves that errors (except for those generated by the data processing area, such as keypunch errors) are only corrected by the user department and subjected to the same controls as the original input. Ironically, error correction is one of the largest single sources of errors in computer systems.

Brown, Johnson's auditing procedures compliance-tested internal control strength IV and show that Werner's system is operating as it was purported to. But what if the opposite were true? Most likely, Brown, Johnson, after investigating the source of the error, would reevaluate internal control with this new information and would have decided to expand the scope of its substantive auditing procedures.

We cited two techniques at the start of this chapter that ostensibly have not yet been covered: specially written programs and generalized audit software. "Ostensibly," because preparing a program in COBOL to perform a parallel simulation is also an example of a specially written program. In fact, the programs Brown, Johnson's computer audit specialists wrote to perform the parallel simulation could also have been written in generalized audit software. As the text explained, generalized audit software enables the non-data processing professional (e.g., an auditor) to prepare programs which use the computer to perform auditing procedures. They generally involve completing specification forms and/or simplified programs, many of which use terms familiar to the auditor, for example, foot, add, subtract, sample, match, search, and so on.

Brown, Johnson & Co. will use a generalized audit software package called System 2170, which it licenses from Peat, Marwick, Mitchell & Co., another firm of certified public accountants, to perform auditing procedure 5:

Obtain and check or prepare an aged trial balance of customer receivables as of an interim date and:

a. Foot the totals and crossfoot selected accounts
b. Compare the total receivable balance with the general ledger
c. Confirm selected accounts: all $10,000 and over; 10% of the rest
d. Prepare a schedule to reconcile the balance as of the interim date to the balance on the audit date; vouch the accuracy of the reconciling amounts (sales, cash receipts, adjusting journal entries)

Steps b and d cannot be performed by use of generalized audit software: they must be performed manually. Independent auditors' procedure 5 (Chapter 3) refers to a weakness and is a substantive rather than a compliance procedure. Its purpose is to enable the auditor to verify account balances as of a given date.

Because of the documentation that System 2170's specification forms automatically provide, our exhibits will consist of these forms and computer output. We have not included all the System 2170 forms, only those needed to explain how Brown, Johnson uses the software to perform its auditing procedures.

Setting up the test—generalized audit software. Brown, Johnson elected to process on a separate service bureau's computer on a weekend, where they can take over the entire system and thereby exercise complete audit control. To do this, they made copies of Werner's applicable files and processed their programs against them.

Turn to Exhibit 4–28, the problem statement. This states Brown, Johnson's audit objectives and relates them to the input, output and computer processing that will be performed. Note that they plan to use the computer to accomplish audit procedure 5a by actually aging the receivable balances as well as footing the total to enable them to make the comparison to the general ledger called for by procedure 5b.

Note also that two changes have been made from the original intent as embodied in the audit program:

- *All* balances will be aged and crossfooted rather than just selected ones.
- The work, and especially the preparation of confirmation requests, will be performed at the audit date (April 30, 1977) rather than at an interim date.

Brown, Johnson decided on this change because (1) the computer offers sufficient speed to permit what in effect is a 100% test of the aging, footing and crossfooting and (2) in view of Werner's generally good internal control over sales, accounts receivable and cash receipts, the time period for compiling the report is more than sufficient.

The first two objectives relate to auditing procedure 5a, the third relates to 5c. This application of System 2170 would not produce the actual confirmations. That will be accomplished by a subsequent System 2170 application, in which the output tape referred to in objective 3 and identified as "ACCTCONF" on the job stream flowchart (Exhibit 4–27) would, with the customer name and address file, be the input. We will not cover the specification forms for the confirmation printing application, but an example of the confirmations appears in Exhibit 4–35.

Our flowcharts show the customer accounts receivable file being on disk. For their processing (and to illustrate a common computer auditing tech-

Exhibit 4–27.   Job Stream Flowchart.

PEAT, MARWICK, MITCHELL & CO.
S/2170
JOB STREAM FLOWCHART

Client	Job No.
73 80	
W E R N E R 0 1	

Client _WERNER MFG., INC._   W.P. No. ___

Division ___   Accountant _R.B._

B.J. + Co.
PMM & Co. Office _CLEVE._   Date _5/16/77_

DESCRIPTION

INPUT FILES:

	INITIAL	SECONDARY
FILE NAME	_MASTACCT_	
SOURCE OF FILE	_CLIENT_	
FILE TYPE	_TAPE_	
SORT REQUIRED?	_NO_	
DISPOSITION	_RETURN_	

PROGRAM:

	PROGRAM
PROGRAM NAME	_WERNER 01_
RUN TYPE	_GENERAL_
STAT OR ATT OPERATIONS?	_NO_

OUTPUT FILES:

	OUTPUT 1	OUTPUT 2
FILE NAME	_ACCTCONF_	
FILE TYPE	_TAPE_	
DISPOSITION	_CONFRUN_	

	OUTPUT 3	OUTPUT 4
FILE NAME		
FILE TYPE		
DISPOSITION		

	OUTPUT 5	OUTPUT 6
FILE NAME		
FILE TYPE		
DISPOSITION		

	OUTPUT 7	SPECIAL
FILE NAME		
FILE TYPE		
DISPOSITION		

PRINTED OUTPUT

	PRINTED OUTPUT
TYPE OF FORM	_STANDARD_
NO. OF COPIES	_2_

Exhibit 4–28. Problem Statement.

PEAT, MARWICK, MITCHELL & CO.

S/2170

PROBLEM STATEMENT

Client	Job No.
WERNER 0 1	

Client _WERNER MFG., INC._   W.P. No. ___—___

Division ___—___   Accountant ___R.B.___

~~B.J. & Co.~~ ~~PMM & Co.~~ Office _CLEVE._   Date _5/16/77_

GENERAL STATEMENT OF AUDIT OBJECTIVES:

1. OBTAIN A FILE DOLLAR CONTROL TOTAL AS OF 4/30/77.

2. PRINT A DETAILED AGED ACCOUNTS RECEIVABLE TRIAL BALANCE INCLUDING SUBTOTALS BY CUSTOMER USING THE FOLLOWING CRITERIA:
   - 0-30 DAYS
   - 31-60 DAYS
   - 61-90 DAYS
   - 91-120 DAYS
   - OVER 120 DAYS

3. TAPE SELECTED SUMMARIZED CUSTOMER RECORDS FOR CONFIRMATION BASED ON THE FOLLOWING CRITERIA:
   - ALL CUSTOMERS WITH BALANCES OF $10,000 AND OVER
   - 10% OF THOSE WITH BALANCES UNDER $10,000

INPUT REQUIREMENTS	REQUIRED OPERATIONS	OUTPUT OBJECTIVES

MASTACCT - TAPE
CUSTOMER NUMBER
INVOICE NUMBER
TRANSACTION DATE
TRANSACTION CODE
EXTENDED COST (AMOUNT)
	INCLUDE CREDITS AND
	  CONVERT AMOUNT TO
	  NEGATIVE
	CONTROL TOTALS
	TEST TRANSACTION DATE
	ACCUMULATE SUBTOTALS
	PRINTDTL
	SUMMARIZE CUSTOMER
	  RECORDS
	SELECT SAMPLE
	TAPE
		PRINTED LISTING:
		  CUSTOMER NUMBER
		  INVOICE NUMBER
		  TRANSACTION DATE
		  TRANSACTION CODE
		  TOTAL BALANCE
		  0-30 DAYS BALANCE
		  31-60 DAYS BALANCE
		  61-90 DAYS BALANCE
		  91-120 DAYS BALANCE
		  OVER 120 DAYS BALANCE
		
		ACCTCONF - TAPE:
		  CUSTOMER NUMBER
		  AMOUNT

Zero = 0   Alphabetic O = Ø   Two = 2   Alphabetic Z = Ƶ

S/2170 - 4 (9/70)

nique), Brown, Johnson has duplicated the file on a reel of magnetic tape. This is frequently done when the client's file is to be processed at another data center.

To conform to System 2170 rules, the tape has been named "MASTACCT" (Exhibit 4–27). The job stream flowchart sets the general flow of work and specifies the input and output. It is a basic rule of effective programming that a detailed program flowchart be prepared before actually writing the instructions (coding) that comprise the program. This is illustrated in Exhibit 4–29. Since the purpose of using System 2170 is to perform auditing procedures with the computer, the program flowchart is cross-referenced to the audit objectives (Exhibit 4–28).

Cross-referencing the program flowchart to the audit objectives serves two purposes:

- It guarantees that all audit objectives are going to be covered by the program (see Exhibit 4–33).
- It makes the subsequent year's job that much easier, as it is sometimes difficult to readily understand what the prior year's auditors did when program documentation is poor.

Note that the flowchart also has another cross-reference, with "L" prefixes. These relate the flowchart elements to the System 2170 operation specifications (Exhibit 4–33), which are like the instructions in a computer program. (System 2170 generates a COBOL program from the information it gets from the specification forms.) Thus, the audit objectives are related directly to the operation specifications. The specifications in Exhibits 4–30, 4–31 and 4–32 give the system detailed information on the format of the input records (customer accounts receivable file) and the tape and printed output, respectively.

Performing the test. Exhibit 4–34 shows an example of the aged trial balance that this application would produce. Brown, Johnson compared the total accounts receivable with the general ledger and the aged balances with the client's aging, preparatory to performing other, manual procedures. For example, note for customer 100240 that a pending credit adjustment has been outstanding for over 120 days. This may require investigation by Brown, Johnson, depending on what decisions they have made on materiality and scope. This aged trial balance would run for several computer printout pages. This is a specially prepared model, presented here on a single page for illustrative purposes.

After printing the aged trial balance, Brown, Johnson used the output tape ("ACCTCONF") to produce confirmations. One of these, for customer 100235, is illustrated in Exhibit 4–35.

Exhibit 4–29. Flowchart.

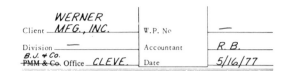

PEAT, MARWICK, MITCHELL & CO.

S/2170

FLOWCHART

Client	Job No.
W E R N E R	O 1

Client __WERNER MFG., INC.__   W.P. No ___

Division ___   Accountant   _R.B._

B.J. & Co.
~~PMM & Co.~~ Office _CLEVE._   Date   _5/16/77_

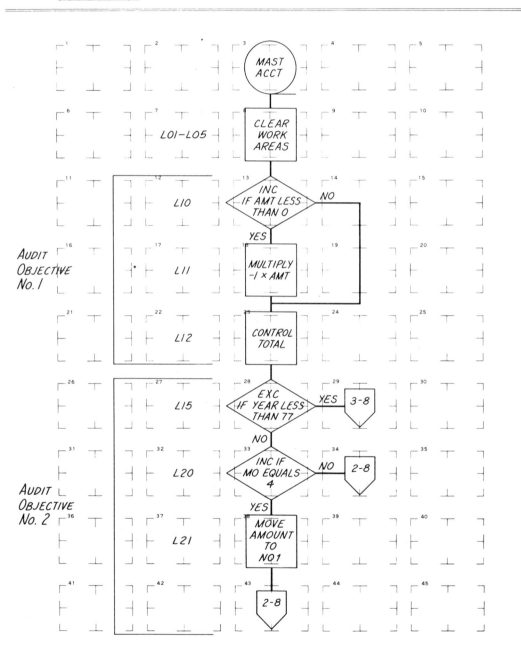

Zero = 0   Alphabetic O = ∅   Two = 2   Alphabetic Z = Ƶ

Exhibit 4–29 (continued)

PEAT, MARWICK, MITCHELL & CO.

S/2170

FLOWCHART

Client	Job No.
W E R N E R O 1	

Client _WERNER MFG., INC._   W.P. No. ——
Division ——   Accountant _R.B._
_B.J. + Co._
PMM & Co. Office _CLEVE._   Date _5/16/77_

AUDIT
OBJECTIVE
No. 2

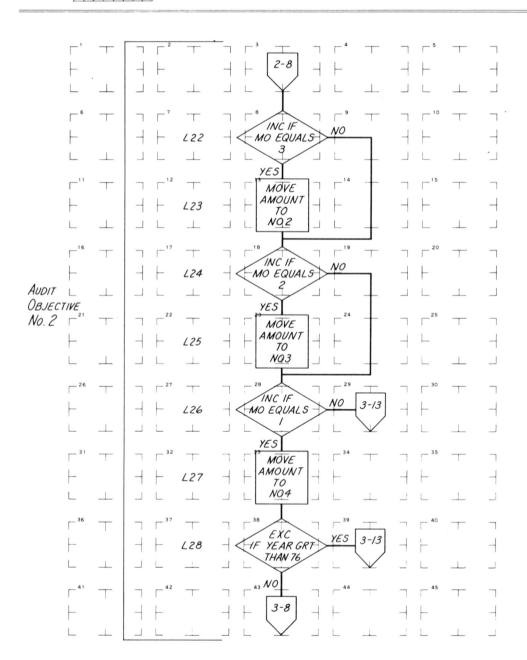

2-8

L22 — INC IF MO EQUALS 3 — NO

YES

L23 — MOVE AMOUNT TO NO.2

L24 — INC IF MO EQUALS 2 — NO

YES

L25 — MOVE AMOUNT TO NO.3

L26 — INC IF MO EQUALS 1 — NO — 3-13

YES

L27 — MOVE AMOUNT TO NO.4

L28 — EXC IF YEAR GRT THAN 76 — YES — 3-13

NO

3-8

Zero = 0   Alphabetic O = Ø   Two = 2   Alphabetic Z = Ƶ

PEAT, MARWICK, MITCHELL & CO.

S/2170

FLOWCHART

Client	Job No.
W E R N E R 0 1	

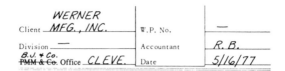

WERNER

Client _MFG., INC._   W.P. No. _—_

Division _—_   Accountant _R.B._

B.J. & Co.
~~PMM & Co.~~ Office _CLEVE._   Date _5/16/77_

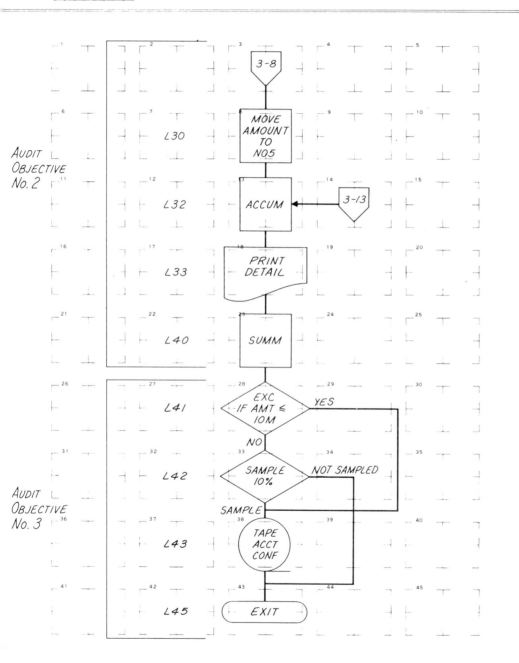

AUDIT
OBJECTIVE
No. 2

AUDIT
OBJECTIVE
No. 3

L30   MOVE AMOUNT TO NO5 (from 3-8)

L32   ACCUM (from 3-13)

L33   PRINT DETAIL

L40   SUMM

L41   EXC IF AMT ≤ 10M   YES

NO

L42   SAMPLE 10%   NOT SAMPLED

SAMPLE

L43   TAPE ACCT CONF

L45   EXIT

Zero = 0   Alphabetic O = φ   Two = 2   Alphabetic Z = Z

Exhibit 4-30. Input Data Specification.

PEAT, MARWICK, MITCHELL & CO.

S/2170

INPUT DATA SPECIFICATION

Client		Job No.
73		80
W E R N E R O 1		

Client __WERNER MFG., INC.__   W.P. No. __—__

Division __—__   Accountant __R.B.__
B.J. + Co.
~~PMM & Co.~~ Office __CLEVE.__   Date __5/16/77__

Page		
1		3
2	0	1

File Name __MASTACCT__

I/S	SEQ.	STARTING POSITION	FIELD	SIZE	# DEC	TYPE	SUMM	LOCATION	CDZ	CODE	FIRST	POS.	NUMBER	OF DIGITS	DESCRIPTION
I	01	0001	06			A	1								CUSTOMER-NUMBER
I	02	0007	05			A									INVOICE-NUMBER
I	03	0012	06	0	N										TRANSACTION-DATE
I	04	0012	02	0	N										TRANSACTION-MONTH
I	05	0014	02	0	N										TRANSACTION-DAY
I	06	0016	02	0	N										TRANSACTION-YEAR
I	07	0018	01	0	N										TRANSACTION-CODE
I	08	0019	09	2	N	S									AMOUNT

Zero = 0   Alphabetic O = Ø   Two = 2   Alphabetic Z = Ƶ

Exhibit 4–31. Output Specification—Tape, Disk or Punch.

PMM & Co. **PEAT, MARWICK, MITCHELL & CO.**

S/2170

OUTPUT SPECIFICATION
TAPE, DISK OR PUNCH

Client	Job No.
73	80
W E R N E R 0 1	

Client _WERNER MFG., INC._   W.P. No. _—_

Division _—_   Accountant _R.B._

B.J. + Co.
~~PMM & Co.~~ Office _CLEVE._   Date _5/16/77_

Page								S - Sequential Disk	File Name		Disk Type
1		4					8	T - Tape	9	16	44
4	0	1	F	0	0	P	T	C - Card	A C C T C Ø N F		

Page		TYPE
1	4	
4	0 1	P

SEQ.	SOURCE FIELD	FIELD SIZE	# DEF	INFORMATIONAL NAME
5 6	7	10	11 12	18 ⋯ 30 ⋯ 40 ⋯ 50 ⋯ 58
0 1	I 0 1	0 6		CUSTØMER-NUMBER
0 2	I 0 8	0 9		AMØUNT
0 3				
0 4				
0 5				
0 6				
0 7				
0 8				
0 9				
1 0				
1 1				
1 2				
1 3				
1 4				
1 5				
1 6				
1 7				
1 8				
1 9				

Zero = 0   Alphabetic O = Ø   Two = 2   Alphabetic Z = Z

S/2170-9 (3/72)

189

Exhibit 4–32.   Output Specification—Printer.

PEAT, MARWICK, MITCHELL & CO.

S/2170

OUTPUT   SPECIFICATION

PRINTER

Client	Job No.
73	80
W E R N E R 0 1	

Client _WERNER MFG., INC_   W.P. No. _—_

Division _—_   Accountant _R.B._

_B.J. + Co._

~~PMM & Co~~. Office _CLEVE._   Date _5/16/77_

Page					File Name	
1	4	5	6	7	8	14
5 0 1	F	0	0	P	P R I N T 0	1

Page	TYPE
1	4
5 0 1	P

SEQ.	SOURCE FIELD	FIELD SIZE	# DEC	EDIT	ACCUM	ROUND	LESS THAN OR EQUAL TO EDITED FIELD SIZE Printer Heading #1	LESS THAN OR EQUAL TO EDITED FIELD SIZE Printer Heading #2
5 6	7	10 11	12	13	14	15	18 29	34 45
0 1	I 0 1	0 6					C U S T	N U M B
0 2	I 0 2	0 5					I N V	N U M
0 3	I 0 3	0 6	0	N			T R A N S	D A T E
0 4	I 0 7	0 1	0	N			T	C
0 5	I 0 8	0 9	2	D	A		T O T A L	B A L A N C E
0 6	N 0 1	0 9	2	D	A		0 - - 3 0	D A Y S
0 7	N 0 2	0 9	2	D	A		3 1 - - 6 0	D A Y S
0 8	N 0 3	0 9	2	D	A		6 1 - - 9 0	D A Y S
0 9	N 0 4	0 9	2	D	A		9 1 - 1 2 0	D A Y S
1 0	N 0 5	0 9	2	D	A		O V E R - 1 2 0	D A Y S

Zero = 0   Alphabetic O = Ø   Two = 2   Alphabetic Z = Ƶ

Exhibit 4–33.   Operation Specifications.

PEAT, MARWICK, MITCHELL & CO.

S/2170

OPERATION SPECIFICATIONS

	Client	Job No.
73		80
	WERNER01	

Client **WERNER MFG., INC.**   W.P. No.   —

Division ——   B.J. + Co.   Accountant **R.B.**

~~PMM & Co.~~ Office **CLEVE.**   Date **5/16/77**

Page
1		3
7	0	1

LINE NO.	OPERATION		OPERANDS 1	2	3	4	5
L01	MOVE		O			NO1	
L02	MOVE		O			NO2	
L03	MOVE		O			NO3	
L04	MOVE		O			NO4	
L05	MOVE		O			NO5	
L10	INCLUDE		I080			LESL12	
L11	MULTIPLY		-1	I08	I08		
L12	FOOT		I08CONTROL-TOTAL				
L15	EXCLUDE		I0677			LESL30	
L20	INCLUDE		I0404			EQUL22	
L21	MOVE		I08			NO1	
L22	INCLUDE		I0403			EQUL24	
L23	MOVE		I08			NO2	
L24	INCLUDE		I0402			EQUL26	
L25	MOVE		I08			NO3	
L26	INCLUDE		I0401			EQUL32	
L27	MOVE		I08			NO4	
L28	EXCLUDE		I0676			GRTL32	
L30	MOVE		I08			NO5	
L32	ACCUM						
L33	PRINTDTL		01				
L40	SUMM						
L41	EXCLUDE		I089999.99			GRTL43	
L42	SAMPLE		10	32871007		L45	
L43	TAPE		ACCTCONF				
L45	EXIT						

Zero = 0   Alphabetic O = Ø   Two = 2   Alphabetic Z = Ƶ

S/2170 - 11 (4/77)

Exhibit 4-34. Aged Trial Balance.

CUST NUMB	INV NUM	TRANS DATE	T C	TOTAL BALANCE	0-30 DAYS	31-60 DAYS	61-90 DAYS	91-120 DAYS	OVER 120 DAYS	
100235	62987	032277	1	4,100.37		4,100.37	0.00	0.00	0.00	
100235	66844	040777	1	63,427.80	63,427.80	0.00	0.00	0.00	0.00	
100235	66905	040977	1	354.85	354.85	0.00	0.00	0.00	0.00	
100235	66906	040977	2	10,000.00-	10,000.00-	0.00	0.00	0.00	0.00	
100235				57,883.02	53,782.65	4,100.37	0.00	0.00	0.00[a]	L01 4
100240	41777	051276	3	1,000.00-	0.00	0.00	0.00	0.00	1,000.00-	
100240				1,000.00-	0.00	0.00	0.00	0.00	1,000.00-	L01 1
•••	•••	•••		•••	•••	•••	•••	•••	•••	•••
175207	60050	026577	1	7,543.27	0.00	0.00	7,543.27	0.00	0.00	
175207	66899	040877	1	10,000.00	10,000.00	0.00	0.00	0.00	0.00	
175207				17,543.27	10,000.00	0.00	7,543.27	0.00	0.00	L01 2
				6,570,967.43	3,709,827.27	2,223,536.35	436,143.40	200,300.40	1,160.01	358

[a]See Exhibit 4-35.

192

Exhibit 4–35. Confirmation.

BROWN, JOHNSON & CO.
CERTIFIED PUBLIC ACCOUNTANTS
2730 LAKEWOOD GROVE AVENUE
CLEVELAND, OHIO 44114

WERNER MANUFACTURING, INC.
27 OAKDALE BOULEVARD
CLEVELAND, OHIO 44114

1J0235

OC001

Our auditors, Brown, Johnson & Co., are making their regular examination of our accounts. In
regard to that examination, your account has been selected for confirmation.
Please compare the information stated below to your records as of **04/30/77**.
Transactions since that date are not to be considered. If the information
is not in agreement with your records please state the difference on the reverse side and return this
form directly to our auditors.

            IF CORRECT, PLEASE SIGN ON THE REVERSE SIDE AND
RETURN THIS DIRECTLY TO OUR AUDITORS.

            BALANCE DUE FROM YOU
        AMOUNTED TO $57,883.02

PALMER AVIATION, INC.
14 AERIAL WAY
WICHITA, KANSAS 67202

WERNER MANUFACTURING, INC.

5
Service Centers and Other Data Processing Services and Organizations

The use of external data processing service organizations increases the processing options available to an organization. It introduces a legally and physically separate organization into the record-keeping process that directly affects the organization's financial and operating records. It also materially changes internal control procedures. As a result, the use of these services may affect the scope of the auditor's examination. Their presence requires that the auditor be familiar with the types of organizations and services being used, the way in which those organizations process their customers' data, the way in which they develop programs and systems, the effectiveness of their internal controls, and the documentation that is developed and maintained by both the client/auditee and the computer service organization.

The use of external data processing services may have a material impact on the client's/auditee's system of internal control and thus is a matter of professional concern to both internal and external auditors. If much of the processing performed under the data processing services is external to the organization, and files and records are maintained at the external service center, the auditor must extend the review of internal control to both the in-house procedures and the procedures executed at the service center. In many audit situations involving external data processing services, physical records such as printed reports, listings, and documents are still available and can be evaluated with traditional audit techniques. In addition, the auditor may access the machine-readable files maintained by the service organization and use the computer itself for evaluating records by developing or obtaining audit programs and processing the machine-readable records. The decision to use the computer facility maintained by the data processing service organization or to seek other facilities available to the auditor is really similar to the kinds of decisions made when an organization has its own equipment.

VARIETY OF DATA PROCESSING SERVICES

The level of services provided by service centers and other data processing service organizations varies widely, and they are purchased for a variety of reasons. Sometimes these services are used by small firms that cannot justify the investment in time and resources to maintain their own center, but can benefit from the use of computerized processing if that processing can be purchased at the right price. In contrast, many large organizations with their own computer center and staff also purchase certain specialized services from outside sources when the applications involved are not suited to their own in-house computer center.

The audit guide *Audits of Service-Center-Produced Records* defines five types of data processing services:

1. Renting of computer time
2. Providing management for computer facilities
3. Processing standard package programs
4. Designing and processing individually tailored systems
5. Providing time-shared computer services [1]

The first service listed, an environment in which the company rents time on a computer and performs its own processing and programming, has few elements of a true service center and can be treated almost in the same way as the company that processes data on its own computer. In fact, many companies that rent computer time from service centers have their own computer facilities to process most of their data. They may rent computer time on a stand-by basis when their own computers are overloaded. Although these situations in reality involve use of a service center, the client/auditee may be so effectively responsible for its own processing that the auditor can treat the company as though it were merely using its own computer in another location, except for the contractual obligations and possible lack of physical security at the service center site.

In facilities management the computer center is physically located on the premises of the customer organization, and the hardware may or may not be paid for by the customer. The staff, however, including systems design, programming and operating personnel, are employees of the service organization. This kind of arrangement is frequently used by companies that feel they do not have the technical expertise to develop and manage the computer services and do not wish to take the time nor expend the resources to develop that expertise. Yet the company usually has sufficient volume of activity and need for computer services so that the total expenditures of an in-house installation are economically justifiable. A facilities management arrangement provides the advantage of an in-house location with its immediate accessibility; at the same time, it frees the user's management from the potential drain on management time related to overseeing the day-to-day supervision and control of the data processing function.

[1] Committee on Computer Auditing, *Audits of Service-Center-Produced Records*, (New York: American Institute of Certified Public Accountants, 1973).

The use of facilities management is also a situation in which some of the normal elements of a service center are missing. In such a case, the auditor must evaluate the internal control procedures of the outside entity in the same manner as if the auditee's own employees were managing the processing. If the party supplying the facilities management services also agrees to purchase the company's excess computer time and sell service center services to others, the auditor must consider this aspect when evaluating internal control, because the data and programs of other companies may be stored in the computer room.

The use of standardized package programs really represents no change at all to the auditor in attempting to evaluate the adequacy of the computer operations and the internal control procedures involved. Assuming that the user exercises adequate care in defining needs and selecting a package that is carefully tested and documented, the control concerns are no different from those that exist when the installation is developing and writing its own application programs. By being willing to do its processing in a standardized, predefined way, the installation normally can purchase one of these programs at a cost less than it would take to develop a program and test the application with its own programming staff.

In many service center arrangements, the service center's employees design the system and write the programs. Although the customer may participate in designing the system, it often does not have the EDP knowledge and background required to evaluate the system's effectiveness or understand the manner in which the system is controlled within the center. The user should, however, "acquire a sufficient knowledge of the system to enable him to provide the necessary input to react to exceptions and differences reported, and to understand the output records." [2] In this arrangement the service organization also processes the customer's data on the service bureau's premises with its own equipment. The service center provides complete data processing service—program design, writing, and execution. A service center serves many customers with its equipment and programming personnel, enabling it to spread the cost of its organization and equipment over many potential users. Thus, it is economically feasible for a small user to buy access to that equipment and programming personnel as needed, with a cost that is much lower than would be required if the organization were to install its own facility.

One change in the audit requirements introduced by the use of a service center is that the processing may be done at a site remote from that of the user. This introduces into the control process the necessity for procedures to prevent loss of information through the transmission to and from the service bureau. Where the customer transmits data to the service center for processing, the center maintains the intermediate data files, prepares summaries

[2] *Audits of Service-Center-Produced Records,* p. 10.

of the data, and sends the results of processing to the customer. The data may be processed with programs written specifically for the customer or with a standard set of programs maintained by the center for use in processing the records of several different customers.

Since the data in this environment is handled by two completely separate groups of personnel, steps must be taken to insure adequate communication between the staffs involved, so that there is a mutual understanding of the processing to be employed, of the type of data to be handled, and of the controls to be observed. The customer retains the responsibility for establishing the basic description of the processing to be performed, for defining clearly and completely the data to be collected and processed, and for defining the reports and other results to be produced.

In a time-sharing environment, the service facility does not directly handle or process either the user's programs or the user's data—it simply provides the processing facility. The customer installs some communication terminal on its premises with which to communicate with a centrally located computer facility. The service organization provides the central processing facility and central storage capacity to hold master files and user programs in an on-line library facility. From a time-sharing service organization's point of view, the system appears as a real-time on-line system. From the customer's point of view, the system appears as a processing system with an input/output device represented by the terminal at its location and a high-speed, sophisticated computer with relatively large amounts of on-line available memory and on-line program library facilities at the central location. The customer prepares and inputs the data, selects and controls the execution of programs, and determines the content and scope of the processing done both to provide operating reports and to perform maintenance and updating of the master files. Customers may write and store their own programs, or they may make use of one of the many standardized programs usually in the library of the time-sharing organization.

Time sharing service organizations lend themselves very well to the concept of third-party review (discussed later in this chapter), for under normal circumstances services provided for other users are quite standardized. The advantage to the small user or the large user with the specialized need is economic. The user gets access to a powerful, sophisticated computer for the relatively low cost of maintaining a terminal and communication facility and the cost of computer usage and file storage.

CONTROLS IN SERVICE CENTER ENVIRONMENTS

The typical controls discussed in Chapter 1 to insure the accuracy of data processing (such as verification, control totals, transaction counts, self-checking digits, consistency checks, limit checks) are relatively unchanged by the use of a service center. However, the introduction of an external service organization represents a division of processing responsibilities for the control procedures between the customer and the external service organization. Controls must be present to insure that the transfer of data from one party to the other does not result in any distortion or loss of data. Thus, additional checking is introduced for both the customer and the external supplier of data processing services to guarantee against that loss.

The customer must establish sufficient controls over the data before sending it to the service center to be able to reconcile the results returned from the service center to the data originally furnished. These transmission controls can take the form of control or batch totals, document counts, copies of the source data from which the transactions are recorded, or transaction logs. The exact form will depend upon the way in which the customer transmits the data to the service center. These controls may take the form of a manually calculated batch total submitted with the documents. In cases where the transaction data is transmitted to the service center electronically, control totals developed by the customer may be transmitted. In addition to the customer-generated controls that can check both the transcription and transmission process, the terminal equipment may generate control data to check the transmission further.

The division of responsibilities created by the contractual relationship suggests that periodic reports on the contents of master files should be made to the customer. Frequently, these master files are maintained by the service organization. The transactions submitted by the customer organization are employed to perform updating operations and to produce reports that are returned to it. Under these circumstances, service organizations should submit to the customer periodic reports showing the current contents of the master files and a summary of changes made to them. The traditional techniques for checking master files are periodic printout and review, periodic tests against physical counts, or other external evidence.

The customer and the service center should establish carefully defined procedures for recording errors and for controlling their correction and resubmission. These procedures represent a combination of activities for both parties. The techniques mentioned earlier can identify errors. Once the errors are identified, they must be corrected by the customer or with its approval. The erroneous data must often be returned to the customer. It is important for logs to be kept of the error items returned to the customer for correction and resubmitted by it for processing. The fact that two different parties are involved complicates the process of detecting and correcting errors and requires formalized procedures to prevent loss or duplication of the data items in error.

The customer's organization should maintain a proper separation of responsibilities. The individual who reconciles control totals and data received from the service center should not prepare the source documents or other data to be sent to the service center. The customer organization should assign definite responsibility for periodic review of the master files or the control information sent from the service organization. The individual assigned this responsibility should not be the person who generates the original source data. Although separation of responsibilities is desirable, it should also be recognized that the customer of a service organization may be a small firm without adequate staff to provide for optimum separation of duties.

The fact that the service organization is external to the customer's organization provides a degree of segregation between the record-keeping process and the custody of the assets. However, this protection is not complete without adequate control procedures instituted by both the customer organization and the service center. If the customer has inadequate control over the authorization of transactions or subsequent review of processing results, the access that service center programmers and operators have to critical files and programs may represent a potential area for manipulation of the customer's information and access to some of its assets.

AUDIT CONCERNS IN SERVICE CENTER ENVIRONMENTS

The auditor is directly concerned with external computer services only in those cases where the data being processed has audit significance. The extent of the auditor's concern with and review of the service organization is dependent upon the materiality of the application, the adequacy of the controls maintained by the customer organization, and the nature and adequacy of the controls at the service organization.

For an internal audit, external computer services will probably be judged to have audit significance if they include any processing and/or processing controls which have impact on the accuracy of the financial data, protection of the assets, or the efficiency of operations. In a financial audit, the definition of audit significance usually would only affect those external services which have an impact on the financial statements. *Audits of Service-Center Produced Records* defines the general criteria for external auditors conducting financial audits as follows:

> A review of controls at the service center should be considered when the financial data processed by the service center has a material effect on the client's financial statements, unless the user controls relied upon, which are external to the service center, are adequate to provide assurances that errors and irregularities may be discovered with reasonable promptness, thus assuring the reliability and integrity of the financial records.[3]

If a decision is made to rely on the system, the auditor must establish a thorough understanding of the controls and procedures in effect for the pre-

[3] *Audits of Service-Center-Produced Records*, p. 9.

liminary review of internal control; otherwise, only a general understanding is required. An excellent starting point for such a review is systems documentation. If that is adequate and up-to-date, it can provide an excellent insight into the system under examination. An important part of that documentation should be the formal agreement between the customer and the service center. To properly protect the interests of the customer, the agreement with the service organization should include the following provisions:

1. Description of the processing to be performed
2. Content and format of input, output, and management reports
3. Procedures for handling errors
4. Protection of customer's records
5. Right of the auditor to examine and test the system and records
6. Backup provisions by the service center
7. Customer's responsibilities for data preparation, input controls, and maintenance of master files
8. Designation of prime contact personnel with the center
9. Charges for services rendered
10. Procedures for conversion of customer's data to record formats required by the center
11. Liability of the center for errors and loss of data files
12. Ownership of programs and data files
13. Form and frequency of billing
14. Special provisions for payments to the center when special programs are being written

If after the preliminary review of internal control the auditor decides to depend upon that internal control, compliance tests must be performed. Among the common compliance tests recommended in the audit guide when a service center is involved are the observation of procedures and tracing of batch totals of data to reconciliations, control totals, and financial statements.[4]

Another common compliance test in the service center environment is the use of a test data procedure. After preparation and submission of test transactions, the auditor analyzes the output prepared by the program and determines whether the processing has been carried out correctly by the program. The use of test transactions in an environment with external data processing services has the same advantages and disadvantages as in those environments where the computer services are provided in-house. It can be time-consuming and difficult to prepare an adequate group of test transactions. The auditor must confirm that the program being tested is the actual program and system normally used for processing. Anonymity is the best technique for insuring that the normal processing program is the one used for the test data. This means that the test transactions must be introduced along with normal cus-

---

[4] *Audits of Service-Center-Produced Records,* p. 33.

tomer transactions and should not be separately identified. If this technique is used, however, the danger to customer files is increased; under these circumstances, the potential exists for distorting its master files. Thus, the use of test data requires a thorough knowledge of the system and a high level of technical proficiency by the auditor.

The auditor may also use computer audit programs to test customer files, to validate control records maintained by either the service organization or the customer, or to validate the contents of the files. Further, these programs may process client input and file data to validate the results of the center's processing. Procedures may be designed to serve the dual function of compliance and substantive testing.

When external data processing services are used, the auditor's attention must be divided between the records and documentation at the customer's site and those located at the service organization. Except for this division of responsibility and distribution of financial data, external computer services do not basically change the kinds of data processing or the audit concerns involved. The audit procedures involved can be performed by either manual or automated procedures and are similar to those followed with an in-house installation. The audit guide provides several examples of automated procedures which are quite similar to those already described in chapters 3 and 4. They are:

1. Examination of records for quality, completeness, consistency, and incorrect or unusual items
2. Selecting and printing samples
3. Testing calculations and making computations
4. Summarizing data and performing analyses of the totals
5. Comparing data maintained in separate files for correctness and consistency
6. Comparing audit data with company records

THIRD-PARTY REVIEWS OF EXTERNAL DATA PROCESSING SERVICES

The tests for compliance and the subsequent evaluation of the system of internal control require a careful review and test of the procedures in effect at the service organization. The procedures and controls in effect at the service organization can generally be divided into two groups—those procedures that are employed only for a particular customer and have no significance or application to the general operation of the service center or to the needs of other customers of that service center, and those procedures and controls that have general application or use for all the customers.

To avoid the duplication of effort and expenditure of time involved in the individual review of the service organization's general controls by the auditors of all individual customers, the service organization or a number of its customers may engage a third-party auditor to review the system at the service organization and to issue a report on it. The use of a third-party audit is equally appropriate for the external and the internal auditor. The report of the third-party auditor should describe in detail the system in effect at the service organization, the controls exerted by that organization, and the tests made by the third party of the system and controls in effect at the service organization. The report of the third-party auditor should provide a statement as to the scope of the examination and the time period covered. In addition, the report should include, where appropriate, an opinion as to the compliance of the system with its description and, where appropriate, comments regarding any material weaknesses in internal control.

A third-party auditor's report pertains only to the controls and procedures in effect in the service organization. It does not cover the procedures and controls peculiar to a particular customer's requirements. It does not eliminate the requirement for an individual review of a customer's controls and procedures by its independent and internal auditors. Although the auditor of a customer of a service organization may use the report of an independent third-party auditor in the evaluation of the customer's internal control, the auditor remains responsible for evaluating the internal control of the total system as it affects the customer's financial records.

To be useful to an auditor, the third party evaluating and describing the system of the service organization should be an independent auditor whose services are performed in accordance with the generally accepted auditing standards in effect in any professional audit engagement. The rationale for use of the report of a third-party auditor in formulating an opinion of internal control is expressed by the following statement in *Statement on Auditing Standards No. 1:*

> Independent auditors of one entity or organization unit may be concerned with internal accounting control of another because it is relevant to the scope of their examination. It may be presumed that these groups include persons whose training and experience or intimate knowledge of the organization should provide a reasonable basis for understanding the nature and effectiveness of internal accounting control and the auditor's evaluation of it. Consequently, it is evident that reports on internal accounting control can serve a useful purpose for management, regulatory agencies, and other independent auditors.[5]

Since the responsibility for evaluation of an organization's internal control rests with that organization's auditor, the auditor must determine the extent to which the third-party auditor's report on the service organization's system

---

[5] Committee on Auditing Procedure, *Statement of Auditing Standards No. 1: Codification of Auditing Standards and Procedures* (New York: American Institute of Certified Public Accountants, 1973), par. 640.04.

will be depended upon and the extent to which that system will be tested directly by the auditor. The report of the third-party auditor takes the form of an opinion about whether the system's operation and controls conform to the system description for the time period under review. This report would not include an evaluation of the adequacy of the controls for a specific user of the service center. The individual user's auditor is "responsible for evaluating the controls in his client's system, including the elements of control at the service center." [6]

If the third-party review is performed and the customer's auditor relies on it, the service center could avoid having the auditors of each of their customers visit the center to review and test the system and its controls. Third-party review, however, does not free the customer's auditor from the requirements that substantive tests on the accounting records maintained at the service center be performed. The customer's auditor may choose to rely upon third-party auditor's reports in the review and evaluation of internal controls, but the auditor may also visit the service center for the substantive testing of accounting records. Particularly in those instances where the service organization performs an extensive number of procedures and control techniques that are especially designed for an individual customer, the latter's auditor may find it necessary to perform additional tests of compliance and additional review procedures at the service organization to complement those reviews and tests conducted on its procedures.

WERNER MANUFACTURING, INC.—CASE STUDY

The next portion of the case study shows how a wholly owned subsidiary of Werner, Starr Products, processes its data at a service bureau and what internal control and auditing considerations such a system involves. It also illustrates the third-party review letter and how it is used by the auditor.

CONTROLS AND AUDITING IN A SERVICE CENTER ENVIRONMENT

On February 21, 1978, Werner Manufacturing purchased all the outstanding capital stock of Starr Products Corporation, a manufacturer of oil and air filtering devices for aircraft engines. Werner purchases almost all of its oil and air filtration needs from Starr, about forty percent of whose net sales are to Werner.

Werner is accounting for Starr as a wholly owned subsidiary and, for the present, Starr is continuing to maintain its own general ledger. Starr sends regular reports to Werner.

---

[6] *Audits of Service-Center-Produced Records*, p. 39.

Although Starr is material to Werner's consolidated financial statements, its use of computers is not as extensive as Werner's. The systems it has computerized are:

- Sales, accounts receivable and cash receipts
- Manufacturing and perpetual inventory of raw materials and finished goods
- Factory and administrative hourly payroll

Starr does all its own systems development and computer programming, but does not have a data center. Instead, processing is done at a service center, Consolidated Data Services, Inc. by service center personnel.

In this portion of the case study, we are going to look at how Starr's sales, accounts receivable and cash receipts system works. You will note that Starr sends, as part of its reporting package, daily sales registers, cash receipts books and aged accounts receivable trial balances to Werner.

To enable Werner to reflect Starr's sales and cash receipts in its daily (computer-generated) reports to management (on a memo basis), Starr also sends daily transaction tapes to Werner for processing at Werner's data center. To do this, Starr and Werner systems analysts and operations personnel worked together to make changes in Starr's record layouts. This was helped by the fact that Consolidated also uses an IBM S/370–145 to process Starr's data.

Note that we are following the same general format used in Chapters 1 and 3 for Werner Manufacturing's system:

- System flowchart to explain the processing sequence and identify application control strengths and weaknesses (Figure 5–1, pp. 216–229)
- Narrative, in tabular form, to describe the application control strengths and weaknesses identified on the flowchart and to explain their audit significance (Table 5–1, pp. 230–233. Read Figure 5–1 and Table 5–1 now.)
- Narrative to explain the general controls
- General narrative to explain auditing in a service bureau environment by relating the application and general control strengths and weaknesses to substantive and compliance auditing procedures

The audit guide *Auditing Service-Center-Produced Records* and the procedures of independent and internal auditors will be discussed.

We saw in the previous chapters that general controls affect the evaluation of application controls. This principle holds for service center situations as well. In the next few pages we are going to describe Consolidated's general controls. Then we will see how they impact the application controls just covered and the auditing procedures performed by Werner's independent and internal auditors.

Look at Consolidated's data center layout and organization chart (Figures 5–2 and 5–3, pp. 234–236).

Our vehicle for covering Consolidated's general controls will be a third-party review letter issued by a CPA firm: Bellows, Ronan & Co. Since third-party review letters can be long, we will reproduce only those parts of Consolidated's that apply to this case study. To highlight strengths and weaknesses, supplementary comments are provided in brackets. These would normally not be found in an actual third-party review letter. The third-party review letter follows:

Third-Party Review Letter.

BELLOWS, RONAN & CO.
Certified Public Accountants
431 Jackson Street, S. E.
Cleveland, Ohio 44115

Consolidated Data Services, Inc.
27–19 Fortieth Street
Cleveland, Ohio 44115

Gentlemen:

We have reviewed and tested to the extent we considered necessary the accompanying description of the system, procedures and controls of Consolidated Data Services, Inc. during the period from January 9, 1978 through January 27, 1978.

Our review and tests were limited to the activities of Consolidated Data Services, Inc. and did not include review or consideration of procedures preformed by customers of the service center.

In connection with our review and tests, as discussed further in our attached supplemental report, we performed the following procedures:

1. Reviewed the overall organization and the procedures for documenting program changes, file protection and security of user records

2. Reviewed program documentation

3. Reviewed controls related to the input, processing and output phases of the applications

4. Observed, on a test basis, operations on each shift

5. Tested processing under normal operating conditions

Our attached supplemental report includes a description of the controls, a description of the scope of our review and a description of the tests performed and the results of those tests.

In our opinion, the controls of Consolidated Data Services, Inc. during the period January 9, 1978 through January 27, 1978 conformed with the accompanying descriptions.

Since our review and tests were limited to the attached system description and related procedures performed by Consolidated Data Services, Inc. and did not extend to procedures performed by customers or to other procedures performed by Consolidated, we express no opinion on the adequacy of internal accounting controls as they apply to either a specific customer of Consolidated Data Services, Inc. or Consolidated itself.

This report is intended solely for distribution to auditors of customers served by Consolidated Data Services, Inc. Distribution to other parties is not authorized.

Very truly yours,

BELLOWS, RONAN & CO.

Description of the System, Procedures and
Controls

January 27, 1978

Index

Note: The index shows the page numbers used in this book.

Description of the System, Procedures and Controls

January 27, 1978

General Operations

Consolidated Data Services, Inc. (Consolidated), located in Cleveland, Ohio, provides the following data processing services to its customers:

- Programming, where Consolidated, working with the customer's personnel, writes programs to their specifications. Consolidated prepares complete documentation (system and program flowcharts, record layouts, report layouts, run manuals, source code), programs and testing of completed programs to insure they process properly. Testing is done jointly with the customer. Frequently, the programs are modifications of existing program packages (payroll, order entry, inventory, accounts receivable, sales, accounts payable, purchases) that Consolidated has developed. All programs and documentation become the customer's property when accepted.
- Processing, where Consolidated processes customers' data using programs it developed (see above) or those supplied by the customer. In addition to the programs themselves, Consolidated maintains a complete copy of the system documentation and appropriate master file generations. Processing is performed and output is delivered to the customer on an agreed-upon schedule.
- Renting of computer time, where Consolidated permits customer personnel to process their programs and data on its computers. This is done on an "as machine time is available" basis and usually takes place during the evening or on weekends. Each customer removes its programs, files and output from Consolidated's premises after its processing is completed. This service is generally used by customers when their own computer installations are overloaded.

Consolidated provides up to $100,000 fidelity bond coverage on its employees.

Consolidated does not employ an internal auditor, but the president and majority stockholder monitors compliance with established control policies. [This is a strength. General controls do not require an internal auditor, but someone in authority to regularly review compliance with controls.]

Organization and Physical Security

Consolidated employs a president (majority stockholder), data center manager (in charge of day-to-day operations), a keypunch and operations supervisor, nine keypunch operators, four computer operators, three programmer-analysts, a unit record equipment operator, and a control clerk.

There is no file librarian; the computer operators control the file library. We noted that the file library, which opens directly onto the computer room, is open when customers are renting computer time. Consolidated's computer operators sometimes leave the computer room when customers are processing. In addition, programmer-analysts have full access to the file library when they operate the computer to test the programs they are developing. [This is a serious weakness. Look at the organization chart. Organizational separation of the operations and programming functions is weak, as both report to the operations supervisor and the programmers have ready access to the equipment. Further, as the data center layout and the foregoing show, access to the equipment and the file library is not well controlled. Finally, there are no effective safeguards to prevent customers who are renting machine time, and who are therefore in the computer room, from entering the file library. Security in this area is lax. See also the description of Consolidated's file protection and security procedures.]

Access to Consolidated's facilities is limited. During normal business hours, visitors must register at the building's single entrance. Access to the building after normal business hours requires passage through a locked gate and a door which must be opened by the security guard. Access to the computer room is also limited. The doors to the computer room are locked and only Consolidated employees have combinations in the form of coded plastic cards. There is also an elevator entrance to the computer room. An alarm will automatically sound if this elevator is used after normal hours. During normal hours, the door from the elevator entrance to the computer room is locked. The computer room has temperature and humidity monitoring devices in continual operation. [These are sound access control procedures. See, however, the description of the weak file library control procedures.]

Documentation Procedures

Documentation standards and procedures have been established for applications developed by Consolidated and for which they do the processing. These include: problem statements, system flowcharts, record layouts, program source listings, operator instructions, approval and change forms, and descriptions of input and output requirements. As program changes are made, the above applicable documents are prepared for the change. Operator instructions are incorporated into run manuals as changes are implemented. Run manuals include: operator instructions, special switch settings, console messages and responses, input and output files, and printing requirements.

New programs or changes to existing programs require testing, the extent of which is determined by the nature of the change and the programmer-analyst. Test data is processed against a designated test environment in which programs other than the test program are processing. Data is entered and the affected daily reports are produced. Test data and results are then submitted to a programmer-analyst for review and approval. After a program change has been approved, test data is retained for a week and then is discarded.

Consolidated has offsite storage of object programs which are updated daily. There is no offsite storage of documentation. However, Consolidated plans to periodically microfilm all documentation for offsite storage.

Program Change Procedures

Program changes or additions must be submitted on Consolidated's data processing service request form, which may be initiated by a customer or by a programmer–analyst. Program requests are reviewed at a weekly staff meeting. Those requests determined feasible and appropriate are approved. The form is then given a number, entered into a log and the change is assigned to a programmer-analyst. A copy of the approved form is also sent to the person making the request.

When the programmer-analyst has completed the required documentation and testing, he submits the work to another programmer-analyst for review and approval. Upon approval, the work is submitted to the data center manager for review and approval. After approval, the new program is cataloged to the resident library. After the new program is cataloged, the program request form is completed, entered into the log and filed numerically. A copy of the completed form is also sent to the person initiating the request.

Actual cataloging of the new program is performed by operations personnel. The completed and approved program request form serves as the operator's authority to implement the program.

Control over superseded programs is provided using the program name. Changes to existing programs are cataloged under the old program name, thus removing the old program. [Documentation and program change procedures are effective for good control, *except* for the fact that program changes may be initiated by a programmer-analyst without the user's knowledge or approval.]

File Protection and Security

Consolidated's policy provides file reconstruction in the following manner:

- Daily transactions are copied to tape and retained 35 days.
- Daily transactions are copied daily to a quarter-to-date tape with 380 days of transactions being retained.
- Other transactions are saved for 14 days and are merged weekly to a quarter-to date tape with 380 days of transactions being retained.
- End-of-month balance tapes are retained for 12 months.

Through this series of backup files, Consolidated can reconstruct 35 days of transactions, balances and reports and one year of application transactions and balances.

Backup files necessary to restore a system (including customers' data) are stored in an offsite storage vault. Historical information could be generated from users' hard-copy reports in the event of destruction of the history files.

Tape files are externally numbered and internally labeled. A daily listing of tape numbers and contents is printed and is controlled by the control clerk. Tapes are stored in a fireproof vault which serves as Consolidated's library. Tape movements in and out of the library are controlled and recorded by the computer operators. Internal labels and retention dates are processed automatically by the operating system.

Access to tape files is limited by the absence of external tape labels. Access to disk files or current work files is limited because the location of data on the files is controlled by the operating system and would require extensive manual decoding to locate desired data.

Backup is provided by the existence of a second computer at another service center in Cleveland. In the event of the destruction of the existing physical facilities, access to these facilities and relocation of the data would be required to provide uninterrupted service. [File protection and security procedures are effective for good control. See, however, the description of the file library access control procedures.]

Input Procedures

[Our primary purpose in presenting this third-party review letter is to describe and evaluate Consolidated's general controls. We have already looked at the application controls as they affect Starr's sales, accounts receivable and cash receipts system. We are going to describe the input, processing and output controls for a secondary purpose: to illustrate a third-party review letter.]

The following input procedures relate to the applications Consolidated processes for its customers.

All input is delivered to the control clerk, who either prepares batch control totals or checks those prepared by customers. After establishing batch control, the input is sent to keypunching. All keypunching is keyverified by a different operator.

When processing is complete, output is sent to the control clerk for comparison with the batch control totals. Input control totals can be established by the customer at the input source and subsequent reports produced by Consolidated enable the customer to balance such totals.

Input transactions are copied to tape files, with the tape file being subsequently used for backup.

Processing Procedures

- General:
  In addition to requiring that programs generate batch control reports, Consolidated strongly encourages its customers to agree to including edit and reasonableness tests. Thirty-five of the forty-one applications that Consolidated processes have edit and reasonableness tests; all generate batch control total reports.

We utilized limited test data (see appendix) for testing each application that Consolidated processes. The test data included valid and invalid transactions and was processed on Consolidated's equipment during normal business hours, under the appropriate operating system. The invalid transactions were rejected by the system, while the valid transactions were properly reported.

Internal header and trailer labels (including expiration dates) are created for files and are automatically processed by the operating system for applications. This helps prevent accidental destruction of the files. Customer master files are accessible at designated times during normal business hours, and, at other than normal business hours, on special request.

- Master file changes:
  Changes to customer's master files other than through regular dollar transactions (e.g., adding customers to or deleting them from an accounts receivable master file) are subject to the same controls as dollar transactions. Master file changes are authorized by customers through specially coded forms. Consolidated provides the customer with a daily list (depicting both old and new data) of master file changes as recorded by the system. In addition, customers are provided with a monthly listing of their master files.

- Error correction:
  Error detection is performed by the control clerk (control total differences) and by the edit and reasonableness tests in the programs. If a transaction fails the edit and reasonableness tests, it is rejected and appears on an error report. Errors are corrected by the customer and resubmitted as part of a subsequent batch of input. [This is an important control strength, as data center personnel are not permitted to either initiate transactions or correct errors without the customer's involvement.]

Output Procedures

All customer output, including regular and special reports, is controlled by the control clerk as to validity (see Input Procedures) and number and distribution of copies.

A daily schedule of output reports by customer is prepared by the operations supervisor and approved by the data center manager. It is then given to the operator and control clerk. The control clerk obtains the reports and acknowledges receipts on his daily schedule. The clerk scans the output for propriety and compares the control totals with the batch controls and account balances supplied by the customer.

Imbalances are not corrected by the operator or control clerk. The control clerk informs the operations supervisor of the error and they locate its source. The affected customer is also informed of the error at this time. When the appropriate corrective action has been determined, the customer is again notified of the source of the problem and what corrective action is needed.

At the end of a processing run, the control prepares output for distribution. Reports are separated by customer and compared with the schedule of output reports to insure that all output has been received. The control clerk then packages the reports by customer and distributes the packages through normal delivery channels.

Recommendations

Access to the file library is not properly controlled (see Organization and Physical Security). We recommend that someone who does not report to the operations manager be designated file librarian and that only he and the data center manager have access to the library.

Blank presigned dividend checks for several customers are stored in a secured room. The control clerk maintains a log of checks used and in inventory. We suggest the control numbers in the log be periodically checked to the inventory of checks on hand by the president of Consolidated.

During our visit we noticed an incomplete box of blank disbursement checks for one customer in the computer room. There was no log control of these checks. All checks should be controlled and accounted for through the log.

Appendix

In the section titled Processing Procedures—General, we referred to testing using limited test data. We created two hundred test items to simulate regular daily transactions and thirty to simulate master file changes [Since this portion of the third party review letter is for illustrative purposes, it will be somewhat shorter than what we would normally expect.]

Batch Totals

Inserted transactions with batches before they were delivered to the control clerk to intentionally cause the batched transactions not to agree with the batch control totals.

Master File Changes

Added and deleted master file records with forms not properly approved; changed master file balances to reflect unauthorized credits and other adjustments.

Input Format Edit Functions

Entered a transaction using incorrect field entries.

Input Validation Functions

Entered transactions against nonexistent master file records.

Computation Functions

Entered transactions which produce incorrect results to test edit and reasonableness routines.

At this point, let's review what we've covered:

- We reviewed Starr Products Corporation's sales, accounts receivable and cash receipts system—the entire system, including the processing at Starr and at the service center. In connection with this review, we also evaluated the application controls.
- As we learned in earlier chapters, general controls are extremely important. If they are weak, they may partially or completely offset strong application controls. We have just reviewed the general controls in the service center. To complete the general controls picture, we must now review the general controls in Starr itself.

As we have seen, all transactions are initiated by Starr. Further, any errors detected at the service center are referred to Starr for correction. An exception would be errors which are attributable to keypunching.

Starr's systems development group has been given responsibility for searching out opportunities for computerizing accounting applications. When they find areas they feel should be computerized, they report them to the Data Processing Committee for consideration.

If the Data Processing Committee feels the idea has merit, a project development team is formed to conduct a feasibility study. The team consists of a systems analyst, a representative of the prospective user department, and a member of the controller's department. Since its acquisition by Werner Manufacturing, the team also includes one of the latter's EDP internal auditors and systems analysts.

As the project develops, the new system is well documented and controlled at each stage. Werner's internal auditors have concluded that Starr's systems development controls are generally strong and that its written specifications for computerized systems are adequate. Further, all new systems and systems changes (including program revisions) are reviewed by user departments, which must approve them in writing *before* implementation. Systems testing is a joint effort of the user department, EDP systems personnel, Consolidated's personnel, and Werner's EDP internal auditors (see Documentation Procedures in the third-party review letter).

For purposes of this case study, therefore, the reader may assume that Werner's independent and internal auditors have concluded that EDP general controls at Starr are strong.

We are now ready to cover the substantive and compliance auditing procedures that Werner's independent and internal auditors use on Starr's sales, accounts receivable and cash receipts system.

Werner's independent and internal auditors met to plan the annual audit of Starr, just as they did for the annual audit of Werner itself. Several points were discussed and they decided on and carried out the following plan:

- The third-party review letter shows a major area of weakness in file security, although other controls appear to be strong. The letter was studied by the independent auditors, who decided to contact Bellows, Ronan & Co. to discuss their review of Consolidated's controls before relying on the descriptions.
- The independent auditors interviewed the engagement partner at Bellows, Ronan, Carl M. Bellows, and the staff auditor who performed the review of Consolidated's controls. Then, with Bellows and his staff auditor present, they reviewed the working papers and the auditing procedures performed. Bellows, Ronan cooperated fully.
- Based on this visit, they concluded that Bellows, Ronan is independent of Starr, their audit was completely performed by qualified personnel, and their descriptions could be relied upon.
- With this point determined, the independent auditors decided to audit Starr's sales, accounts receivable and cash receipts system using the same general methods they had used for Werner's:

  - The internal auditors reviewed and compliance-tested the general controls; then the independent auditors reviewed and tested the internal auditors' procedures.
  - The independent auditors performed compliance tests on the application controls and substantive tests on balances and amounts.

- In performing their compliance tests of the general controls, the internal auditors did not rely entirely on the third-party letter. They visited Consolidated to perform auditing procedures designed to satisfy themselves that the controls did not change between the period covered by the review (January 9–27, 1978) and their audit. There were some minor changes, but the controls were essentially the same.

  The auditing procedures performed by the internal auditors were similar to those performed on Werner's general control strengths (described in Chapter 3).

- The independent auditors, in view of the weakness in file security, decided to expand the scope of their substantive auditing procedures further than they would have if these controls had been strong.

  In carrying out their procedures, they acted just as they did in auditing Werner. For example, they used the computer to perform some auditing procedures on computerized files. Since those files are at Consolidated, that is where they performed their procedures.

  As with the auditing procedures performed by the internal auditors, these were similar to those performed on Werner itself (see chapter 3).

The "authoritative basis" for the use Werner's auditors made of the third-party letter is contained in Chapter 4 of *Audits of Service-Center-Produced Records*. Exhibit A of that chapter contains an example of a third-party letter for an on-line savings and mortgage loan system processed by a service center. Since it refers to a system which is applicable to banks and savings and loan associations, it differs materially from the one we used in this case study.

The next and final chapter deals with minicomputers and distributed processing systems.

Operation	Personnel	Sales Department

1. Sales orders come in by mail or telephone. Sales clerk prepares a six-part prenumbered sales order form. Copies 1–5 are sent to the credit department; copy 6 is retained at the sales order log—kept in numerical sequence. Sales orders are prepared with unit prices as well as quantities. Orders subsequently rejected are so noted on copy 6; the log thereby accounts for all sales order numbers.

Personnel: SALES CLERK

2. Each sales order is reviewed for credit clearance by the credit clerk by tracing the total of the order to the daily accounts receivable trial balance. If there is a question, the order goes to the credit manager for clearance.

Copy no. 5 of the sales order is marked with the credit decision and signed. Copy 1 is filed in the credit department.

Personnel: CREDIT CLERK/ CREDIT MANAGER

3. If the order is refused, the customer is advised by the credit manager that it is being backordered until the unpaid balance is brought down sufficiently to permit the sale not to exceed the credit limit.

Personnel: CREDIT MANAGER

4. If the order is accepted, copy 1 is sent to the customer as acknowledgement. Copies 2 and 3 are sent to the warehouse, while copy 4 is placed in the open order file.

Personnel: SALES CLERK

Note: File Symbols:
D = Date
N = Numerical

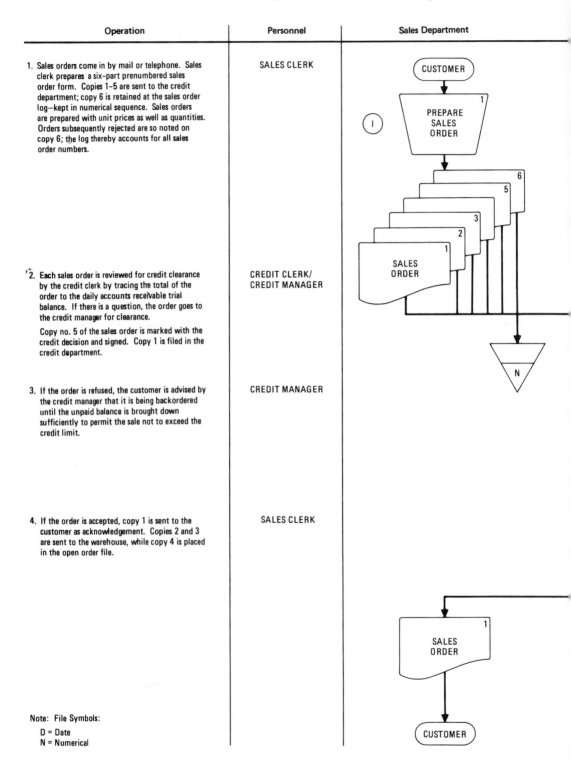

Figure 5–1. Sales, Accounts Receivable, Cash Receipts—Starr Products Corporation.

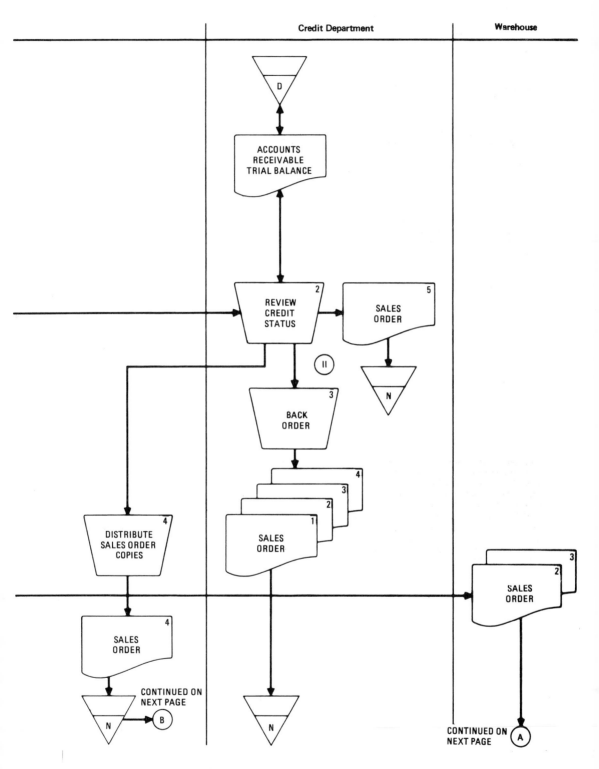

Operation	Personnel	Sales Department	

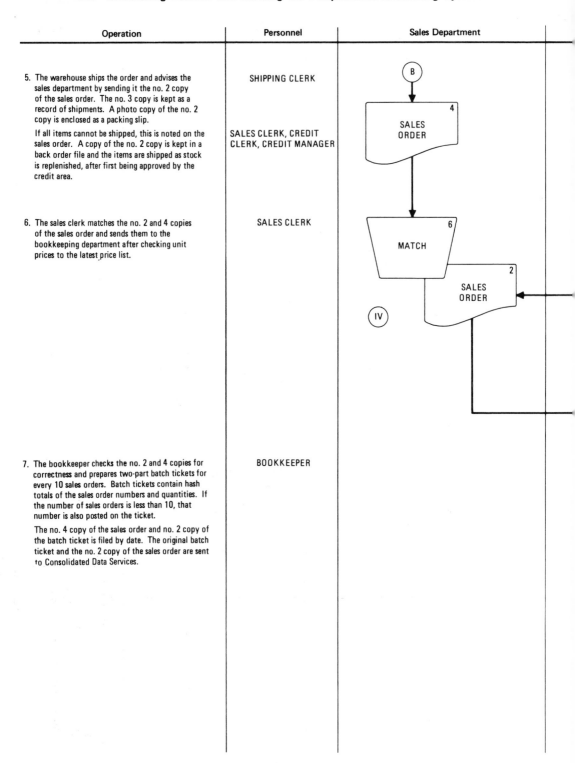

5. The warehouse ships the order and advises the sales department by sending it the no. 2 copy of the sales order. The no. 3 copy is kept as a record of shipments. A photo copy of the no. 2 copy is enclosed as a packing slip.

   SHIPPING CLERK

   If all items cannot be shipped, this is noted on the sales order. A copy of the no. 2 copy is kept in a back order file and the items are shipped as stock is replenished, after first being approved by the credit area.

   SALES CLERK, CREDIT CLERK, CREDIT MANAGER

6. The sales clerk matches the no. 2 and 4 copies of the sales order and sends them to the bookkeeping department after checking unit prices to the latest price list.

   SALES CLERK

7. The bookkeeper checks the no. 2 and 4 copies for correctness and prepares two-part batch tickets for every 10 sales orders. Batch tickets contain hash totals of the sales order numbers and quantities. If the number of sales orders is less than 10, that number is also posted on the ticket.

   BOOKKEEPER

   The no. 4 copy of the sales order and no. 2 copy of the batch ticket is filed by date. The original batch ticket and the no. 2 copy of the sales order are sent to Consolidated Data Services.

Figure 5–1 (*continued*)

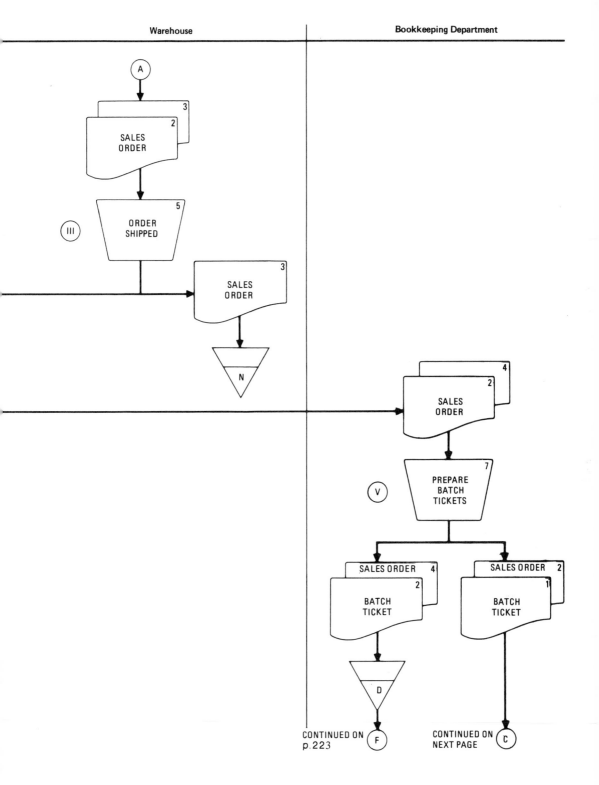

Warehouse

Bookkeeping Department

CONTINUED ON p.223

CONTINUED ON NEXT PAGE

Operation	Personnel	
		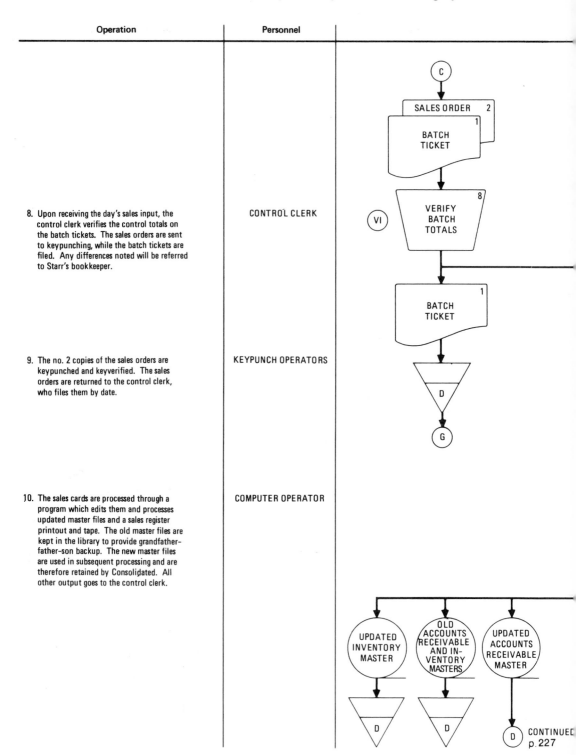
8. Upon receiving the day's sales input, the control clerk verifies the control totals on the batch tickets. The sales orders are sent to keypunching, while the batch tickets are filed. Any differences noted will be referred to Starr's bookkeeper.	CONTROL CLERK	
9. The no. 2 copies of the sales orders are keypunched and keyverified. The sales orders are returned to the control clerk, who files them by date.	KEYPUNCH OPERATORS	
10. The sales cards are processed through a program which edits them and processes updated master files and a sales register printout and tape. The old master files are kept in the library to provide grandfather-father-son backup. The new master files are used in subsequent processing and are therefore retained by Consolidated. All other output goes to the control clerk.	COMPUTER OPERATOR	

Figure 5–1 (*continued*)

Consolidated Data Services

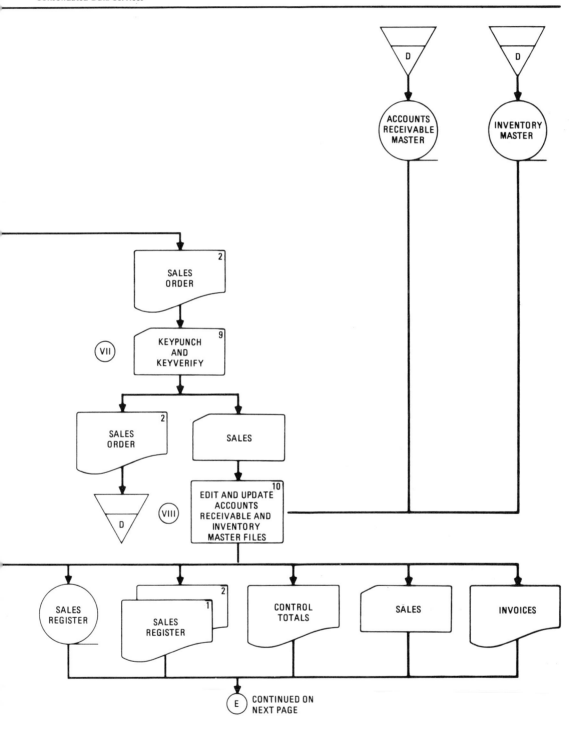

CONTINUED ON
NEXT PAGE

Operation	Personnel	

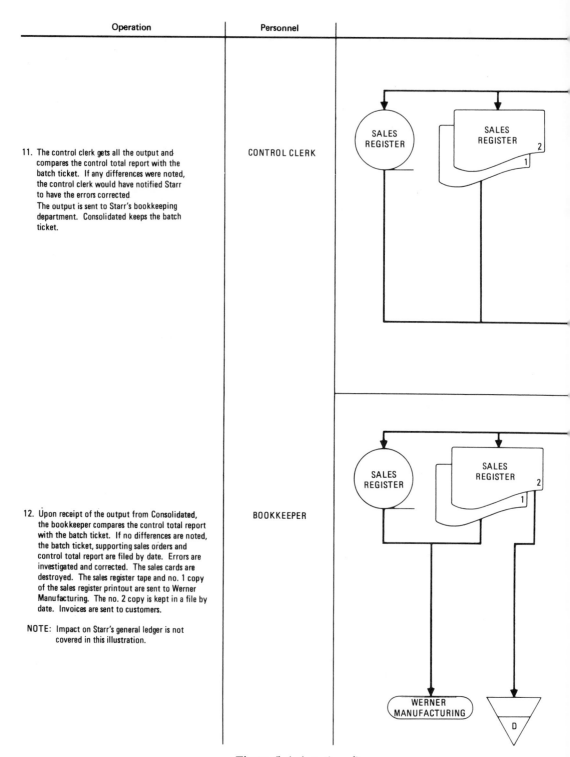

11. The control clerk gets all the output and compares the control total report with the batch ticket. If any differences were noted, the control clerk would have notified Starr to have the errors corrected
   The output is sent to Starr's bookkeeping department. Consolidated keeps the batch ticket.

CONTROL CLERK

12. Upon receipt of the output from Consolidated, the bookkeeper compares the control total report with the batch ticket. If no differences are noted, the batch ticket, supporting sales orders and control total report are filed by date. Errors are investigated and corrected. The sales cards are destroyed. The sales register tape and no. 1 copy of the sales register printout are sent to Werner Manufacturing. The no. 2 copy is kept in a file by date. Invoices are sent to customers.

NOTE: Impact on Starr's general ledger is not covered in this illustration.

BOOKKEEPER

Figure 5–1 (*continued*)

Consolidated Data Services

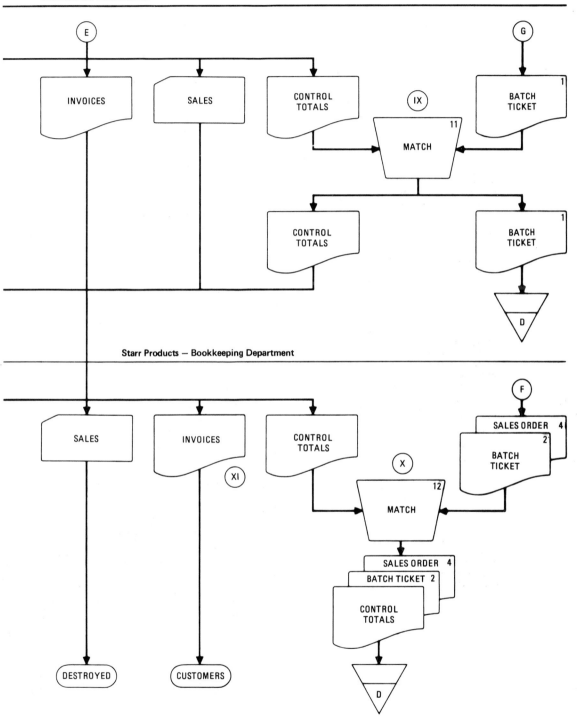

Starr Products — Bookkeeping Department

Operation	Personnel	Bookkeeping Department	Consolidated Data Services

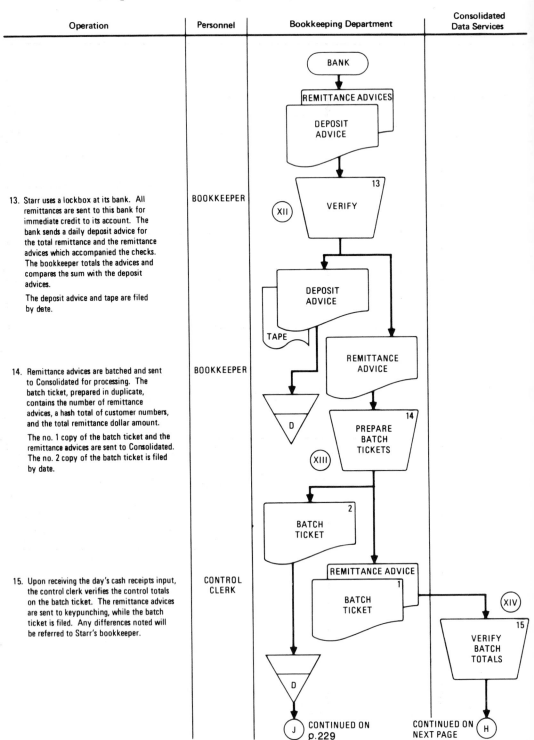

13. Starr uses a lockbox at its bank. All remittances are sent to this bank for immediate credit to its account. The bank sends a daily deposit advice for the total remittance and the remittance advices which accompanied the checks. The bookkeeper totals the advices and compares the sum with the deposit advices.

The deposit advice and tape are filed by date.

14. Remittance advices are batched and sent to Consolidated for processing. The batch ticket, prepared in duplicate, contains the number of remittance advices, a hash total of customer numbers, and the total remittance dollar amount.

The no. 1 copy of the batch ticket and the remittance advices are sent to Consolidated. The no. 2 copy of the batch ticket is filed by date.

15. Upon receiving the day's cash receipts input, the control clerk verifies the control totals on the batch ticket. The remittance advices are sent to keypunching, while the batch ticket is filed. Any differences noted will be referred to Starr's bookkeeper.

CONTINUED ON p.229

CONTINUED ON NEXT PAGE

Figure 5–1 (*continued*)

Chart continued
on pages 226–229

Operation	Personnel	

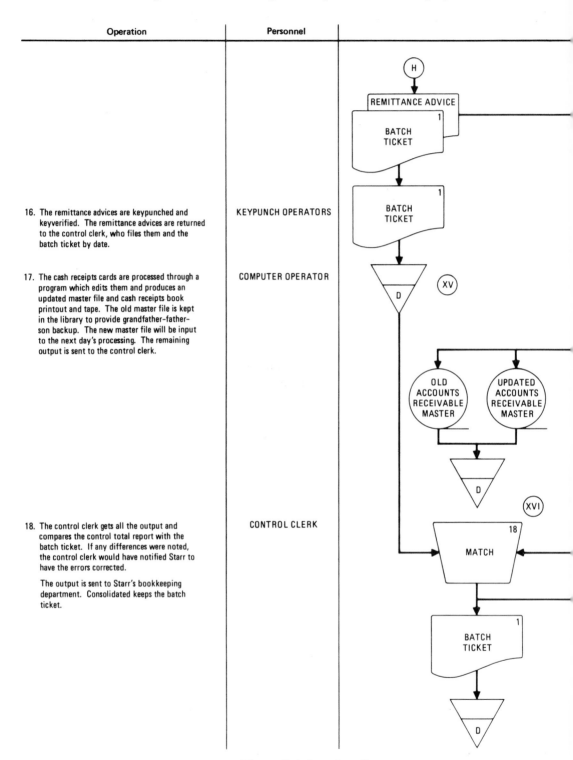

16. The remittance advices are keypunched and keyverified. The remittance advices are returned to the control clerk, who files them and the batch ticket by date.

(Personnel: KEYPUNCH OPERATORS)

17. The cash receipts cards are processed through a program which edits them and produces an updated master file and cash receipts book printout and tape. The old master file is kept in the library to provide grandfather-father-son backup. The new master file will be input to the next day's processing. The remaining output is sent to the control clerk.

(Personnel: COMPUTER OPERATOR)

18. The control clerk gets all the output and compares the control total report with the batch ticket. If any differences were noted, the control clerk would have notified Starr to have the errors corrected.

The output is sent to Starr's bookkeeping department. Consolidated keeps the batch ticket.

(Personnel: CONTROL CLERK)

Figure 5–1 (*continued*)

Consolidated Data Services

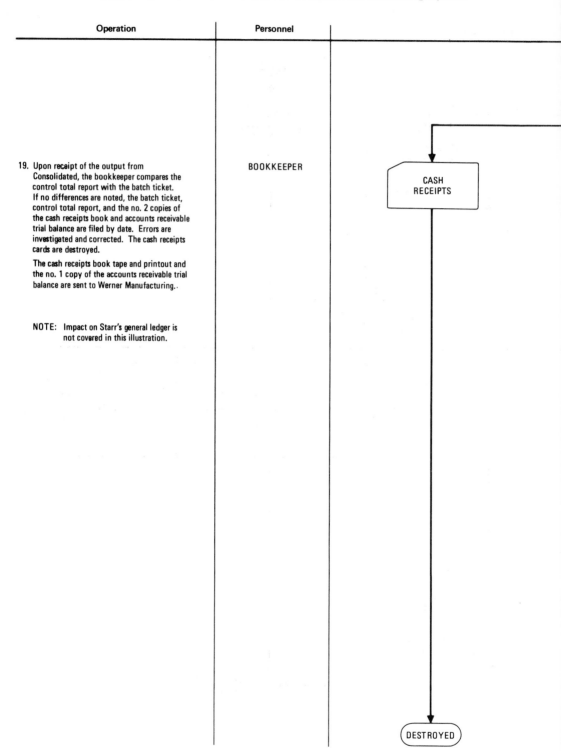

Operation	Personnel	

19. Upon receipt of the output from Consolidated, the bookkeeper compares the control total report with the batch ticket. If no differences are noted, the batch ticket, control total report, and the no. 2 copies of the cash receipts book and accounts receivable trial balance are filed by date. Errors are investigated and corrected. The cash receipts cards are destroyed.

The cash receipts book tape and printout and the no. 1 copy of the accounts receivable trial balance are sent to Werner Manufacturing..

NOTE: Impact on Starr's general ledger is not covered in this illustration.

BOOKKEEPER

CASH RECEIPTS

DESTROYED

Figure 5–1 (*continued*)

Bookkeeping Department

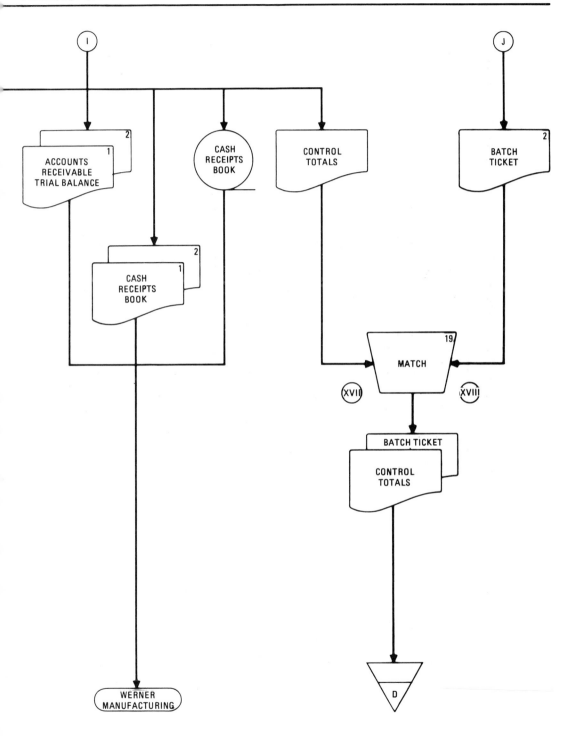

Table 5–1. Sales, Accounts Receivable, Cash Receipts System—Starr Products Corporation.

OPERATION	S	W	INTERNAL CONTROL PROCEDURES/IMPLICATIONS	AUDIT IMPLICATIONS
I. All sales orders are prenumbered and one copy kept in a numerical sequence file as a log.	X		A sales order, once it is written on a sales order form, stands a good chance of not being lost or misplaced. In addition, the disposition of every sales order can be readily checked and any break in numerical sequence investigated.	Sales orders are properly recorded and each is carried through to an actual sale or is rejected.
II. Each sales order is subjected to a credit check by the credit clerk and if there is a question, by the credit manager. Each signs a copy of the sales order as evidence of review.	X		Sales are not accepted until the prospective customer's credit status has been checked and found satisfactory. Even if a customer is technically unacceptable (for example, because the current order would cause his balance to exceed the credit limit), the order is not automatically rejected. It goes to the credit manager for review. Thus, the system provides for final review by a responsible official with both knowledge and authority to waive discretionary limitations.	Accounts receivable are collectible when recorded.
III. Sales orders are not processed until the goods are actually shipped.	X		Transactions are not sent to Consolidated Data Services for processing until the warehouse generates a shipping advice (no. 2 copy of sales order). This insures that sales, accounts receivable and inventory files will not be updated until the sale transaction is completed.	Accounts receivable and sales are properly stated and are collectible when recorded.
	X		If portions of an order cannot be filled, the out-of-stock items are backordered. They are shipped when the inventory is replenished and the credit area has given its approval. This insures that backordered items will not be shipped to a customer whose credit position has deteriorated since the order was originally received.	Accounts receivable and sales are properly stated and are collectible when recorded.

IV.	Before completed sales documents are sent to Consolidated Data Services for processing, the shipping advice is compared with the sales order and prices are checked.	X	Since the sales clerk prepared the sales order, including the pricing, someone else should check the prices for accuracy.	Accounts receivable and sales may not be properly stated.
V.	Sales orders are batched and control totals accumulated before the input is sent to Consolidated Data Services.	X	The user (Starr) establishes the means by which computer-generated output can be checked for accuracy and completeness. (See X below.)	Accounts receivable and sales are properly stated when recorded.
VI.	Consolidated Data Services has its own control group, which checks the accuracy of the user's batch totals before passing on the input for computer processing.	X	A group organizationally separate from operations establishes the means to control the accuracy and completeness of computer-generated output. (See IX below.)	Accounts receivable and sales are properly stated when recorded.
VII.	All kepunching is 100% verified by a second person.	X	Minimizes the chance of keypunch errors and resulting erroneous accounting information.	Recording of sales results in proper recording of sales and cash receipts.
VIII.	Input is edited for reasonableness (correct customer numbers, inventory items, and so on) before it is permitted to update the accounts receivable and inventory master files.	X	Checks the input for reasonableness to insure that data with errors is not permitted to affect the master files. Any errors will be corrected by the user before the affected transactions are processed again.	Accounts receivable and sales are properly stated when recorded.

Table 5–1 (continued)

OPERATION	S	W	INTERNAL CONTROL PROCEDURES/IMPLICATIONS	AUDIT IMPLICATIONS
IX. Output goes to the control clerk, who compares the control total report with the batch totals.	X		Output is checked for accuracy and completeness before it is sent to the user. Any differences are resolved with the user before the affected transactions are processed again. (See VI above.)	Accounts receivable and sales are properly stated when recorded.
X. Starr checks the output received from Consolidated Data Services to its batch totals.	X		The user employs its control totals to insure that the output received from Consolidated Data Services is accurate and complete. (See, however, XI below.)	Accounts receivable and sales are properly stated when recorded.
XI. Neither the control clerk at Consolidated Data Services nor the bookkeeper at Starr checks the invoices or the sales register to the no. 4 copies of the sales orders.		X	Even though the control totals agree with the batch totals, it is possible for the individual customer data to be incorrect. For example, a sale of a certain item to one customer may have been erroneously (perhaps due to a computer program error) posted to another's account. In such case, the totals would be correct. Some comparison of invoices and entries in the sales register with underlying sales orders (no. 4 copy) is needed.	Accounts receivable master file data may be incorrect.
XII. Remittance reports from the bank lockbox are checked for clerical accuracy.	X		Since the remittances are sent directly to the bank, there is less danger of cash receipts being misappropriated by Starr's employees. To reduce the danger of clerical error, the bookkeeper totals the remittance advices to be certain they equal the deposit.	Cash receipts are deposited to company accounts.
XIII. Remittance advices are batched and control totals accumulated before the input is sent to Consolidated Data Services.	X		The user establishes the means by which computer-generated output can be checked for accuracy and completeness. (See XVII below.)	Recording of sales results in proper recording of receivables and cash receipts.

	S/W		
XIV. Consolidated Data Service's control group checks the accuracy of the user's batch totals before passing on the input for computer processing.	X	A group organizationally separate from operations establishes the means to control the accuracy and completeness of computer-generated output. (See XVI below.)	Recording of sales results in proper recording of receivables and cash receipts.
XV. Input is edited for reasonableness (correct customer and invoice number, etc.) before it is permitted to update the accounts receivable file.	X	Checks the input for reasonableness, to insure that data with errors in it does not affect the master files. Any errors will be corrected by the user before the affected transactions are processed again.	Recording of sales results in proper recording of receivables and cash receipts.
XVI. Output goes to the control clerk, who compares the control total report with the batch totals.	X	Output is checked for accuracy and completeness before it is sent to the user. Any differences are resolved with the user before the affected transactions are processed again. (See XIV above.)	Recording of sales results in proper recording of receivables and cash receipts.
XVII. Starr checks the output received from Consolidated Data Services to its batch totals.	X	The user employs its control totals to insure that the output received from Consolidated Data Services is accuate and complete. (See, however, XVIII below.)	Recording of sales results in proper recording of receivables and cash receipts.
XVIII. Neither the control clerk at Consolidated Data Services nor the bookkeeper at Starr checks the cash receipts book to the remittance advices which are kept by Consolidated.	X	Even though the control totals agree with the batch totals, it is possible for the individual customer data to be incorrect. For example, a remittance from one customer may be erroneously credited to another's account. In such a case, the totals would be correct. Some comparison of invoices with remittance advices is needed.	Accounts receivable master file data and the cash receipts book may be incorrect.

Note: S = Internal Control Strength
W = Internal Control Weakness

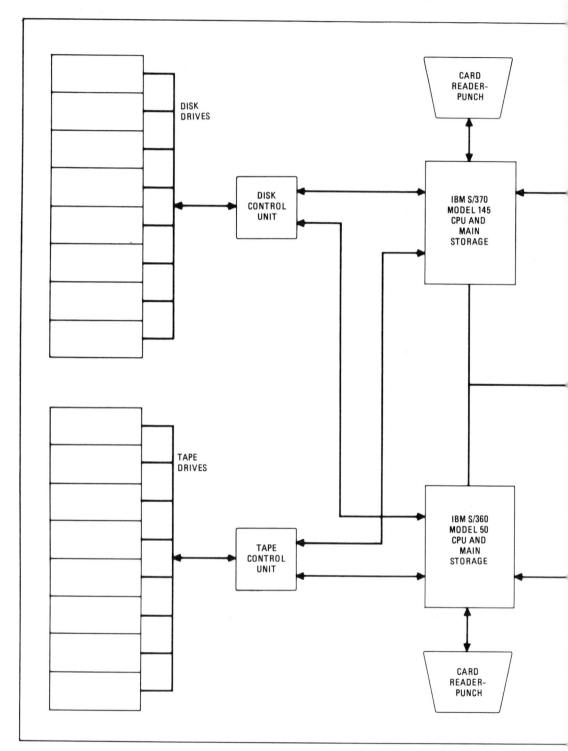

Figure 5–2.　Data Center Layout—Consolidated Data Services, Inc.

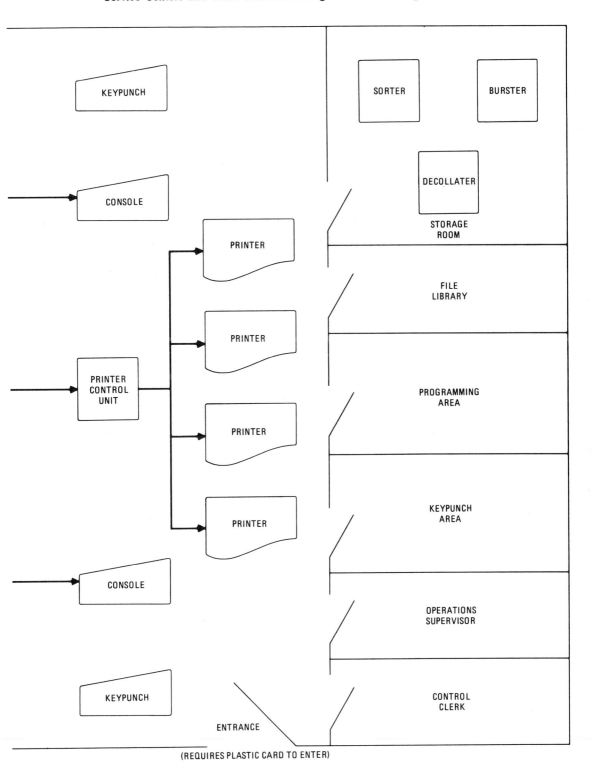

KEYPUNCH

CONSOLE

PRINTER

PRINTER

PRINTER
CONTROL
UNIT

PRINTER

PRINTER

CONSOLE

KEYPUNCH

ENTRANCE

(REQUIRES PLASTIC CARD TO ENTER)

SORTER

BURSTER

DECOLLATER

STORAGE
ROOM

FILE
LIBRARY

PROGRAMMING
AREA

KEYPUNCH
AREA

OPERATIONS
SUPERVISOR

CONTROL
CLERK

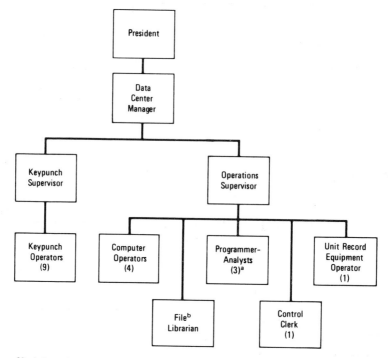

^aOne is also a systems programmer.

^bProposed. At present, the operators control the file library, which should be locked when they are not present.

Figure 5–3.   Organization Chart—Consolidated Data Services, Inc.

6
The Audit and Control of Distributed, Interactive and Integrated Systems

Advanced systems have been defined as those systems which possess one or more of the following characteristics: data communications, data integration, automatic transaction initiation, unconventional or temporary audit trail.[1] These characteristics are not unique to large-scale systems and in fact have been incorporated in many small processing systems. Furthermore, they may be implemented in either batch processing environments or real-time environments.

These techniques make systems potentially faster, more efficient, and more versatile. It is possible to move data collection closer to the source of transactions thereby eliminating a lot of previously necessary data handling activities. In some cases data acquisition can be handled automatically without any human intervention. The use of integrated files or data base systems can eliminate the duplication of information that previously existed in separate application files and can facilitate more efficient access and updating of those integrated files. These advantages make it possible to use automated systems in all aspects of an organization's operations and to make information available on a sufficiently timely basis to be an important resource in the decision-making process.

While these technological advances offer promise for increased efficiency and effectiveness, they also represent the need for new approaches to control and security. Communication techniques that allow for remote collection of data at the user site also produce the opportunity for unauthorized access to the processing system if adequate controls are not implemented to protect against that danger. Elimination of intermediate processing and automatic generation of transactions may eliminate previously available documents and thus change the traditional audit trail. In order to enjoy maximum benefit from the efficiencies of the techniques available in advanced systems, it is necessary to develop control procedures which will protect the integrity of these systems and the data processed. Systems using data communications and data bases can operate in either a real-time or batch processing mode.

[1] *Management, Control and Audit of Advanced EDP Systems,* (New York: American Institute of Certified Public Accountants, 1977), p. 5.

Most installations use a mixture of the two. Thus, an installation may use real-time processing for inquiries and batch processing for updating. Another approach would be to do all processing in real-time. Both processing approaches, however, may employ the advanced technology of data communications and data base systems.

REAL-TIME PROCESSING SYSTEMS

A real-time system may be defined as "one which controls an environment by receiving data, processing them, and returning the results sufficiently quickly to affect the functioning of the environment at that time.[2] Another definition of real-time systems is "one or more digital computers and other devices used to participate in, control, or monitor a business, industrial, or scientific process while this process is actually taking place."[3] Both of these definitions stress the characteristic of immediate response, and it is this characteristic and this characteristic alone that distinguishes a real-time system from a batch processing system. In effect, a real-time system views each transaction as a batch of one and must be prepared with all of the necessary equipment, processing programs, and data files necessary to recognize, record, process, and respond to that transaction as it occurs.

A real-time environment is geared to a short reaction time. The goal is to provide a response from the initial recording and processing of a transaction in time to affect the operations of the business or the subsequent activities in a process control or scientific environment. The most important implication for control considerations is the elimination of the time interval that usually exists in a batch processing system between the point at which the transaction takes place and the point at which it is entered into the processing cycle. In a batch processing system, that time delay provides opportunities to examine each individual transaction in detail, to develop certain balancing control totals for a group of such transactions, and to edit data not only for internal consistency within a transaction but also for consistency between groups of transactions. The real-time approach, in which a transaction enters the processing system and begins to affect master records immediately as it occurs, imposes increased requirements for editing and validation techniques as part of the initial recording process.

There is a technical distinction between an on-line system and a real-time system in the sense that the term real-time applies only in those instances where the computer reacts to the input data immediately, processes that data as it is received, and takes the action appropriate to the particular transaction. It is possible to have on-line computer systems that are not real-time. In that

---

[2] James Martin, *Design of Real-Time Computer Systems* (Englewood Cliffs, New Jersey: Prentice-Hall, 1967), p. 5.
[3] Franz E. Ross, "Internal Control and the Audit of Real-Time Digital Systems," *The Journal of Accountancy* (April 1965), p. 46.

case, the auditor would have to be concerned with the problems of appropriate controls of the remote devices and control of the transmission process, but some of the traditional batch controls would be appropriate. On the other hand, a real-time system must also be an on-line system, and added to the control problems mentioned for remote locations and transmission is the additional need for complete validation of the data as it is in fact entered into the system and used.

Some real-time systems do not update or change data files but are merely inquiry systems. In this kind of real-time environment, the primary control emphasis is upon identification of the user and the user's authorized access to certain parts of the information system. The validation procedures of the input data itself are much less critical than they would be in a real-time application in which updating is actually taking place. When real-time updating is employed, the need for control procedures is extended beyond simple identification of the user and the user's right to certain data and must include procedures which actually attempt to verify and edit the data itself.

Updating in a real-time environment usually involves a direct-access device to store the master files. This results in *destructive updating,* a technique in which the updated or changed version of a record is written on the same physical space previously occupied by the original master record, thereby destroying the original record. This is to be contrasted with the *non-destructive updating environment* in which the updating process produces a whole new copy of the master file and leaves the old generation intact. Whenever destructive updating is employed, the need exists for procedures to provide backup copies of the master file by periodic dumping or some form of logging.

REMOTE INPUT/OUTPUT AND DATA COMMUNICATIONS

Advanced systems frequently employ input/output devices which are at locations remote from the central processing unit. The remote devices are usually connected to the computer through telecommunication lines which are leased from a common carrier. The communication lines are available at various speed ratings and are usually either *dial-up lines* (the connection is completed by use of a normal dialing procedure) or *leased lines* (dedicated service, the user has exclusive use of the communication line). The remote locations of the input/output devices make it more difficult to control access to the system than in an installation where all input devices to the computer exist within the controlled environment of the physical installation itself. Thus, techniques have to be introduced to identify the users of the I/O devices and to control their access to the central processing system and its information files.

This need for control of access exists in any environment but is especially critical when input/output devices that have entry to the processing system are at locations physically remote from that of the central processing unit. It should be stressed that the use of remote input/output devices and telecommunication lines does not make a system a real-time system. If a group of transactions are collected at a remote location and transmitted at one time to a central location, this is a batch processing system. The characteristic that makes the use of these telecommunication lines part of a real-time system is recording, transmitting, and processing the transaction immediately as it occurs.

There are a great variety of devices available for use as remote input/output operations. Some of these devices are manually operated terminals in which the operator uses a keyboard or some other device, such as a light pen, to actually record the data for transmission, usually one record at a time. Other devices are essentially high-speed transmission devices which read preprepared documents (cards, magnetic tape, or other machine-readable records) and usually transmit these documents a group or batch at a time. When such high-speed devices are in use, they are usually employed in some form of remote job entry and are usually involved in a batch processing application. Table 6–1 provides some insight into the variety of remote input/output devices available.

Some installations use telecommunication lines to communicate with remote locations in an off-line environment. In off-line activities, data is not transmitted directly to the computer but is transmitted to another device located at the installation, such as a magnetic tape handler or a card punch, and the machine records thus received are held for later processing. In other installations, the remote devices are linked through the communication lines directly with the central processing unit. In still other applications, the data communication lines can be used to link two computers which can communicate with each other. An increasingly popular configuration is one in which a network of small computers, usually used for local processing, can be linked to large central computers so that the sharing of information and processing can occur throughout the network thus created. In such configurations, conventional files are frequently replaced by data bases. This approach is called *distributed processing.*

The use of remote input/output devices in data communications is available in both large and small systems. It has the effect in many applications of moving the data capture function closer to the source of the data and the original user. This technology also makes it possible to move information from one processing system to another automatically.

Remote input/output devices and data communications do not change the requirements for physical protection of the equipment and data files as discussed in an earlier chapter. However, the existence of remote input/output devices by which access can be gained to the files of the system through long distance transmission lines does present a potential control problem. First, there are many more potential access points compared with the relatively few devices in a system without remote terminals, and second, the remote location of these input/output devices makes the physical control

Table 6–1.   Common Terminal Devices.

DOCUMENT TRANSIMISSION TERMINALS	HUMAN INPUT TERMINALS	ANSWERBACK DEVICES AND DISPLAYS
Paper-tape readers/ punches	Typewriter-like keyboard	Typewriter
Card readers/punches	Special keyboard	Printer
Magnetic card readers	Matrix keyboard	Teleprinter
Badge readers	Lever set	Passbook printer
	Rotary switches	Display screen
Optical document readers	Push buttons	Display tubes
Magnetic-ink character	Teleprinter	Light panel
readers	Telephone dial	Microfilm or film-strip
Mark-sensing devices	Touch-tone telephone	projector
Microfilm	keyboard	Big display boards
		Graph plotter
		Strip recorder
Plate readers	Light pen with display	Dials
Facsimile machines	tube	Telephone voice
	Coupled stylus	answerback
Magnetic-tape units	Facsimile machine	Facsimile machine
Tape cassettes	Plate reader	
Magnetic disks	Badge reader	

From: James Martin, *Introduction to Teleprocessing,* © 1972, p. 3. Reprinted by permission of Prentice-Hall, Inc., Englewood Cliffs, New Jersey.

of the devices more difficult. Procedures for identification and authorization of users of the remote devices are necessary.

INTEGRATED FILES AND DATA BASE SYSTEMS

Up to this point, we have been considering conventionally structured files, that is, a separate file for each application or group of applications (for example, a customer master file, an open invoice file, an inventory file and a price list file for the sales, accounts receivable and cash receipts system). All are entirely separate files; they are located in physically different areas in the storage media.

This system has the advantage of simplicity: a given file contains all the data items needed for the programs that process it. However, it also has disadvantages:

- Some of the information in one file is also contained in other files. This is redundant and may be undesirable if enough data is involved, as it will take up valuable storage space.
- Several files may contain different versions of data common to both of them. This happens when not all files are updated by current trans-

actions on a timely basis or when the various updating programs produce different results.

These disadvantages can be mitigated by integrating the data items into a few common files, perhaps even a single file, called a *data base*. These data remain on-line and are processed by all the programs in a given system. For example, there may be a data base for the sales, accounts receivable and cash receipts system, another for the purchases, accounts payable, cash disbursements system and yet another for the payroll-personnel system. Or, there may be one data base for everything: all systems access the same data base.

Data integration results in the combination of the data records for several different operations with similar information into single comprehensive sets of records. This process of creating single comprehensive records and thus a single comprehensive file minimizes the necessity for duplicate operations and duplicate records. These integrated sets of data records, called the data base, become the master file for a number of different applications.

The processing for a data base is characterized by the fact that a single document describing a transaction is used to initiate the updating of all records or data elements associated with that transaction and affected by it. Although this results in an elimination of redundancy within the master files and more efficient handling of all facets of the transaction, it places a very heavy responsibility on the installation for maintenance of that single data base. Under this approach all of the pertinent master information and historical data is contained within one single master file or data base, and erroneous processing or inadvertent destruction of that single data base can have more serious implications for an organization than the destruction of an individual application master file that is only one of several master files for a firm. Data bases can be updated or integrated on either a real-time or a batch-mode basis.

Access controls for the data base should encompass both those activities that can effect a change in the files (updating) and those activities that simply involve reading the data files (inquiry). The data files represent a real asset whose value can be diluted as much by unauthorized access and reading as by incorrect updating. Access controls become even more critical when the data base is maintained on-line, making the information accessible to all devices within the computer system. This is to be contrasted with files that are maintained on an off-line basis, such as tape, and require an actual mounting of the data file before they can be interrogated through the computer. If the on-line data base exists in a system which has remote terminals, access controls must be concerned with all users having access to either the remote terminals or to the central processing facility.

In an integrated data base containing many different data elements from different applications, individuals may have authorization to access specific modules or elements within the data base. A carefully constructed system of authorization for access to each data element in the system must be established to prevent improper access or manipulation by persons without legitimate reason for accessing the information. Thus, an authorization system is an essential control in a data base environment which supports the necessary segregation of functions. Furthermore, responsibility for each data element in the data base must be established and assigned. A good security system must not only control which data elements a user is entitled to access but also the operations that may be performed. Control should be exercised over which programs a user is allowed to execute. Whether an existing record in the file may be updated or simply read, whether the user is authorized to add a new record, or whether the user is authorized to eliminate or delete a record from the data file must all be made a part of the system specifications and operating controls.

Another function that must be carefully controlled within the installation is the identification of those individuals who have the right to change the access authorizations within the system or execute those programs that interpret or otherwise update the user identification routines. Once a system of identification has been worked out so that the processing routines and the data files the individual user may access have been identified, it is important to protect the integrity of these identification codes or passwords. Individual users must be impressed with the importance of maintaining the confidentiality of their password, and steps must be taken to prevent unauthorized access to the identification scheme. One of the easiest ways to gain access to the password or identification code of another is to allow those passwords to be printed on a terminal during the normal processing performed on that terminal.

Passwords or identification codes should not be made available to the computer operators or systems programmers on a normal basis. Consideration should be given to periodic rearrangement or changing of the passwords in order to prevent publication of the passwords. Installation management must control access to the identification codes and processing programs to prevent systems programmers from either gaining access to that information or modifying it for their own use. The installation management should exercise continual care in reviewing the operations of the computer to insure that knowledgeable operators have not themselves attempted to access the data.

In addition to identifying legitimate users and preventing unauthorized access to the data files, a file security system should also provide regular notification to the operations management or the security officer of the installation when unauthorized attempts to access the data base are made. Attempts to gain unauthorized access can be handled immediately by techniques that lock the terminal keyboard or simply fail to respond to these initial inquiries. In the case of critical information, such an attempt could cause a message to be relayed to an appropriate security officer who could investigate the terminal in question.

In addition to preventing access, it is desirable to maintain a log of unauthorized attempts to access the data files in order to determine whether there is some pattern involving a particular user, a particular terminal location, or a particular element of the data base. If a pattern can be discerned, the opportunity to identify the illegal user or strengthen the security system is enhanced. In the case of a particularly sensitive element, it may be desirable to maintain a log of all accesses to the records within that data element. This log can then be periodically reviewed to assess the way that segment of the data base is being used as well as to review the efficiency of the control procedures maintained for that file.

As with any other data files, provision must be made to provide adequate backup for the data base system. Since data base systems are usually recorded on direct-access devices and processed by destructive updating, which does not provide a grandfather-father-son backup procedure, it is necessary to make some provision to produce backup copies of the file periodically. This can be done either by periodic dumping or by an adaptation of a logging procedure. As each update takes place within the data base, a log can be constructed before processing the transaction to create a copy of the master record. After processing, a copy of the updated master record would be made. If any disruption of processing takes place or if the data base were physically damaged, it would be possible to use the latest file dump or the reconstruction log (whichever technique is used) to reconstruct the physical data base.

In a data base environment, the organization and maintenance of the master data is separated from the application programs. A separate group of software programs, called the *data base management system,* organizes, records, and retrieves data elements from the data base making specific elements available to the application programs when updating is necessary. This is in contrast to the approach used when individual application files are created and maintained by the application programs themselves. This separation of function causes some change in the approach to maintenance and protection of the data files. Many installations use a data base administrator whose responsibilities are to develop the organization of the data base, including identification of the elements and the logical relationships of the individual data elements to each other and to the various applications systems. The data base administrator is also responsible for the documentation of the data base and the implementation of the control and security measures developed for that data base system.

In organizations large enough to support staff specialization, the data base administrator represents a separate individual or staff. It should be recognized, however, that many small installations employing minicomputers also use the data base approach. While the separation of responsibilities makes it desirable that a different individual act as data base administrator from the person operating the system and developing application programs, that separation may not be possible. If this is the case, then alternative controls must be instituted to compensate for that lack of segregation of responsibilities.

IMPLICATIONS FOR THE AUDIT TRAIL

While the form of the audit trail may change substantially, there is no reason why the audit trail should disappear or become unusable. If careful thought is given to the need for audit trails at the time the system is being designed, they can be implemented in the system. In most instances, the introduction of sufficient controls and records to provide an adequate audit trail is mutually beneficial to the installation and to the auditor. Usually the same techniques that provide adequate audit trail are valuable to the installation for its own control and reconstruction purposes.

One change that may occur in the audit trail is in the availability of original source documents. In some instances, as in the case of automatic transaction initiation, the source document may not exist. In other instances, the traditional source document exists but is stored at locations remote from the central processing facility and in a different sequence from that recorded. Some transactions initiated at remote locations (whether batched or processed in a real-time environment) are previously recorded on a traditional source document before transmission to the computer. In these instances, new methods for relating transactions to the source document must be developed.

If the installation maintains a transaction log which records appropriate identifying information for the transaction as well as user codes and terminal identification codes, the transaction log can be used both as a control tool and as an audit trail, facilitating the process of tracing the results of processing back to original source documents. The transaction log can be sorted daily by part number and user code or terminal code to print daily transaction journals in forms that will facilitate verification of the previous period's activities. Transaction logs can also be summarized by type of transaction to provide or confirm summary information for control accounts. Not only can a transaction log for all transactions of a given type be printed, but these transactions can also be sorted by master record or control field to print a summary of all the activity occurring to a particular master record (or account) for a given period from a specified terminal or user department.

The technique of updating an integrated data base in which one transaction is used to perform all updating to all affected data elements simultaneously can cause difficulty in associating individual source documents or transactions with specific summary records. The problem is one of ordering the source documents for those transactions in such a way that they are easily accessible for audit purposes without requiring a search through thousands of documents that may be stored in a sequence other than that which is currently needed. Transaction logs containing identifying information (such as transaction date, transaction number, and files to which a transaction has been posted) allow the auditor to use the computer to reorder that information and to group it for convenient use. Thus if an auditor wants to look at all of the transactions posted against a particular account on a particular day, the transaction log can be used to produce a listing of that information. As part of that listing, the specific location of the supporting documents for the transaction can be indicated.

In many applications, manual generation of a separate source document and subsequent transcription of the data into machine-readable form has been eliminated. Frequently the initial recording of a transaction is done directly at the terminal transmitting to the central processing unit, thus eliminating the original source document. In these circumstances, one form of protection against destruction of the audit trail is to generate hard copy as a result of the data recording process. This can be done by attaching a printer/typewriter capability to the terminal or by requiring some manual logging procedure at the terminal. These procedures would be employed in addition to the transaction log being recorded at the central computer as transactions are transmitted.

It is also possible to use the data generated for an audit trail as a reconstruction tool. This can be accomplished by making the logs all-inclusive, containing the contents of each master record both before and after updating as well as the contents of the transaction. The log can be recorded on any medium although the most efficient would be the machine-readable form most accessible to the recovery routines. By copying the contents of the data base master record before updating, the full text of the transaction, and then the contents of the data base record after updating, the log makes it possible for a recovery routine to determine all transactions that were in the process of updating when a failure occurred. The records containing information regarding the contents of data base records allow restoration of any data base segment involved in the failure. Serious failures, in which the full file is destroyed, are still handled best by the latest file dump. But even in that instance the log would be useful, for it would provide the source of those master records that had been updated by transactions after the last dump.

Maintenance of the audit trail in machine-readable form facilitates the use of the computer by the auditor. This, however, increases the need for adequate technical proficiency on the part of the auditor so that these machine-readable records can be appropriately interrogated and evaluated. In addition to understanding computer-assisted audit techniques, the auditor must also consider the timing of audit procedures. Frequently these machine-readable trails are not maintained indefinitely. If this is the case, the auditor must make provision for either saving the data or changing the timing of audit procedures to coincide with the existence of these trails. This is true of both the internal and external audit procedures and may provide the basis for a greater coordination between the efforts of the internal and the external auditors.

GENERAL CONTROLS

The introduction of distributed, interactive, or integrated processing characteristics does not change the nature of the general controls discussed in Chapters 1–2. The organization and operation controls, documentation and systems controls, hardware controls, access controls, and data and procedural controls continue to be an essential part of the internal control of any system. In some instances, however, the techniques employed to provide these controls may be affected by the existence of the characteristics discussed in this chapter.

The use of data communications, on-line integrated files, and the availability of interactive processing generally results in a great deal of automatic processing of a transaction after its introduction into the system. This will increase the significance of the programmed system's controls and the controls dealing with the transaction-initiation function. Separation of the responsibilities for initiating transactions and processing them remains imperative as the data-capture function is moved closer to the user group through the use of remote terminals.

The use of a transaction log, control totals, or internal program checks that verify the accuracy of the transaction itself are all more meaningful when provision is made for independent input records in the user departments. This does not necessarily mean that the system should be forced to reproduce copies of source documents or to generate unnecessary printed matter. It does require that the system provide for carefully controlled access to the input terminals and for the assignment of responsibility to the user department for authorization and subsequent verification of transactions used to process data.

Proper identification of the user and control of access to data files in program and processing libraries is another area of increased significance. This is a particularly sensitive issue in an on-line environment, featuring on-line program libraries and integrated data files in a processing system also containing multiple remote I/O devices. Because so much of the processing is automated, protection of the integrity of the program libraries—both application programs and systems support programs, such as the operating system—is critical. Logs should be maintained of all accesses to those program libraries and of any changes made to the libraries. Periodic tests should be made of the program library to insure that unauthorized changes have not in fact occurred. Authorized changes to the program library should be properly documented indicating the nature of the change and the authorization for the change.

The installation should be prepared to react to any unexpected emergency occurring within the processing environment. Correction routines should be in operation to handle normal errors within transmission or processing procedures. In addition, preplanned procedures and programs should be available to handle major failures and the resulting restart activities. Restarting a distributed system with multiple input/output operations or a real-time updating operation requires a sequence of operations that frequently is quite demanding. The potential for losing transactions or for repeating others is great, and the potential for operator error is increased under the duress of an emergency situation if the operator has not been thoroughly trained in a pre-determined and tested plan of action for emergency situations. Similarly, good processing control requires that adequate attention be given to the need for file reconstruction and for the preservation of sufficient file and transaction information to allow for reconstruction of the data base in an acceptable time frame.

Once detected, error conditions within the system must be corrected. This may require reintroduction of corrected data. Error-correction procedures are complicated when the transactions are initiated at a remote location or when the updating is taking place in a real-time environment. There is the frequent possibility that erroneous data may have already been used to update files by the time it is recognized as erroneous.

When data is introduced from remote locations, the system should be designed to notify the terminal user of the disposition of each transaction. Then should a system failure occur, the terminal user will be aware of those transactions that have been processed and of those transactions that have not been processed and require additional operator action such as reentry into the system.

APPLICATION CONTROLS

The use of programmed self-checking digits, existence checks, combination checks, completeness checks, and reasonableness checks provides a method by which individual transactions can be examined for accuracy by the computer before the transaction is used in processing. If the processing is being done in a batch mode, these programmed checks can be implemented in an edit program which checks all of the transactions at one time. In a real-time environment these checking procedures must be included in the data entry program itself since the nature of real-time processing is to process a transaction as soon as it occurs. Again, it should be recognized that the nature of an application control is not changed by the existence of remote terminals or integrated on-line files. The decision to apply this technology in either a batch-mode or real-time environment, however, will affect the timing of some of these application controls.

Accumulative control totals, record counts, or logs of transactions continue to be effective control tools. In the case of batch processing environments, these accumulated totals can be used to balance data prior to the next processing step. In the case of real-time processing, these totals are not accumulated until after the processing has been completed. But they continue to be useful, for they provide a means to verify that all transactions have in fact been recorded and subsequently processed. In the real-time mode, as transactions are entered over a period of time, they can be posted to accumulative totals. At the end of the specified period of time, the accumulated control totals can be compared with similar controls being maintained at the initiation point. The balancing operation can be facilitated by procedures that identify the terminal and/or the user and can accumulate controls by these subdivisions. The presence of these balancing or control totals can be used both to verify application controls and to check on the transmission accuracy of the communications network. Remember that in a real-time environment these control totals or batch totals are used after the fact. They should always be used as a supplement to the data verification procedures implemented before the transaction is used in processing.

These control totals can usually be accumulated as a by-product of the transaction log. While the transaction log can be used for balancing and improving the total processing performed over a period of time, it usually provides no protection against the omission of original transactions; the log simply contains copies of original transactions actually entered through the input terminals. Further, if an erroneous transaction goes by the input controls and is allowed to enter the system, it would be reflected as it was entered on the transaction log. If independent controls are maintained on the actual transactions and the control totals (calculated either through an accumulation routine or totals from the transaction log) are compared with these independently developed control totals, a better control exists for determining that all transactions have in fact been entered into the system.

In those instances where the system itself generates a transaction (as in the automatic reorder function in an inventory control system), it is important that the system document the existence of that machine–generated transaction by producing some hard-copy memorandum that can be verified by an independent check of the activity.

All transactions must be properly authorized by the user department. Listing all transactions processed during a preceding period and returning the list to the supervisor of the original department facilitates verification of the authorization of all processed transactions. Similarly, restrictions of terminals to authorized users can also constitute approval of the documents generated by that terminal.

Controls must also be instituted to prevent loss of transactions. The control totals mentioned previously represent one approach. Still another that can be employed is to provide serial numbers for each transaction. In some cases this can be done by the terminal operator. Thus, as each operator sends a message, a serial number is attached to the message. As the computer receives the message, it can check that the serial number from each message received is one higher than the serial number from the previous message received from that particular operator or that particular terminal. A variation on this approach is to allow the computer itself to generate a serial number which is attached to each transaction and recorded on the transaction log.

The use of serial numbers allows the system to keep track of all transactions entered into the system. If a hardware or software breakdown occurs, or if the application program malfunctions, the system has a means of identifying the fact that a transaction has not been properly processed. System-generated control or serial numbers can be used in the same way that serial numbers or preprinted numbers are used on normal source documents. For those computer systems that contain electronic clocks, the serial number can be expanded to include a time designation as well.

AUDITING TECHNIQUES

Audit objectives are not changed by the introduction of distributed processing, data communications, or integrated data base systems. As discussed throughout this book, the auditor's responsibilities include a proper study and evaluation of the system of internal control, execution of appropriate compliance tests if reliance is to be placed on internal control, and execution of appropriate substantive tests of the financial data.

Whenever possible, the auditor should seek independent evidence of processing controls or data accuracy. Techniques such as confirmations and inventory counts are still most appropriate. However, systems containing the features discussed in this chapter tend to reduce the amount of independent source data and manual intervention. As a result, control procedures and data generation tend to be more heavily dependent upon processing controls within the system. The auditor will tend to be more heavily involved in systems testing procedures and in the use of computer-assisted audit techniques to access machine-readable data that is no longer available in alternative form. Consequently, the auditor must also be concerned with protection of these audit procedures or audit data as they are produced by the system. Further, the audit trail or audit access will tend to be reduced unless deliberately provided in the system.

Auditors can continue to use computer-assisted techniques that operate on historical data and compliance testing techniques which use simulated or test data. In addition, however, the ability to use live data on a real-time basis in both the compliance and substantive tests is greatly facilitated by the availability of the system characteristics discussed in this chapter. The ability to use live data on a real-time basis requires that a prewritten audit program be executed as the data is being processed. This audit program may be incorporated into the operating system or the application program. Successful use of such a technique, however, requires that sufficient controls exist to prevent modification or circumvention of the audit programming in place. This approach requires considerable advance planning and usually can be successfully implemented only if the auditor has appropriate input at the systems design stage.

Table 6–2 (pp. 252–253) summarizes the computer-assisted audit techniques which are available. It should be noted that these techniques are not substantially different from those discussed in Chapter 5. However, the timing or relative advantage of one technique over another may in fact be affected by the existence of a data communication or on-line facility.

WERNER MANUFACTURING, INC.—CASE STUDY

In the last segment of our case study, Werner converts to a distributed processing system and encounters some additional processing, internal control and auditing problems.

CONTROLS AND AUDITING IN A DISTRIBUTED PROCESSING ENVIRONMENT

This section will illustrate some of the auditing and control problems posed by distributed processing systems. The components of a distributed processing system can include minicomputers, a full-scale computer, a data communications network, and common data bases. This immediately tells us that there may be three sets of internal control problems in addition to those we would normally expect:

1. Minicomputers are generally small installations with relatively few supporting individuals. This may mean weak controls caused by an inability to properly segregate duties.
2. Data communications networks introduce another element, telephone lines, by which data are transmitted between computers. This creates another medium in which data may be accidentally (or intentionally) lost or distorted.
3. A common data base brings in a number of control problems, such as data integrity, audit trails, input/output controls, data recovery, file maintenance, file access, the role of the data base administrator (DBA).

CONVERSION TO DISTRIBUTED PROCESSING

Assume it is 1979 and Werner has completed a conversion to a distributed processing system. As the revised configuration charts (Figures 6–2, 6–3, 6–4 and 6–5) show, each of the regional locations has a minicomputer (IBM System/3 Model 6) that communicates with the Cleveland data center via

Table 6-2. Techniques Matrix.

	TECHNIQUE	CAPABILITY SUPPLIED BY	USED BY	DATA USED	PURPOSE	ADVANTAGES	DISADVANTAGES
Techniques using live data on a real-time basis	Transaction tagging	Vendor or application system designer	Auditors and managers	Live accounting	Compliance and substantive test	Full range of selectivity	Adds to overhead of system, special programming
	Real-time notification	Systems programmer or vendor	Auditors and managers	Live accounting and system	Compliance test and control	Control and timeliness	Cost
	Audit log	Systems designer	Auditors and control personnel	Live accounting and system	Compliance and substantive test	Specified transactions logged for audit review	Cost
	Monitoring	Vendor	Auditors and managers	Live system	Review actual system activity	Shows what has happened	Requires technical knowledge to interpret
Techniques using historical data	Audit language and programs	Vendor and system designer, software house, manufacturer or audit firm	Auditors and managers	Historical and live	Compliance and substantive test. Perform wide variety of audit tests	Retrieves data for audit purposes. Relatively easy to use, not expensive	Requires some programming knowledge by auditor. Presently limited to types of files that can be accessed.
	Simulation	Auditors, internal and external with program copy	Auditors	Historical	Determine accuracy of data processed	Permits comparison with real processing	Extensive use can be large consumer of machine resources

Technique					
Extended records	Design of client applications	Auditors and managers	Historical	Provide complete audit trail for audit and management purposes	Provides complete account history	Very costly use of machine resources at present
Techniques using simulated data: Integrated test facility	Auditors, mostly internal	Auditors	Dummy	Compliance test	Relatively inexpensive	Must be "backed out" very carefully
Program analysis technique	Special software, contractor or vendor	Auditors and programmers	Usually dummy	Authentication of program operation / Check of key points in program execution	Gives better understanding of application; gives assurance controls are functioning	Needs auditor knowledge of programming, may be expensive; useful only in certain circumstances.

From: *Management, Control and Audit of Advanced EDP Systems*, Computer Services Guideline, American Institute of Certified Public Accountants, 1977, p. 24.

telephone transmission lines. The equipment at the Cleveland data center (IBM S/370–145) did not change. This configuration is known as a *star network*. The regional locations perform certain processing steps on their minicomputers and transmit certain data to the central computer at Cleveland, where a data base common to the entire revenue system is maintained. Conversely, certain data generated at the Cleveland data center is transmitted to the regional locations.

One immediate result of the conversion to distributed processing was a sharp increase in Werner's data processing budget from $740,500 per year (Chapter 1) to $1,002,100 (Table 6–3) per year.

As you can see, the entire increase is due to the change in equipment and staff at the regional locations and the presence of the DBA. For simplicity, we will assume that the old staff was retrained to handle the new (data base) file organization and no net increase in salaries, aside from the DBA's, or software costs resulted. This may not be true in real life.

What did Werner get for the additional expense of $261,600 per year? To answer that question, we will construct a scenario, starting with the decision to use distributed processing.

At about the time Werner completed its purchase of Starr Products, the president, B. T. Summers, was attending a computer symposium for chief executive officers. One of the speakers was Charles Woodhull, who described

Table 6–3.   Data Processing Budget—Distributed Processing—Werner Manufacturing, Inc.

ITEM	AMOUNT
• Components of IBM System/3 Model 6 at each remote location:	
• IBM 5406 Central processor	$ 11,000
• IBM 5444-M1 Disk drive—2 units	4,500
• IBM 3741-M2 Data entry system	2,500
• IBM 5213-M3 Printer	3,300
• IBM 2265-M2 CRT display	2,300
• IBM 2074 BSCA communications I/O device [a]	3,600
Total hardware	$ 27,200
• Salaries (2 persons)	35,000
• Supplies	6,000
• Overhead and miscellaneous	6,000
Total per remote location	$ 74,200
• Total for 3 locations	$ 222,600
• Data base administrator (DBA)	45,000
• Cleveland data center [b]	734,500
Total	$1,002,100

[a] Housed in the central processor.
[b] See Chapter 1 for breakdown of budget and hardware configuration.

the new technology (data communications, data bases, and so on) in computers and the benefits it offers when applied to distributed processing systems.

Summers was very interested in Woodhull's presentation, as he wants Werner's executives to use the most modern management techniques. Summers considers computers to be an essential part of modern management, and although he doesn't understand their technical aspects, he tries to keep up with the latest developments in the field.

During the symposium, Summers talked at some length with Woodhull who told Summers that Werner's data processing was somewhat behind the times. In response to Summer's question, Woodhull gave these reasons for his opinion:

"1. All processing is done at the central data center in Cleveland, with results sent back to the regional sites. This is contrary to the latest trend in data processing which provides for some processing (that which is needed by that location) to be performed at remote locations. The results may be transmitted to the central data center for further processing and dissemination. Conversely, data from the central data center is transmitted to the regional locations. By allowing remote locations to process data which they need, the results will be available sooner and decision making expedited.

2. Files at the central data center are organized conventionally, with files for receivables, open orders, accounts payable, and so on. This frequently involves a certain amount of unwanted redundancy and slower processing. The latest concept is to have one large file, called a data base, where each element of information is stored only once. This data base is accessible by all programs.

3. Conventional processing systems are staffed by people who think in conventional terms. They may lack the imagination needed to accommodate the expanding information needs of the modern corporation. Modern management techniques need modern, forward-looking people as well as modern technology."

Summers was attracted by the last point; it struck a responsive chord—his predilection for his executives' use of the most modern management techniques. He decided to talk to J. T. Brown, the vice president of Information Systems, about these ideas as soon as possible.

*   *   *   *

Brown listened attentively to Summers' explanation of Woodhull's remarks. He then countered with this statement:

"We've looked into distributed processing and decided it did not offer us enough to justify the expense of a conversion. In fact, it would cost us considerably more a year to support it. Our present system uses teleprocessing and gives us timely management information.

"Keep in mind we have not been computerized very long. We played it conservatively and computerized the accounting system only when we were sure doing so was cost-effective. You kept very close to the conversion projects, which was the best thing to do, so you know the decision processes we went through. You also know how much we've invested in our present system and that we haven't begun to earn it back. I think the accountants call it amortization.

"Computerization, while it involves a special technology, is like any other business decision. So is the decision to convert from one computer system to another. It must be approached as dispassionately as possible, with the benefits and costs evaluated carefully.

"For the reasons I've outlined, we feel that distributed processing is not for Werner, at least not for the present. If you would like us to present and explain our findings and conclusions, we'll be happy to do so. I'm sure you'll see we've considered the situation very carefully."

Summers had little to say in reply to Brown's reasoned response, but he was still not satisfied with it. He had it in his mind to use the latest technology that Woodhull expounded.

*   *   *   *

Werner did convert to a distributed processing system. Because of the frustration of having his logical arguments virtually ignored, Brown retired.

Summers hired Woodhull to replace him, and the conversion process began. See the new organization chart (Figure 6–1).

DESCRIPTION OF THE SYSTEM

Read the system flowchart (Figure 6–2) for a description of the system. For now, concentrate on understanding the system. Note we are again using the procedure established in previous chapters. First we describe the system, then we identify its internal control strengths and weaknesses. Finally, we discuss the procedures used by the independent and internal auditors.

COMPARISON WITH PREVIOUS SYSTEM

Before we review Werner's internal control strengths and weaknesses in its new system, we will compare it with the system it replaced.

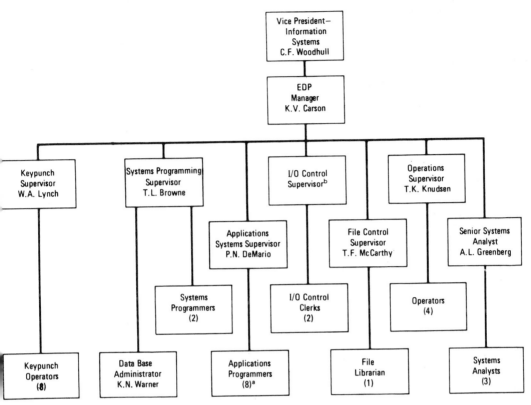

aTwo three-person teams, each headed by a lead programmer.

bProposed. Plan is to set up this function in about six months.

Figure 6–1. Data Processing Organization Chart—Distributed Processing—Werner Manufacturing, Inc.

- Werner now has a "hybrid system." For example, the three regional locations no longer have an open order file, but the Cleveland sales office does. Cleveland's open order file is a vestige of the previous system. This part of the system was not changed completely because it uses the full-size computer system at the Cleveland data center.

  One must wonder how this situation is defended by Charles Woodhull. It is not only inconsistent with his apparent philosophy of a system's providing more and timely information, it indicates a failure to fully complete the conversion to the new processing system.

- Looking at the system's output, it is evident that it produces no more information than did the system it replaced. This seems strange in view of the cost of converting and the increased annual cost of the new system. One must wonder if the conversion was worth the price.

- Under the previous system, if the inventory at the selling location was not sufficient to fill an order, the quantities at the other locations could

Operation	Personnel	Regional Sales Office[a]

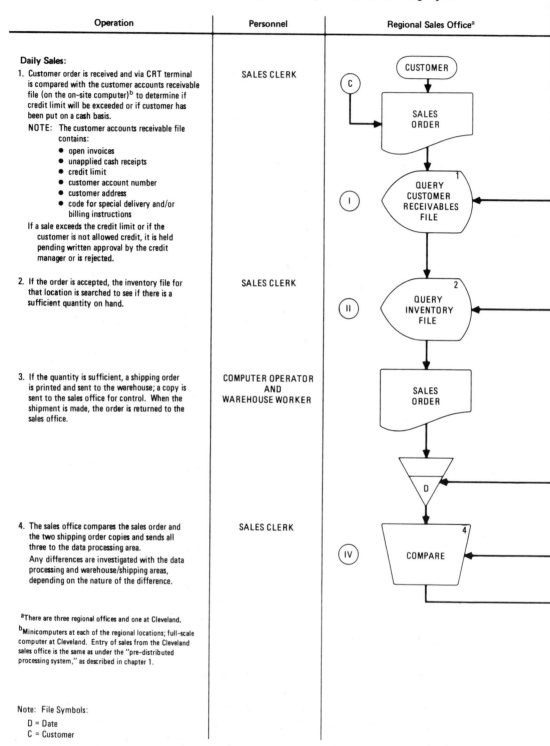

Daily Sales:

1. Customer order is received and via CRT terminal is compared with the customer accounts receivable file (on the on-site computer)[b] to determine if credit limit will be exceeded or if customer has been put on a cash basis.

   NOTE: The customer accounts receivable file contains:
   - open invoices
   - unapplied cash receipts
   - credit limit
   - customer account number
   - customer address
   - code for special delivery and/or billing instructions

   If a sale exceeds the credit limit or if the customer is not allowed credit, it is held pending written approval by the credit manager or is rejected.

   SALES CLERK

2. If the order is accepted, the inventory file for that location is searched to see if there is a sufficient quantity on hand.

   SALES CLERK

3. If the quantity is sufficient, a shipping order is printed and sent to the warehouse; a copy is sent to the sales office for control. When the shipment is made, the order is returned to the sales office.

   COMPUTER OPERATOR AND WAREHOUSE WORKER

4. The sales office compares the sales order and the two shipping order copies and sends all three to the data processing area.

   Any differences are investigated with the data processing and warehouse/shipping areas, depending on the nature of the difference.

   SALES CLERK

[a]There are three regional offices and one at Cleveland.

[b]Minicomputers at each of the regional locations; full-scale computer at Cleveland. Entry of sales from the Cleveland sales office is the same as under the "pre-distributed processing system," as described in chapter 1.

Note: File Symbols:
   D = Date
   C = Customer

Figure 6–2.   Sales, Accounts Receivable, Cash Receipts—Distributed Processing—Werner Manufacturing, Inc.

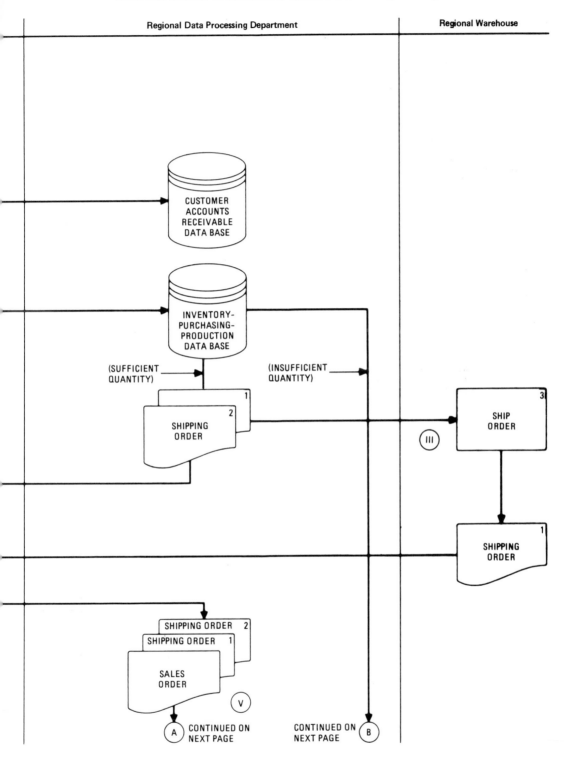

Operation	Personnel	Regional Sales Offices

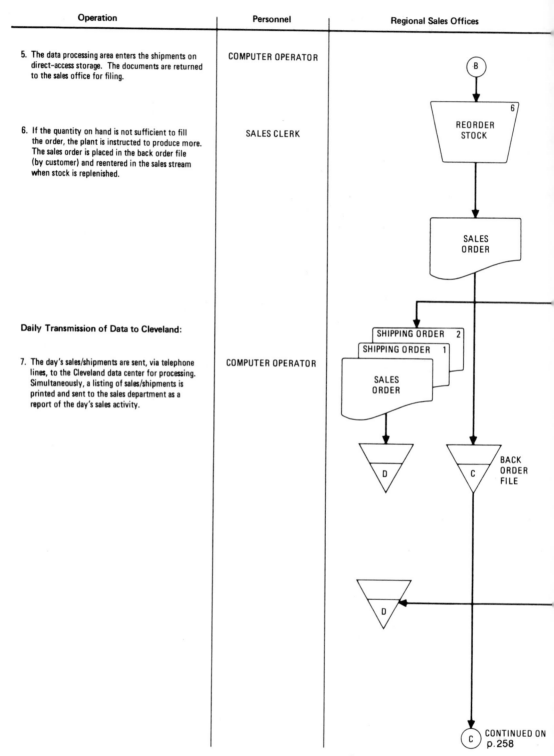

5. The data processing area enters the shipments on direct-access storage. The documents are returned to the sales office for filing.

COMPUTER OPERATOR

6. If the quantity on hand is not sufficient to fill the order, the plant is instructed to produce more. The sales order is placed in the back order file (by customer) and reentered in the sales stream when stock is replenished.

SALES CLERK

Daily Transmission of Data to Cleveland:

7. The day's sales/shipments are sent, via telephone lines, to the Cleveland data center for processing. Simultaneously, a listing of sales/shipments is printed and sent to the sales department as a report of the day's sales activity.

COMPUTER OPERATOR

CONTINUED ON p. 258

Figure 6–2 (*continued*)

Regional Data Processing Department

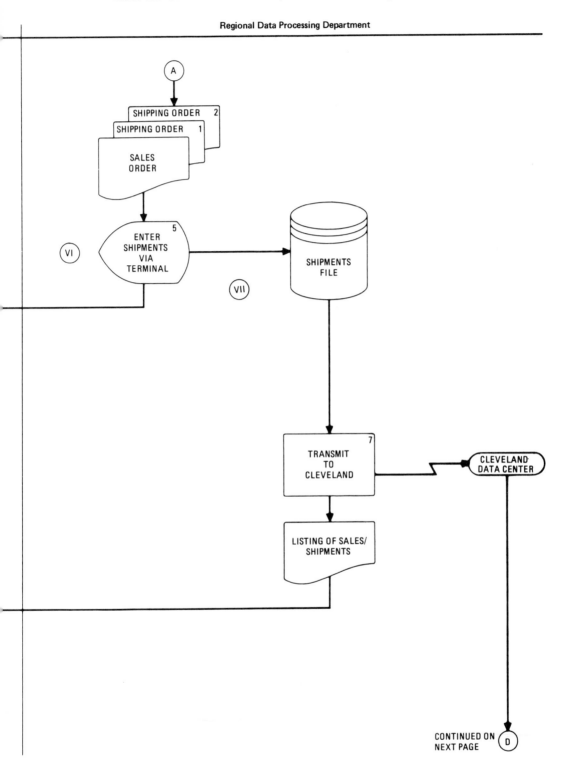

Operation	Personnel	Cleveland Data Center

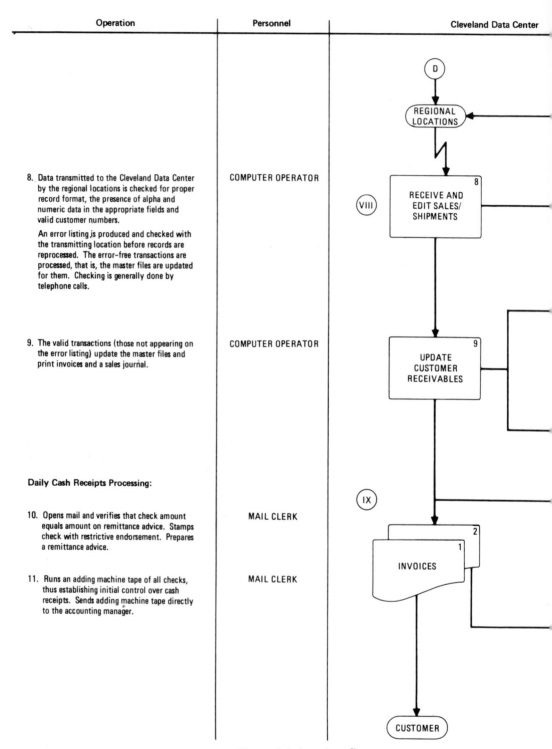

8. Data transmitted to the Cleveland Data Center by the regional locations is checked for proper record format, the presence of alpha and numeric data in the appropriate fields and valid customer numbers.

   An error listing is produced and checked with the transmitting location before records are reprocessed. The error-free transactions are processed, that is, the master files are updated for them. Checking is generally done by telephone calls.

   COMPUTER OPERATOR

9. The valid transactions (those not appearing on the error listing) update the master files and print invoices and a sales journal.

   COMPUTER OPERATOR

Daily Cash Receipts Processing:

10. Opens mail and verifies that check amount equals amount on remittance advice. Stamps check with restrictive endorsement. Prepares a remittance advice.

   MAIL CLERK

11. Runs an adding machine tape of all checks, thus establishing initial control over cash receipts. Sends adding machine tape directly to the accounting manager.

   MAIL CLERK

Figure 6–2 (*continued*)

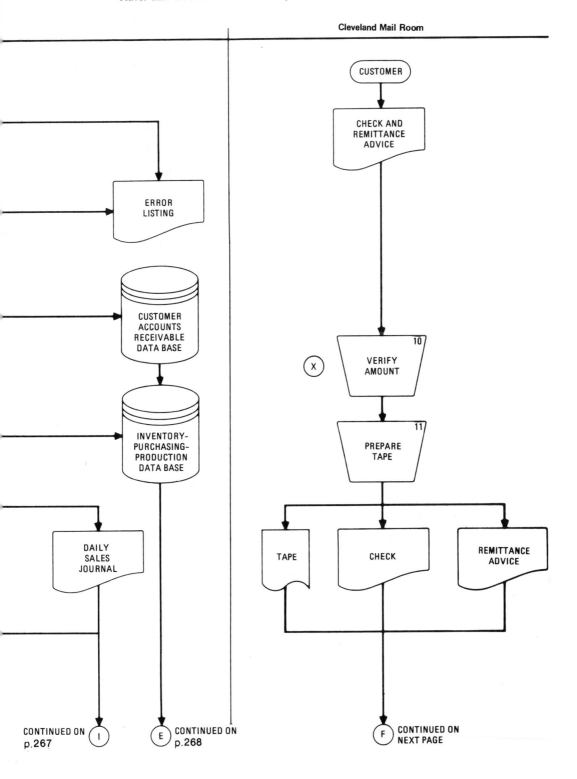

Cleveland Mail Room

CUSTOMER

CHECK AND
REMITTANCE
ADVICE

ERROR
LISTING

CUSTOMER
ACCOUNTS
RECEIVABLE
DATA BASE

INVENTORY-
PURCHASING-
PRODUCTION
DATA BASE

X

VERIFY
AMOUNT 10

PREPARE
TAPE 11

DAILY
SALES
JOURNAL

TAPE

CHECK

REMITTANCE
ADVICE

CONTINUED ON
p.267 I

E CONTINUED ON
p.268

F CONTINUED ON
NEXT PAGE

Operation	Personnel	Accounting Department — Cleveland
		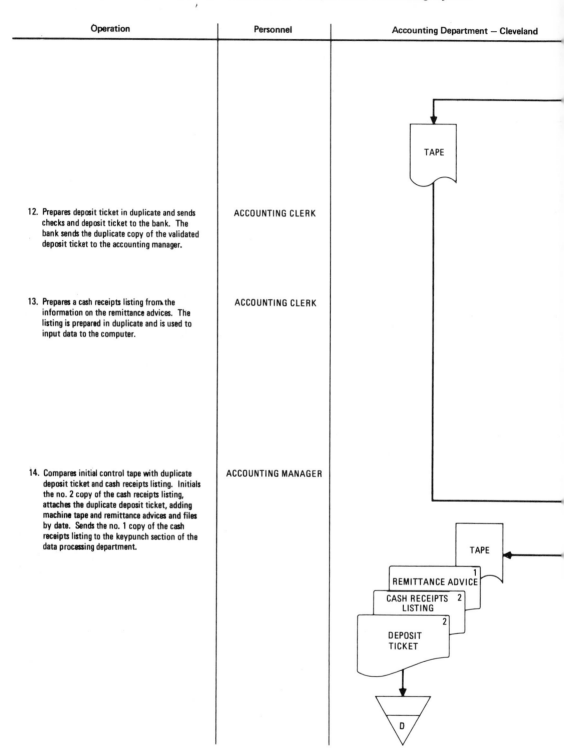
12. Prepares deposit ticket in duplicate and sends checks and deposit ticket to the bank. The bank sends the duplicate copy of the validated deposit ticket to the accounting manager.	ACCOUNTING CLERK	
13. Prepares a cash receipts listing from the information on the remittance advices. The listing is prepared in duplicate and is used to input data to the computer.	ACCOUNTING CLERK	
14. Compares initial control tape with duplicate deposit ticket and cash receipts listing. Initials the no. 2 copy of the cash receipts listing, attaches the duplicate deposit ticket, adding machine tape and remittance advices and files by date. Sends the no. 1 copy of the cash receipts listing to the keypunch section of the data processing department.	ACCOUNTING MANAGER	

Figure 6–2 (*continued*)

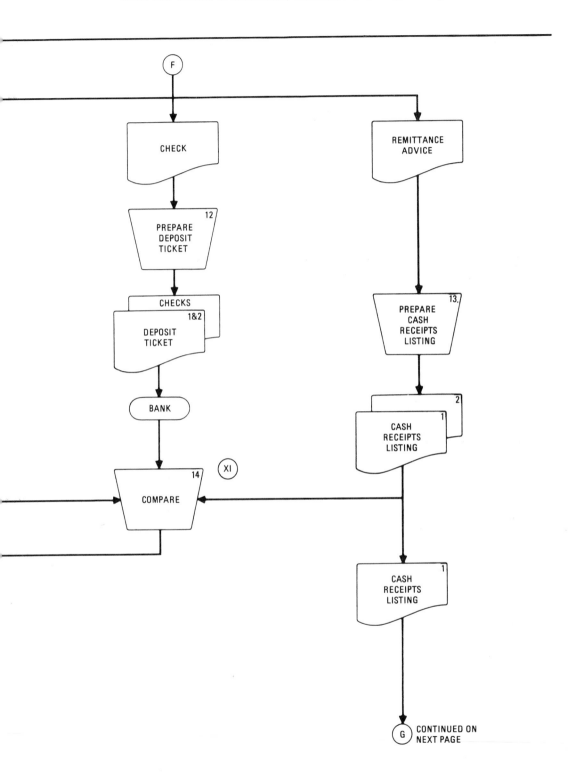

Operation	Personnel	Cleveland Data Processing Department
15. Keypunches and keyverifies cash receipts information from the cash receipts listing.	KEYPUNCH OPERATORS	
16. Runs a listing of cards punched and compares total with cash receipts listing. Corrects errors. Files cash receipts and transaction listing by date.	COMPUTER OPERATOR	
17. Runs program to process cash receipts and update customer accounts receivable file. A daily cash receipts book is printed, filed and posted to the general ledger at the end of the month. The punched cards are kept until the monthly accounts receivable trial balance is reconciled to the general ledger; then they are destroyed. The sales journal is posted at this time.	COMPUTER OPERATOR	
18. Reconciles bank statement monthly. Bank statements are received unopened directly from the mail clerk.	CONTROLLER'S SECRETARY	
19. Approves bank reconciliation and files by date.	CONTROLLER	

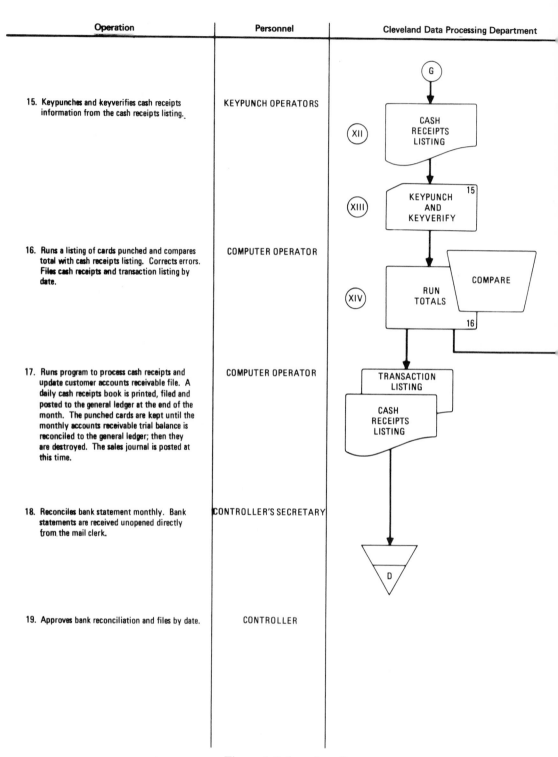

Figure 6–2 (*continued*)

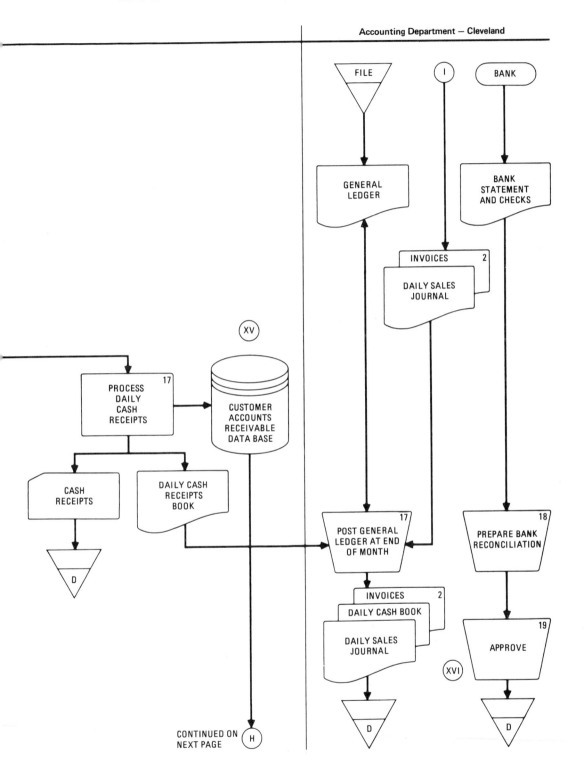

Operation	Personnel	Cleveland Data Center

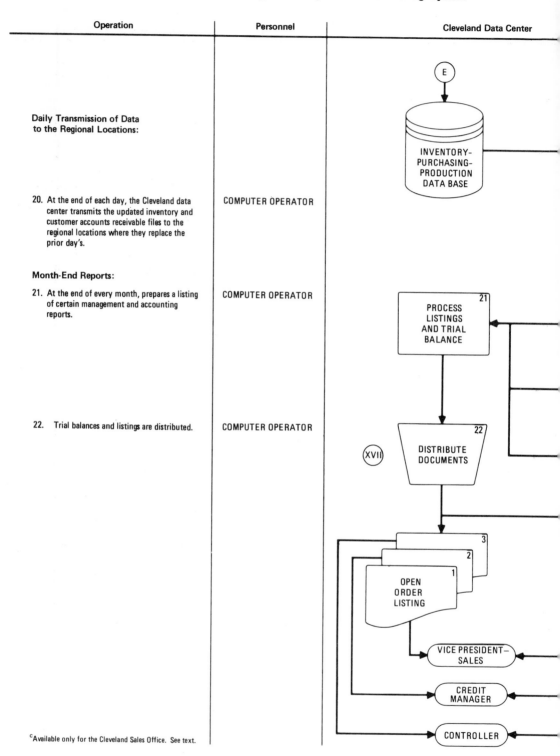

Daily Transmission of Data to the Regional Locations:

20. At the end of each day, the Cleveland data center transmits the updated inventory and customer accounts receivable files to the regional locations where they replace the prior day's. — COMPUTER OPERATOR

Month-End Reports:

21. At the end of every month, prepares a listing of certain management and accounting reports. — COMPUTER OPERATOR

22. Trial balances and listings are distributed. — COMPUTER OPERATOR

cAvailable only for the Cleveland Sales Office. See text.

Figure 6–2 (*continued*)

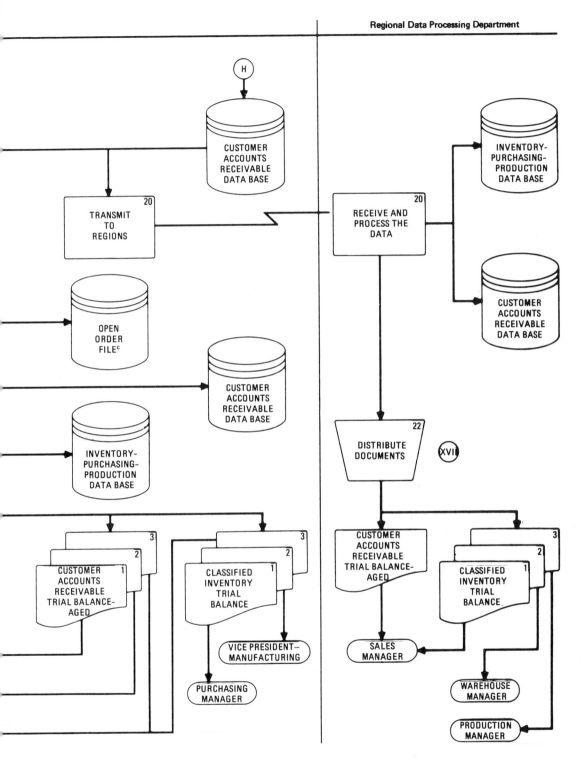

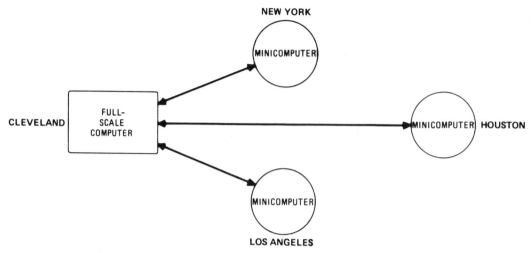

Figure 6–3. Configuration—Distributed Processing—Werner Manufacturing, Inc.

be ascertained to see if the order could be filled from them. The new system does not have this capability. If a quantity is short, the local plant is "automatically" instructed to produce more. This is obviously a managerial decision, but one must wonder whether it will lead to excess quantities of items at one location while others have shortages. An important production decision has been made a purely local one, ostensibly because of the new computer system's limitations.

• The previous system generated replenishment notices as soon as the perpetual inventory for a backordered item was restored. This "automatically" notified the sales people that action had to be taken. The new system does not have this capability. Further, the previous system generated a back order notice, a copy of which was sent to the customer. The new system does not have this capability. In the new system, the customer may never be notified the order is being held up pending the replenishment of stock. Further, if a close watch is not kept over the back order file, the order may not be filled within a reasonable time after the stock has been replenished. This may lead to customer dissatisfaction and a loss of sales.

• The conventional master files have been replaced by data bases, but there are at least two such data bases, plus conventional files, such as those for open orders and shipments. Presumably there has been some concentration, for example, sales, cash receipts and customer receivables data are in one data base, while purchasing, production, payables and inventory data are in another. A reading of the system flowcharts, however, should create some doubt in the reader's mind about whether this system is using these data bases in such a way as to materially reduce processing time. We have not considered other accounting systems, such as payroll, but one suspects there are other data bases in existence. Woodhull stressed the desirability of a single data base to eliminate unwanted data redundancy and reduce processing time.

In view of this and the continued existence of such conventional files as open orders for the Cleveland sales office, it appears that Woodhull's distributed processing system has yielded only minor benefits (if indeed there are any) over the one it replaced.

- Although it is obviously an on-line system and affords users the ability to query master files by remote terminals, it is not a real-time system. Master files are updated once a day in batch mode. It therefore affords the user the opportunity to take advantage of the conventional batch-mode controls which we studied in connection with the previous system (see Chapter 1). The previous system also used on-line batch-mode processing and afforded on-line enquiry.

The critical tone of this portion of the case study is not intended to be a blanket condemnation of distributed processing systems. We are illustrating two very important things:

1. A system, any system, must be carefully thought out and designed with close cooperation among management, systems personnel and the users. It must also be clearly justifiable in economic terms. It is a business decision, just like any other.
2. A system with relatively weak internal control impacts the auditors' work. In Chapter 1 we reviewed a system with effective controls and saw how the auditors' reliance on control strengths affected the scope and nature of their auditing procedures. In this chapter we will see how auditing procedures are affected when the system's internal controls are ineffective.

INTERNAL CONTROL—APPLICATION CONTROLS

Now that you understand the system, go back through the flowchart again. This time, refer to Table 6–4 whenever you come to a circled roman numeral.

The table reiterates the operation, states whether it is a control strength or weakness, and explains the implications for the overall system of internal control and the audit.

INTERNAL CONTROL—GENERAL CONTROLS

Assume the EDP internal auditors reviewed the controls in Werner's new distributed processing system. Their review covered operational efficiency as

Cleveland Data Center

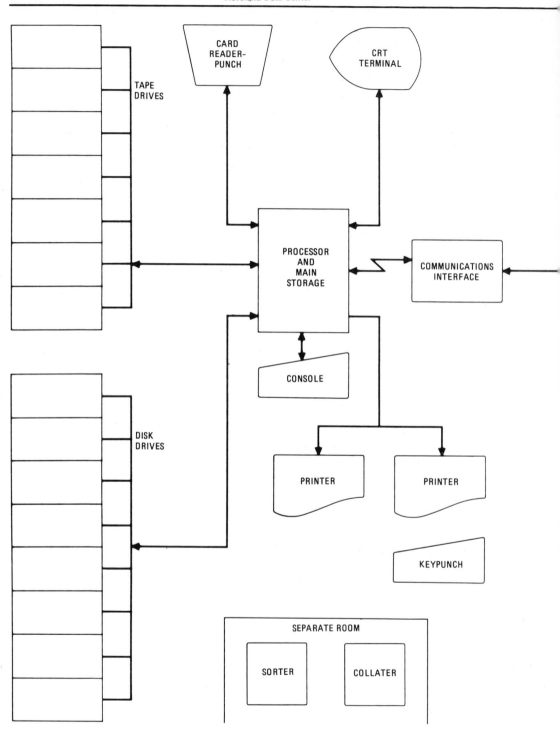

Figure 6–4.   Computer   Hardware   Configuration—Distributed   Processing—Werner Manufacturing, Inc.

Remote Locations: New York, Houston and Los Angeles

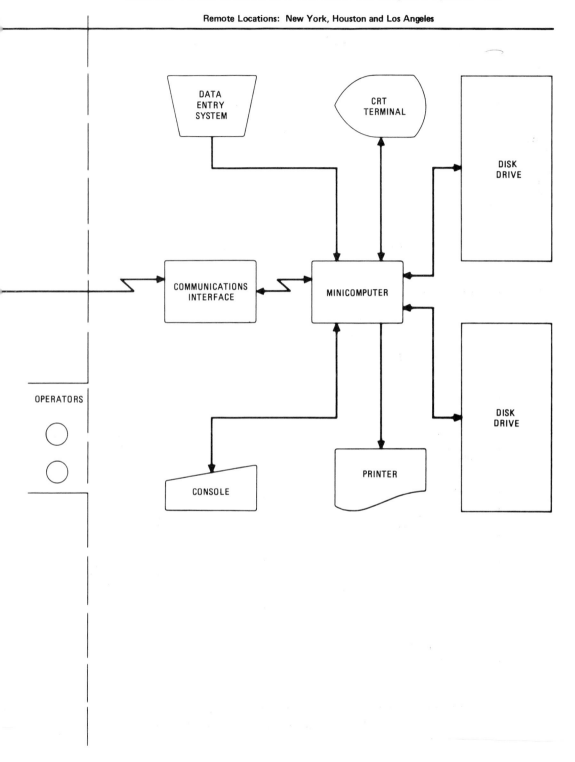

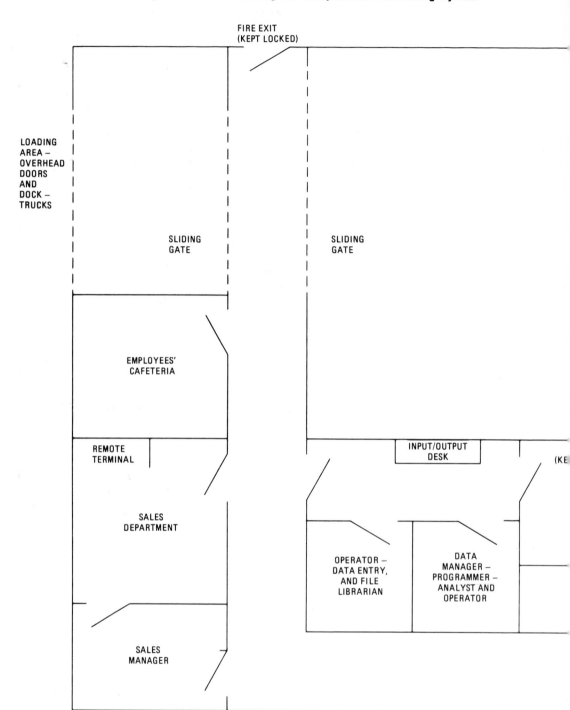

Figure 6–5. Layout of Regional Data Centers—Distributed Processing—Werner Manufacturing, Inc.

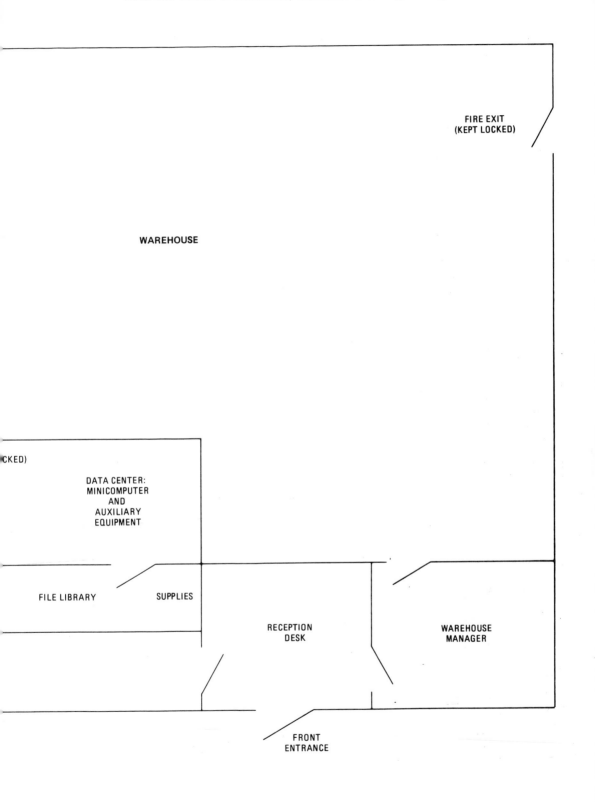

Table 6–4. Sales, Accounts Receivable, Cash Receipts—Distributed Processing—Werner Manufacturing, Inc.

OPERATION	S	W	INTERNAL CONTROL PROCEDURES/IMPLICATIONS	AUDIT IMPLICATIONS
I. Status of the customer's account is determined before any significant processing takes place.	X		Customer accounts are checked before the orders are accepted. Credit review is therefore timely and effective.	Accounts receivable are properly stated and collectible.
		X	The terminal in each regional sales office is in an open location, available to all sales clerks. Terminals have keys, but these are generally left in the machines until closing time, when they are locked up in someone's desk. User numbers, keys and passwords are given to sales clerks, but user numbers and passwords are not changed or keys always taken back when a clerk leaves the firm. In some offices, the user numbers and passwords are written on the terminal itself. The sales office door is not locked at night. No additionl passwords are needed to access the customer file.	Unauthorized persons may have access to the company's confidential customer files, particularly after closing time.
	X		Access to customer files from the sales office terminals is limited to "read only" operation.	Even after the customer file has been accessed, the terminal operator can only read data. The security system prohibits data from being deleted, added or changed in any way.
	X		The computer maintains a log of valid and invalid access attempts and describes the transactions performed.	Enables the company to review accesses and transactions. The log also provides a hard-copy trail of transactions from each terminal and provides the auditor with a ready means of reviewing activity.
II. Before shipping orders are prepared, the inventory files are queried to determine if there is sufficient quantity on hand.	X		The order process does not continue unless the order can be completed. Thus there is no danger a back order will be erroneously treated as a sale.	Accounts receivable and sales are not overstated.

III. One copy of the shipping order is sent to the warehouse, which sends it to the sales office after the goods are shipped. Neither sales nor shipping orders are prenumbered for control.	X	The warehouse does not keep any documentary evidence of the authority to ship, nor does it keep a record of such shipment.
		The warehouse does not have any copy of authorization to ship merchandise. It cannot re-create an audit trail if there is a need for one. The warehouse relies on the daily classified inventory trial balance for control over quantities; it keeps no independent perpetual inventory record. The classified trial balance does show movements by quantity and cost.
IV. The warehouse copy of the shipping order is compared with the sales order and a control copy of the shipping order by the sales clerk before being sent to the data processing department.	X	This is a good internal control procedure, but not if it is performed by the same sales clerk who prepared the original sales order. There is no guarantee that this would not be the case here.
		Sales could be misstated after the shipment of inventory by the sales clerk's preparing an entirely new set of documents. Since the warehouse keeps no independent record of its shipments, there would be no way to reconstruct the transaction.
V. Sales orders are sent to the data processing department without an independent check of prices.	X	The system is designed so that the computer prices the order when it is entered by the data processing department as a shipment/sale. There is no opportunity for an authoritative review by the user department of the prices stored in the computer before the master files are updated and invoices rendered. The computer has complete control.
		Sales and accounts receivable may be misstated.
VI. Input is sent directly to the data entry operator for entry on key-to-disk equipment and processed.	X	A fundamental input control is missing. The user department has no input control totals with which to check that (1) all items have been entered, (2) no unauthorized transactions have been entered, (3) transactions have been entered correctly, or (4) processing has been performed correctly. This situation is made more serious because invoices are sent to customers by Cleveland and copies are kept in the Cleveland accounting department. The regional sales office does not see the invoice at all under normal processing.
		There is no assurance that all items shipped have been recorded, that sales and receivables are properly recorded, or that sales and related costs are properly matched.

Table 6–4 (continued)

OPERATION	s	w	INTERNAL CONTROL PROCEDURES/IMPLICATIONS	AUDIT IMPLICATIONS
VII. Sales orders are not processed until the goods are actually shipped.	X	—	The data processing department does not update the appropriate master files (data bases) until the sales transaction has been completed.	Accounts receivable are collectible when recorded.
VIII. Input to data bases is accepted as long as the customer number is valid and the fields contain appropriate alpha and numeric data.		X	The computer is not being used to perform edit and other logic checks. The quantities ordered of certain items could be checked for reasonableness. The total of the order could be matched against the credit limit as a final check against the credit process being circumvented.	Accounts receivable, sales and inventory may be distorted and sales and related costs not properly matched.
IX. Output is distributed by the computer operators.		X	No input/output control group exists.	Computer-produced data is not verified before being posted to the general ledger or sent to customers, nor is there any assurance that sensitive output is not being sent to unauthorized persons. Accounts receivable and sales may be distorted and uncollectible.
X. Checks are restrictively endorsed in the mail room as soon as received.	X		Minimizes the chance for irregularities in cashing checks.	Cash receipts are deposited to company accounts.
XI. Initial control tape is compared with the duplicate deposit slip and cash receipts listing.	X		Insures that all receipts are accounted for and deposited in the bank promptly.	Cash receipts are properly recorded to appropriate accounts.
XII. Input is sent directly to the keypunch operators for conversion to machine-readable format.		X	See explanation for item VI above and item XIV, which is a mitigating strength, below.	Computer processing may take place using incorrect input. The entire control procedure over computer processing of cash receipts lies in the data processing department; there is no independent check by the user group until the bank account is reconciled.

	S	W	Purpose	Comment
XIII. All keypunching is 100% verified by a second person.	X		Minimizes the chance of keypunch errors and resulting erroneous accounting information.	Recording of sales results in the proper recording of receivables and cash receipts.
XIV. A daily listing of transactions is printed and compared with the cash receipts listing.	X		Insures that all cash receipts have been input to the computer. (See, however, XII above.)	Recording of sales results in proper recording of receivables and cash receipts.
XV. Output is distributed by the computer operator.		X	There is no input/output control group. (See XII.)	Computer-produced data is not verified before being posted to the general ledger, nor is there an assurance that sensitive output is not being sent to unauthorized persons.
XVI. A person independent of the daily recording of cash receipts and disbursements reconciles the bank account. The reconciliation is reviewed and approved by the controller.	X		This enables the controller to detect unauthorized use of company funds and bank and accounting errors.	Cash receipts are deposited to company accounts.
XVII. Trial balances of accounts receivable and inventory and a listing of open orders is sent to responsible persons for review.	X		Gives knowledgeable persons in the user groups an opportunity to review results of a month's processing for reasonableness.	Sales, accounts receivables and inventory are properly recorded; sales and related costs are properly matched.

Note: S = Internal control strength.
W = Internal control weakness.

well as the general and application controls and the report (Exhibit 6–1) contains their conclusions and recommendations in both areas.

In some cases, dollar amounts and other facts were invented to illustrate the form and content of an audit report. They are not always based on information you have seen in preceding sections of this book. Since the study was ordered by B. T. Summers after he was questioned sharply by the audit committee of the board of directors, the internal auditors' report is addressed to him. The report contains bracketed references to facts in the case study to make it easier to understand the source of certain information.

Exhibit 6–1. Evaluation of Distributed Data Processing System.

WERNER MANUFACTURING, INC.
INTEROFFICE MEMO

Printed in U.S.A.

TO OFFICE	B. T. Summers—President	**Date** **Steno**	April 27, 1979
FROM OFFICE	F. L. Bouchard—Chief Internal Auditor	**Enc.**	
CC:		**Contract No.**	
SUBJECT	Distributed Data Processing System	**Your Letter Dated:**	

As you requested, we audited the new (distributed) data processing system to evaluate:

- Internal control effectiveness
- Operational efficiency

Our examination included the system's general controls and the application controls for the sales, accounts receivable and cash receipts application. It covered the period March 26, 1979 (when the new system became operational) through April 20, 1979. Our findings follow; since we have one general recommendation, it appears at the end of this report.

Data Bases

The proposal for the new system called for the conversion of the old system's conventional files to a single data base for the entire company. Our examination disclosed that in the sales, accounts receivable and cash receipts system alone there are two "data bases" and two files being accessed on-line:

- Customer Accounts Receivable Data Base
- Inventory—Purchasing—Production Data Base

- Shipments File
- Open Order File

The first three files are at the Cleveland Data Center and the regional locations; the open order file is used only at the Cleveland Data Center.

Our review of the "data bases" disclosed that they are really on-line master files organized in much the same way the master files were in the old system. The conversion did combine some of the individual files in the old system into larger files, but these are not data bases as that term is used in state-of-the-art data processing.

Poor System Design—Hybrid System

The present system is a hybrid one because it does not work the same at all locations. For example, the Cleveland sales office has an on-line open order file, but the regional locations do not. The old system, which had an open order file, was not completely converted at the Cleveland location because it was decided to have that sales office use the full-scale computer at the data center. Since the system was already in place and there was to be no change in hardware, the system designers decided to let Cleveland process with portions of the old application system. New equipment, including minicomputers and data communication devices, were installed at the regional locations, and new software was designed for them. Thus, the new system includes elements of the old. Discussion with user and systems group members of the design team revealed that the decision to retain the old system to process Cleveland sales office transactions was made at the last minute, partly because the project was running behind schedule and considerably over budget. Our review of project documentation disclosed that the new system became operational four months later and cost $18,000 more than originally projected. It did not, however, include integration of Starr Products' processing and complete conversion of Cleveland data center operations, as originally proposed.

The new system costs $261,600 per year more than the old one did, not counting amortization of the cost of the conversion. We feel that the new system does not yield benefits that justify this increase in cost. In fact, we noted the following operating deficiencies in the new system:

- It produces less information than did the old system. For example, it does not produce back order notices, nor does it print replenishment notices when inventory of a backordered item is restored to the proper level. Thus, customers are not notified of the status of their order and back orders may not be filled unless Werner's employees keep a close watch on the status of back orders. The old system automatically generated this information.
- If the inventory at a given location is not sufficient to fill an order received by that location's sales office, the new system does not query the other locations to see if the order can be filled from them. The old system did. Indeed, if the quantity is insufficient to fill an order, the new computer system generates an order to produce more of that item, regardless of the quantities

that may be on hand at the other locations. We noted several items that were overstocked at one or more locations that were being automatically ordered at others. We calculate this situation is costing Werner approximately $10,000 per year for the items selected for our examination.

- The new system is on-line and affords the user the ability to query the status of certain master files via CRT terminals. However, as with the old system, the new updates its files once daily in batch mode. We feel that the cost of the new system and the technology available under it, warrants providing for updating master files in real-time mode, with proper internal controls to provide for data integrity.

Position of the Data Base Administrator

Although the data bases are in reality on-line files organized conventionally, there is a data base administrator. However, the data base administrator's position [see figure 6–1] indicates a lack of appreciation for the proper role of this person. The organization formed to accommodate the new system places the data base administrator under the systems programming supervisor, an addition to the organization as it existed under the old system.

The data base administrator is charged with maintaining the organization's data. Although the title is singular, it is frequently applied to a number of persons possessing various skills. Where a true data base has been formed, the organizational structure of the data processing area may be changed significantly, and some of the functions performed under the conventional system may be transferred to the data base administrator.

Because Werner's data processing organization remains substantially as it was under the old system, the structure of the firm's data resources have in fact changed little. Indeed, our examination reveals that the formation of the position of data base administrator is a change with little real meaning except to support the illusion that a true data base has been created.

Starr Products System Unchanged

The conversion to the new system did not change Starr's data processing system at all. Its data is still processed at a service center. The proposal for the new system stated that Starr's system would be integrated into Werner's.

We understand that this integration was deferred so that the new system could become operational.

Separation of Duties

The regional data centers are staffed by two persons who perform the computer operating, programming, file librarian and data entry functions interchangeably. [See figure 6–5.] Consequently, there is no separation of duties within the data processing area at the regional locations.

Access to Data, Files and Equipment

The door to the computer room at the regional data centers is generally locked, but we observed several occasions during which the door was left open when both data processing employees were out of the office. We also noted that non-data processing personnel were allowed in the computer room when the data processing employees were present.

Input and output is left on a table in an unlocked part of the data processing area. This is done to permit input documents to be dropped off and to enable recipients of output to pick it up when convenient for them. Further, the CRT terminal is kept in the sales department which is unlocked; we observed at the Houston and Los Angeles locations that access numbers and passwords were written on the terminals and that the key was left in the terminal at all times.

Access to equipment, files and data at the Houston and Los Angeles regional locations is generally unrestricted.

Control over Systems Development

The system development process for the old system [see case study for Chapter 2] was very sound, in that it provided for effective controls at each step in the process and involved top management, the internal auditors, users, the controller, and systems and procedures specialists.

We reviewed the project documentation for the conversion to the new system for the sales, accounts receivable and cash receipts application and discovered that:

- The user groups were never consulted about or agreed to the need for the conversion. Conversion rationale was based largely on a desire to utilize the latest computer technology and system configuration.
- Internal auditing was not involved in any phase of the design process until implementation. At that time, the department raised serious questions about the effectiveness of internal controls and the conversion of files. (See my memo to you dated March 15, 1979 and the following comments on weaknesses in internal control.*)
- Systems testing of individual program modules was properly performed to insure that they processed properly and that all controls were operational. Integration of those modules into the system was not performed properly, however, and the first live processing run resulted in delays of up to three hours. This was due to the new programs' contending with others for use of the computer system's resources, for example, main memory, on-line storage, print queues, and so on.
Review of the data processing department's schedules and overtime records disclosed that $34,000 in overtime has been expended in correcting these problems since the system was made operational. Further, several payrolls have had to be processed at other, off-premise data centers to meet the payroll deadlines.

* Not reproduced in this book.

- Users and data processing operations personnel have not been adequately trained to use the new system. Consequently, errors are 143% above the rate experienced under the old system.

System Documentation

Werner's documentation standards are high and have been observed in the past, so that they have constituted an internal control strength. We reviewed the documentation for the new system and discovered:

- It does not conform to Werner's established documentation standards.
- System and program flowcharts do not contain up-to-date revisions. In some cases, programs contain code for which there is no documentary support.
- System changes are not being supported by change orders. Consequently, it is not possible to determine whether they were properly reviewed and authorized before implementation. Discussion with systems and applications programmers disclosed that some changes were made "on the fly" to correct unanticipated processing problems. These changes were not documented. Consequently, it is not possible to get an accurate description of either the operating system or several programs from the system documentation.
- Processing problems have been made more serious by the inadequacy of the operator's instruction manual. During the period audited, 67 hours were lost correcting problems because remedial action was not clearly stated in the operator's manual. In some cases, the systems and applications programmers had to come in on weekends to help solve the problems.

Control Weaknesses in the Sales, Accounts Receivable and Cash Receipts Application

[Note to reader: This section is included to complete the report. However, since the weaknesses have already been explained in detail on the system flowchart and the pages which follow it, there is no point in repeating that information here. The general subject areas are listed below, and you are referred to the specific weakness by the roman numeral reference on the system flowchart.]

- Control Over Shipments—III and IV
- Check of Pricing—V
- Input Controls—VI and XII
- Master File Updating—VIII
- Output Control—IX and XV

Recommendation

In view of the internal control weaknesses and operational inefficiencies in the new (distributed) data processing system, we recommend that it be abandoned and Werner return to the previous system.

Our reasons for this rather drastic recommendation are:

- The additional annual cost of $261,600 (not including amortization of conversion cost) is not accompanied by any discernible benefits to Werner.
- The new system yields less operating information than the old one did.
- We estimate the cost to correct the internal control weaknesses and bring the new system up to the old system's operational efficiency would be $275,000 and would take four months. Conversion back to the old system would cost $54,000 and take one month.
- Because of the lack of internal control, the independent auditors do not plan to rely on the system in setting the scope of their audit work. (See their preliminary review report dated April 7, 1979.*) We discussed the effect of this nonreliance with them and found that they estimate this will increase their audit fee $10,000 over last year's.

We will be happy to discuss our findings in greater detail with you.

AUDITING PROCEDURES

Internal auditors.   The internal auditors reviewed the new computer system and prepared the report you just read. We will assume they performed their normal auditing procedures on the old system during the year.

Independent auditors.   The independent auditors received a copy of the internal auditors' report and reviewed their working papers in connection with the *SAS No. 9* review. You will recall that *SAS No. 9* requires that the independent auditors evaluate the internal auditors' work to see whether they can rely on it as an internal control strength and whether they can use the internal auditors to perform certain auditing procedures.

Based on their review of the report, the independent auditors concluded that the general and application controls in the new system, which is the one in effect on the audit date (April 30, 1979), are extremely weak and do not afford them a basis for restricting the scope of their substantive auditing procedures.

Consequently, substantive auditing procedures will be more extensive than in the past. In fact, there may be little (or no) compliance audit work, since auditors do not perform compliance tests on internal control weaknesses. You will recall from their report that in estimating the additional $10,000 audit fee, the internal auditors referred to a preliminary review the independent auditors performed and a report they issued, dated April 7, 1979. Refer to Chapter 3 for a discussion of the independent auditors' procedures in past years.

* Not reproduced in this book.

Index

Index